teach®
yourself

latin american
spanish
juan kattán-ibarra

For over 60 years, more than
40 million people have learnt over
750 subjects the **teach yourself**
way, with impressive results.

be where you want to be
with **teach yourself**

For UK order enquiries: please contact Bookpoint Ltd, 130 Milton Park, Abingdon, Oxon OX14 4SB. Telephone: +44 (0) 1235 827720, Fax: +44 (0) 1235 400454. Lines are open 9.00–18.00, Monday to Saturday, with a 24-hour message answering service. You can also order through our website www.madaboutbooks.com

For USA order enquiries: please contact McGraw-Hill Customer Services, P.O. Box 545, Blacklick, OH 43004-0545, USA. Telephone: 1-800-722-4726. Fax: 1-614-755-5645.

For Canada order enquiries: please contact McGraw-Hill Ryerson Ltd, 300 Water St, Whitby, Ontario L1N 9B6, Canada. Telephone: 905 430 5000. Fax: 905 430 5020.

Long renowned as the authoritative source for self-guided learning – with more than 30 million copies sold worldwide – the *Teach Yourself* series includes over 300 titles in the fields of languages, crafts, hobbies, business, computing and education.

Teach Yourself Latin American Spanish is also available in the form of a pack containing this book and cassette. If you have been unable to obtain the pack, the cassette can be ordered separately through your bookseller.

British Library Cataloguing in Publication Data
A catalogue entry for this title is available from The British Library.

Library of Congress Catalog Card Number: on file

First published in UK 1994 by Hodder Headline Ltd, 338 Euston Road, London, NW1 3BH.

First published in US 1994 by Contemporary Books, a Division of The McGraw Hill Companies, 1 Prudential Plaza, 130 East Randolph Street, Chicago, IL 60601 USA.

This edition published 2003.

The 'Teach Yourself' name is a registered trade mark of Hodder & Stoughton Ltd.

Typeset by Transet Limited, Coventry, England.
Printed in Great Britain for Hodder & Stoughton Educational, a division of Hodder Headline Ltd, 338 Euston Road, London NW1 3BH by Cox & Wyman Ltd, Reading, Berkshire.

Impression number   10 9 8 7 6 5 4 3 2 1
Year   2008 2007 2006 2005 2004 2003

acknowledgements

The author would like to thank Juan Luzzi Montes de Oca, from Chile, for his assistance in the preparation of the second edition of this book, and for the artwork on pages 33, 83 and 155 (bottom).

Every effort has been made to obtain permission for all material used. In the absence of any response to enquiries, the author and publisher would like to acknowledge the following for use of their material: diario *El Heraldo* and *Revista Tiempo Libre,* (Mexico), Oficina de Turismo (México), diario *El Mercurio,* Carey Internacional, Cascada Nature Expeditions, Economy Tour, restaurante La cocina de Sebastián (Chile), parrillada Casa Brava, Mobli Market (Colombia).

Thanks are also due to Radio Mar FM (Mexico), for use of material on the recording that accompanies this book.

About the author

Juan Kattán-Ibarra was born in Chile and has travelled extensively in Latin America and Spain. He has degrees from the University of Chile, Michigan State University, Manchester University and the Institute of Education, London University. He taught Spanish at Ealing College in London and was an examiner in Spanish for the London Chamber of Commerce and Industry and the University of London School Examinations Board. He is now a full-time author.

He is the sole author of *Teach Yourself Spanish, Teach Yourself Spanish Grammar, Teach Yourself Improve Your Spanish, Conversational Spanish, Conversando, Panorama de la prensa,*

Perspectivas culturales de Hispanoamérica, Perspectivas culturales de España, and co-author of *Working with Spanish, Talking Business Spanish, Se escribe así, Sueños – World Spanish 2, Modern Spanish Grammar, Modern Spanish Grammar Workbook*, and *Spanish Grammar in Context*.

iv

acknowledgements

contents

introduction

Welcome to *Teach Yourself Latin American Spanish*!

This is a complete communicative course in Latin American Spanish, which assumes no previous knowledge of the language. It is designed for beginners as well as those who, having done a general Spanish course or one based on Peninsular Spanish, now wish to learn the language spoken in Latin America. The emphasis is first and foremost on *using* Spanish, but we also aim to give you an idea of how the language works, so that you can create sentences of your own.

Although the course has been written especially for people studying on their own, the material and exercises will also lend themselves to classroom use. The 13 units which make up this book provide ample opportunity to learn and practise the language used in practical, everyday situations, such as introducing yourself and others, giving personal information, making travel arrangements, ordering food, shopping, etc. Those travelling in Latin America, for business or pleasure, will find the material in this course particularly useful.

The course covers all four of the basic skills – listening and speaking, reading and writing. If you are working on your own, the audio recording will be all the more important, as it will provide you with the essential opportunity to listen to the Spanish spoken in Latin America and to speak it within a controlled framework. You should therefore try to obtain a copy of the recording if you haven't already got one.

Use it or lose it!

Language learning is a bit like jogging – you need to do it regularly for it to be any good! Ideally, you should find a 'study buddy' to work through the course with you. This way you will have someone to try out your Spanish on. And when the going gets tough, you will have someone to chivvy you on until you reach your target.

Understanding authentic Latin American Spanish

Don't expect to be able to understand everything you hear or read straight away. If you listen to Latin American Spanish audio material, or watch a Latin American programme or film, or are able to get newspapers or magazines, you should not get discouraged when you realize how quickly native-speakers speak and how much vocabulary there is still to be learned. Just concentrate on a *small* extract – either a video / audio clip or a short article – and work through it till you have mastered it. In this way, you'll find that your command of Spanish increases steadily. Look at the **Taking it further** section at the back of the book for sources of authentic Spanish.

The structure of this course

The course book contains

- 13 course units
- self-assessment tests
- a reference section at the back of the book
- an audio recording (which you really need to have if you are going to get maximum benefit from the course)

The course units

The course units are structured in the following way:

Statement of aims

You will be told what you can expect to learn, both in terms of what you will be able to do in Spanish by the end of the unit, and in terms of the language points you will learn to handle.

Presentation of new language

The language is presented through a series of dialogues, two, or more. These are on the recording ▶ and also printed in the book. Some assistance with vocabulary is given before and after each dialogue including, where appropriate, regional variations of words used in the texts. The language is presented in manageable chunks, building carefully on what you have learned in earlier units. Most dialogues are followed by listening comprehension exercises, and there are transcripts of these exercises at the back of the book.

Key phrases and expressions

Key phrases and expressions used in the dialogues and their English translations are listed in the **Key phrases** section.

Description of language forms

In the **Grammar** section you will learn about the forms of the language, thus enabling you to construct your own sentences correctly.

Practice

In this section you will be able to use the language that you have learned. Some of the activities here require mainly *recognition*, but you are also encouraged, right from the start, to *produce* both in writing and in speech, following specific guidelines and models.

Information on Latin American Spanish and aspects of life and customs

At different stages in the course, you will find relevant information on language differences among the various countries, and about aspects of life and customs in Latin America. This information, found in the ⓘ section, is given in English.

Testing yourself

The aim of this section is for you to test yourself and judge whether you have successfully mastered the language.

Reference section

At the end of the book, there are sections that you can use for reference:

- a glossary of grammatical terms
- a grammar summary
- a list of irregular verbs
- a glossary of Latin American terms
- a pronunciation section
- transcripts of listening comprehension exercises
- a key to the activities and 'testing yourself'
- a Spanish–English vocabulary
- an English–Spanish vocabulary
- a 'taking it further' section
- an index of the grammar contents

How to use this course

Make sure at the beginning of each course unit that you are clear about what you can expect to learn.

Dialogues

Read the background information which is given before each dialogue. This sets the scene and the country. There are units based in Mexico (units 1–4), Colombia (units 5 and 6), Chile (units 7–9), Argentina (units 10 and 11) and Peru (units 12 and 13). You will find information on the main pronunciation features in each of these countries in the **Pronunciation** section starting on page 226.

Read, or preferably listen to the dialogue first, before you look at the text, noting the new language forms and vocabulary. You can then check the key words and expressions which follow the dialogue before you read or listen to it again. Do this several times until you feel confident with it, then turn to the accompanying exercise to test what you have learned. You will find the answers in the **Key to the activities** beginning on page 243. If you need an explanation of new language points at this stage, study the relevant paragraphs in the **Grammar** section.

When you listen to the recording, pay special attention to the pronunciation and intonation of the native speakers and try to imitate them. Don't be content with just listening. Spanish may sound fast to you at first, but as you progress through the course you will find it easier to follow the speakers and imitate their speech.

Key phrases

Try learning the key phrases, as these constitute the substance of the unit. You can cover up the English translations and produce the English equivalents of the Spanish. If you find that relatively easy, go on to cover the Spanish sentences and produce the Spanish equivalents of the English. You will probably find this more difficult. Trying to recall the context in which words and phrases were used may help you learn them better.

Grammar

Here the grammatical content of the unit is explained in English and illustrated by means of examples, all with their English translation. The explanations are simple, but if you are daunted by grammar terminology, you can check the **Glossary of grammatical terms** to check the meaning of certain words.

In the **Grammar** section you will learn all major grammatical points, including all main tenses, from the frequently used present tense to the future and past tenses. You will also become familiar with the main grammatical differences between Latin American and Peninsular Spanish. Study the language points and note how they are used in the introductory dialogues as well as in the **Practice** exercises which follow.

Practice

Most of the exercises here are communicative in nature, requiring you to take an active part in them. Work through each one following the instructions that precede them. Some of them are listen-only activities and are there to help you increase your capacity to understand different forms of spoken Latin American Spanish. The temptation may be to go straight to the **Transcripts** in the back of the book, but try not to do this. The whole point of listening exercises is to improve your listening skills. You won't do this by reading first. The transcriptions are there to help you if you get stuck, or used as reading practice only if you do not have access to the recording. The recordings, many of which are authentic interviews, offer a good opportunity to hear speakers from different parts of Latin America.

As you work your way through the exercises, check your answers carefully in the **Key to the activities** at the back of the book. It is easy to overlook your own mistakes. If you have a study buddy it's a good idea to check each other's answers. Most of the activities have fixed answers, but some are a bit more open-ended.

Latin American Spanish

Spanish is the main means of communication for more than three hundred million people, most of them living in Latin America. Latin American Spanish differs from Peninsular Spanish, just as British English differs from American English or from that spoken in other parts of the world. Yet, despite these differences, educated speakers from all over the Spanish-speaking world understand each other.

The main differences between Latin American and Peninsular Spanish are in vocabulary, pronunciation and intonation. Differences in grammar also exist but are less marked. Naturally, there are language variations within Latin America itself, just as there are differences within Spain.

Latin American Spanish has borrowed a number of words from indigenous languages in the region. Some of these terms have found their way into Peninsular Spanish and even other European languages. Words like **tomate**, **chocolate** and **maíz**, among others, have their origin in the Americas. Apart from Spanish words which have acquired a different meaning in Latin America, the region as a whole sometimes shows preference for one Spanish word instead of another. By and large, however, most of the Latin American lexicon is Spanish in origin, and most standard words used in Spain will be understood in Latin America.

Some variations in Spanish within Latin America have their roots in the Spanish colonization of the region; others stem from the influence of Indian languages and from that of non-Spanish settlers, mainly African and European. This has given rise to distinctive linguistic areas within the region. The Spanish spoken in Mexico, for instance, sounds quite different from that spoken in the River Plate region, in countries like Argentina and Uruguay. This in turn differs from that of the Andean countries or that spoken around the Caribbean. In addition to using forms which will be understood in most Latin American countries,

Teach Yourself Latin American Spanish also explains some of the main differences between various forms of Spanish, including references to specific countries or areas, for example Mexico and Central America, the Caribbean, Southern Cone (Argentina, Chile and Uruguay), River Plate (Argentina and Uruguay). Differences in pronunciation and intonation between major regions are demonstrated by means of the recording which accompanies the course. Information on regional differences is given in the **Pronunciation** section at the back of the book (p. 226).

01

¿cuál es su nombre?

what is your name?

In this unit you will learn

- how to use simple greetings
- how to introduce yourself
- how to ask and give personal information

▶1 En un hotel *In a hotel*

A tourist arrives at a hotel in Guadalajara, Mexico. Note the word **tengo** *I have,* and the phrase **¿Cuál es su nombre?** *What is your name?*, a formal way of asking someone's name.

Turista	Buenas noches.
Recepcionista	Buenas noches, señora. ¿Qué desea?
Turista	Tengo una reservación.
Recepcionista	¿Cuál es su nombre, por favor?
Turista	Ana González.
Recepcionista	Ah sí, es la habitación número quince.

buenas noches	*good evening*
¿qué desea?	*can I help you?*
una reservación/reserva	*a reservation*
por favor	*please*
la habitación	*room*
el número	*number*
quince	*fifteen*

ℹ Formal or polite forms of address: señora, señorita, señor

Señora *Mrs, madam,* is used for addressing older and married women. A younger and unmarried woman will be addressed as **señorita,** *Miss.* These two words are used with the first name, the surname or the full name, e.g. **señora María (Miranda).** **Señor** *Mr, Sir,* used for addressing men, can only be used with the surname or the full name, not with the first name, e.g. **señor (Gonzalo) Palma.**

In writing, **señora**, **señorita** and **señor** are normally abbreviated **Sra.**, **Srta.**, **Sr.**, respectively.

Generally speaking in Latin America, strangers and people providing services tend to use these words more often than in Spain, for example **sí/no, señor/a** *yes/no, sir/madam.*

▶2 En el bar *In the bar*

In the hotel bar, a man is looking for someone he has not met before. Key phrases here are ¿**es usted ...?** *are you?*, **soy** *I am*, **yo no soy** *I am not.*

Señor	Buenos días, señorita.
Señorita	Buenos días.
Señor	¿Es usted la señorita Carmen Robles?
Señorita	No, yo no soy Carmen Robles. Soy Gloria Santos.
Señor	Disculpe.
Señorita	No se preocupe.

buenos días	*good morning*
disculpe	*I am sorry*
no se preocupe	*that's all right* (lit. *don't worry*)

ⓘ La señorita, la señora, el señor

In indirect address, **señorita**, **señora** and **señor** are preceded by the Spanish equivalent of *the*: **la** for feminine, **el** for masculine, e.g. ¿**Es usted la señorita Carmen Robles?** *Are you Miss Carmen Robles?* **El** and **la** are not used in direct address, for example greetings, e.g. **Buenos días, señorita.**

▶3 Mucho gusto *Pleased to meet you*

Señor Peña, a Chilean businessman, meets señor Palma, from Mexico.

Señor Peña	Buenas tardes. ¿Usted es el señor Gonzalo Palma?
Señor Palma	Sí, soy yo.
Señor Peña	Yo soy Luis Peña, de Chile.
Señor Palma	Encantado, señor Peña.
Señor Peña	Mucho gusto.
Señor Palma	Siéntese, por favor.
Señor Peña	Gracias.

encantado/a	*pleased to meet you*
	(said by a man / woman)
mucho gusto	*pleased to meet you* (invariable)
buenas tardes	*good afternoon*
¿usted es ... ?	*are you ... ?*
soy yo	*it's me*
siéntese	*sit down*
gracias	*thank you*

ℹ️ Hand-shaking

In a situation like the one in the dialogue, people will normally shake hands. Hand-shaking is much more frequent in Latin America than in English-speaking countries. Even old friends and relatives will sometimes shake hands when meeting or leaving.

▶4 ¿Cómo se llama usted? *What is your name?*

Mónica Lagos and Raúl Molina, both from Mexico, meet at a conference and introduce themselves. Note the way in which they ask each other where they come from: *¿De dónde es usted? Where are you from?*, **Y usted, ¿de dónde es?** *And you? Where are you from?*

Señor Molina	Disculpe, ¿cómo se llama usted?
Señora Lagos	Me llamo Mónica Lagos. ¿Y usted?
Señor Molina	Mi nombre es Raúl Molina.
Señora Lagos	Encantada.
Señor Molina	Mucho gusto, señora.
Señora Lagos	¿De dónde es usted?
Señor Molina	Soy de Monterrey. Y usted, ¿de dónde es?
Señora Lagos	Yo soy de Puebla.

me llamo ...	*my name is ...* (lit. *I'm called ...*)
mi nombre es ...	*my name is ...*
¿dónde?	*where?*
(yo) soy de ...	*I am from ...*

Say it in Spanish

At a party in a Spanish-speaking country you meet someone. How would you answer these questions?:

a ¿Cómo se llama usted?   **b** ¿De dónde es usted?

■ Asking someone's name and saying your name

Note that Spanish uses two alternative ways of asking someone's name in a formal way, **¿Cuál es su nombre?** (see Dialogue 1) and **¿Cómo se llama usted?** *What is your name?* Both are equally common in Latin America. In Spain, you are much more likely to hear the second expression, except in official situations, in which you might hear **¿Su nombre?** *Your name?* To answer, simply say your name or use **Me llamo** (name) or **Mi nombre es** (name).

▶ 5 ¿Cómo te llamas? *What is your name?*

All the people in the previous dialogues have used formal forms of address. **Usted**, *you*, is used to address a person formally. In this dialogue you will learn the familiar form of address, corresponding to **tú**, the familiar word for *you*. Observe the way in which Mark and Nora, two young people, address each other.

Nora   ¿Cómo te llamas?
Mark   Me llamo Mark, ¿y tú?
Nora   Me llamo Nora. ¿De dónde eres?
Mark   Soy inglés, soy de Londres. Tú eres mexicana, ¿verdad?
Nora   Sí, soy mexicana, soy de Jalapa.

¿cómo te llamas?	*what is your name?* (fam)
¿de dónde eres?	*where are you from?* (fam)
inglés / inglesa	*English*
tú eres ... ¿verdad?	*you are ..., aren't you?* (fam)

Say it in Spanish

What questions would you ask to get these replies? Use the familiar form.

a Me llamo Antonio García.
b Soy argentino. Soy de Buenos Aires.

ℹ️ Familiar or formal address?

Latin Americans on the whole are more formal than Spaniards and they use the polite forms of address much more frequently than in Spain. Unless you are speaking to children or friends, it is best to use the **usted** rather than the **tú** form when you first meet somebody, then wait and see what the other person is doing and do likewise. Verb forms and other grammatical words change depending on whether you are using polite (pol) or familiar (fam) address, for example, **¿Cómo se llama usted?** (pol), **¿Cómo te llamas?** (fam) or **¿Cuál es su nombre?** (pol), **¿Cuál es tu nombre?** (fam).

▶ 6 Somos mexicanos *We are Mexican*

A Mexican couple meet a couple from Colombia. Key words and phrases here are **ustedes son** *you are*, and **somos** *we are*.

Colombiano	Ustedes son mexicanos, ¿no?
Mexicano	Sí, somos mexicanos. ¿Y ustedes?
Colombiano	Somos colombianos.
Mexicano	¿Y de qué parte de Colombia son?
Colombiano	Somos de Bogotá.

ustedes	*you* (pol, plural)
¿y de qué parte de ...?	*and what part of ...?*

Key phrases

Greetings

Buenos días.	*Good morning.*
Buenas tardes.	*Good afternoon.*
Buenas noches.	*Good evening / night.*

Introducing yourself and exchanging greetings with people you meet

Soy ...	*I am* (name)
Me llamo ... / Mi nombre es ...	*My name is ...*
Mucho gusto (*invariable*).	*Pleased to meet you.*
Encantado (*if you are a man*).	
Encantada (*if you are a woman*)	

Asking and giving personal information: name, place of origin and nationality

¿Cuál es su / tu nombre? (pol. / fam.)	*What is your name?*
¿Cómo se llama usted / te llamas? (pol. / fam.)	
Me llamo ... / Mi nombre es ...	*My name is ...*
¿Es usted ...? / ¿Tú eres ...? (pol. / fam.)	*Are you (name)?*
(Yo) soy ...	*I am (name).*
¿De dónde es usted / eres tú? (pol. / fam.)	*Where are you from?*
Soy / somos de ...	*I am / we are from ...*
¿Es usted / eres mexicano/a? (pol. / fam.) (m./f.)	*Are you Mexican?*
Somos colombianos.	*We are Colombian.*

Grammar

1 Definite article: *el, la* the (sing)

All nouns (words that name things or people) in Spanish are either masculine (m) or feminine (f) and the word for *the* is **el** for singular masculine nouns and **la** for singular feminine nouns.

el hotel   *the hotel*   **la** habitación   *the room*

2 Gender of nouns: masculine or feminine?

Nouns ending in -o are usually masculine while nouns ending in -a are normally feminine:

el número   *the number*   **la** visita   *the visitor*

But there are many exceptions to the above rule, e.g. **el día** *the day*, **la mano** *the hand*, and there are many nouns which do not end in -o or -a, so it is advisable to learn each word with its corresponding article, **el** or **la** *the*, for example:

el nombre	*the name*	la tarde	*the afternoon*
el bar	*the bar*	la noche	*the evening / night*

Nouns which refer to people will normally agree in gender (masculine or feminine) with the person referred to, and to form the feminine of such nouns you may find it useful to remember these simple rules:

- Change the -o to -a.

  el mexicano (m) *the Mexican* la mexicana (f) *the Mexican*

- Add -a to the consonant.

  el señor (m) *the gentleman*   la señora (f) *the lady*

- But if the noun ends in -ista, the ending remains the same for masculine or feminine.

  el recepcionista (m) / la recepcionista (f) *receptionist*

3 Indefinite article: *Un, una* a/an

The word for *a* is **un** for masculine nouns and **una** for feminine nouns.

  un hotel *a hotel*   una habitación *a room*

4 Adjectives indicating nationality

Adjectives are words which serve to qualify a person or a thing, for example a *Mexican* man, a *good* hotel. Adjectives of nationality, like many adjectives in Spanish, have masculine and feminine forms. To form the feminine from a masculine adjective of nationality or origin change the -o to -a or add -a to the consonant.

Masculine	Feminine
un señor mexicano	una señora mexicana
a Mexican gentleman	*a Mexican lady*
un turista inglés	una turista inglesa
an English tourist	*an English tourist*

Other nationalities (m/f forms)

argentino/a	*Argentinian*
británico/a	*British*
colombiano/a	*Colombian*
cubano/a	*Cuban*
chileno/a	*Chilean*
escocés/escocesa	*Scottish*
galés/galesa	*Welsh*
inglés/inglesa	*English*
norteamericano/a	*American*
(*also* americano/a)	
peruano/a	*Peruvian*
venezolano/a	*Venezuelan*

Note that adjectives of nationality in Spanish are written with small letters.

5 Subject pronouns: *Yo, tú, él ... I, you, he ...*

To say *I, you, he, she,* etc., use the following set of words, which are called *subject pronouns:*

Singular		Plural	
yo	*I*	nosotros/as	*we* (m/f)
tú	*you* (fam)	ustedes	*you* (pl)
usted	*you* (pol)	ellos	*they* (m)
él	*he*	ellas	*they* (f)
ella	*she*		

The main difference between Peninsular and Latin American Spanish is that the latter does not use the familiar plural form **vosotros/as** (*you*). Latin Americans use the plural form **ustedes** in familiar and formal address. In writing, **usted** and **ustedes** are normally found in abbreviated form as **Ud.** and **Uds.** or **Vd.** and **Vds.**

The feminine subject pronoun **nosotras** is used when all the people involved are women. If there are people of both sexes, you need to use the masculine form **nosotros**.

Generally, subject pronouns are omitted in Spanish, except for emphasis or to avoid the ambiguity that may arise with **él, ella, usted,** and the plural forms **ellos, ellas, ustedes,** which share the same verb forms. Consider for example:

Es artista.   *He/she is an artist*
                 or *You are an artist.*

If the context does not make it clear whether you are referring to *he, she,* or *you,* you need to use the corresponding subject pronoun, e.g. **Ella** es artista, *She's an artist.*

In the examples which follow the verb form is sufficient to indicate the person you are referring to, and you would only use a subject pronoun for emphasis or to establish some sort of contrast with something said before.

Soy inglés	*I'm English.*
Yo soy chileno.	*I'm Chilean.*
Somos de Londres.	*We're from London.*
Nosotros somos de Santiago.	*We're from Santiago.*

6 *Ser* to be

Basic personal information, such as name, place of origin, nationality, can be given with the verb **ser** (*to be*).

Soy Gonzalo Palma.	*I am Gonzalo Palma.*
Soy de Monterrey.	*I am from Monterrey.*
Soy mexicano.	*I am Mexican.*

The present tense forms of **ser** are as follows:

Singular		Plural	
yo soy	*I am*	nosotros/as somos	*we are*
tú eres	*you are* (fam)	ustedes son	*you are* (pl)
usted es	*you are* (pol)	ellos, ellas son	*they are* (m/f)
él, ella es	*he, she is*		

To say *it is*, as in *It is a hotel*, use the word **es** on its own: **Es un hotel.**

7 Negative and interrogative sentences

Negative sentences are formed by placing **no** before the verb:

Soy británico.	*I am British.*
No soy irlandés.	*I am not Irish.*

Interrogative sentences can be formed in three ways:

a By reversing the word order in the sentence.

Usted es boliviano.	*You are Bolivian.*
¿Es usted boliviano?	*Are you Bolivian?*

b By using the same word order as for a statement, but with a rising intonation.

¿Usted es ecuatoriana?	*Are you Ecuadorean?*

c By using the word ¿**verdad**? (Lit. *true*) or the word ¿**no**? at the end of the statement.

Tú eres uruguayo, ¿verdad?	*You are Uruguayan, aren't you?*
Ella es cubana, ¿no?	*She is Cuban, isn't she?*

Note that in writing, interrogative sentences carry two question marks, one at the beginning and one at the end of the sentence.

8 Written accent on question words

Note that question words such as **¿dónde?** *where?*, **¿cuál?** *what?*, *which?* carry a written accent.

9 Numbers

0	cero	21	veintiuno
1	uno	22	veintidós
2	dos	23	veintitrés
3	tres	24	venticuatro
4	cuatro	25	veinticinco
5	cinco	26	veintiséis
6	seis	27	veintisiete
7	siete	28	veintiocho
8	ocho	29	veintinueve
9	nueve	30	treinta
10	diez	31	treinta y uno
11	once	32	treinta y dos
12	doce	40	cuarenta
13	trece	45	cuarenta y cinco
14	catorce	50	cincuenta
15	quince		
16	dieciséis		
17	diecisiete		
18	dieciocho		
19	diecinueve		
20	veinte		

Before a masculine noun **uno** becomes **un** and before a feminine noun **una**:

un señor	*one man*
una señora	*one woman*

Note that only numbers from 21 to 29 are written as a single word in Spanish.

Practice

1 It is early morning and you arrive in a hotel in Mexico where there is a room booked in your name. Use the guidelines in English to complete this conversation with the hotel receptionist.

Usted	*Say good morning.*
Recepcionista	Buenos días. A sus órdenes.
Usted	*Say you have a reservation.*
Recepcionista	¿Cuál es su nombre, por favor?
Usted	*Give your name.*
Recepcionista	Sí, es la habitación número veinte.
Usted	*Say thank you.*

2   You are in the bar waiting to meet señora Vargas, whom you have not met before, when a gentleman approaches you. He has obviously mistaken you for someone else. Use the guidelines to complete your part of the conversation.

Señor	Buenas tardes.
Usted	*Say good afternoon.*
Señor	¿Es usted Emilio/a Zapata?
Usted	*No, say you are not Emilio/a Zapata. Say who you are.*
Señor	Disculpe.
Usted	*Say that is all right.*

3   Here comes the person you think you are expecting.

Señora Vargas	Disculpe, ¿cuál es su nombre?
Usted	*Say your name and where you are from.*
Señora Vargas	Yo soy Isabel Vargas, de Veracruz.
Usted	*Say pleased to meet you.*
Señora Vargas	Encantada.
Usted	*Ask señora Vargas to sit down.*
Señora Vargas	Gracias.

4   Here is an informal situation. You are at a party when a stranger approaches you and starts a conversation. Reply accordingly.

Desconocido/a	Disculpa, ¿eres americano/a?
Usted	. . .
Desconocido/a	¡Ah! ¿Y de qué ciudad eres?
Usted	. . .
Desconocido/a	¿Cómo te llamas?
Usted	. . .
Desconocido/a	Me llamo Mario.
Usted	. . .
Desconocido/a	El gusto es mío.

el gusto es mío

| **desconocido/a** | *stranger* |
| **el gusto es mío** | *the pleasure is mine* |

5   You are on your first visit to Latin America and you want to meet people, so be prepared to use greetings and ask some simple questions to make the first contacts. How would you say the following in Spanish? (Use the polite form.)

a   Good afternoon.
b   What is your name?
c   Where are you from?
d   Are you Mexican?
e   What part of Mexico are you from?

6   Read the sentence here written by Roberto Vera about himself, and then write a similar line about yourself.

mi nombre es Roberto Vera, soy colombiano, de Bogotá.

7   Read this form with information about Ana González, and the line which follows.

Nombre:	Ana María
Apellidos:	González Ríos
Nacionalidad:	mexicana
Dirección:	calle Juárez 34, Monterrey

Ana María González Ríos es mexicana. Ana María es de Monterrey.

Use the information in this box to write a similar statement about Pablo Miranda Frías.

Nombre:	Pablo
Apellidos:	Miranda Frías
Nacionalidad:	venezolano
Dirección:	calle Bolívar 65, Caracas

el apellido	*surname*
la nacionalidad	*nationality*
la dirección	*address*

ℹ Surnames

In Spain and in the Spanish-speaking countries of Latin America, people have two surnames. The first surname is that of their father, the second is their mother's. In Ana María's case above, for example, **González** is her father's first surname and **Ríos** is her mother's first surname. The second surname is used in more formal and official situations. Married women add their husband's first surname, preceded by the word **de** (of), to their own name or first surname. For example, if Ana María marries a señor Barros, she will be called **Ana María de Barros** or **Ana María González de Barros**.

▶ 8 Here are two recorded interviews with Mexican women and a brief introduction by someone from Panama. If you are using the recording, listen to each piece as many times as you want until you are confident that you understand what is being said. Then listen again, and as you do so, try to answer the questions below. If you are not using the recording, read the transcripts on page 231, then answer the questions. First study these new words:

el país	country	**para servirle**	at your service

a   What part of Mexico is Initia Muñoz García from?
b   What sentence has been used to express the following: *What country are you from?*
c   What part of Mexico is Clotilde Montalvo Rodríguez from?
d   What sentence has been used to express the following: *Where are you from?*
e   What city is Elizabeth from?
f   How does she express the following: *My name is Elizabeth?*

02

¿dónde está?

where is it?

In this unit you will learn
- how to ask and say where places are
- how to ask and answer questions regarding the existence of something
- how to ask people how they are and say how you are

▶1 En la recepción *In the reception*

Carmen, a Mexican, has come to see her friend Gloria Martín at her hotel in Mexico City. Gloria is from Colombia. Key phrases here are **¿cuál es ...?** *which is ...?* and **está en ...** *she is in ...*

Carmen	Buenos días. ¿Cuál es la habitación de la señorita Gloria Martín, por favor?
Recepcionista	Un momentito. (*Looking at the register*.) La señorita Martín está en la habitación número cincuenta, en el quinto piso. Allí está el elevador.
Carmen	Gracias. Muy amable.

un momentito	*just a moment*
el piso	*floor*
quinto/a	*fifth*
allí	*(over) there*
el elevador / ascensor	*lift*
muy amable	*that's very kind*

▶2 En la habitación número cincuenta *In room fifty*

Gloria greets her friend Carmen. Key phrases here are **¿Cómo estás?** *How are you?*, **¿Cómo están?** *How are they?*, **Estoy bien** *I'm fine* (lit. *well*), **Están muy bien** *They are very well*.

Gloria	Hola, Carmen. ¿Cómo estás?
Carmen	Estoy bien, gracias. ¿Y tú, cómo estás?
Gloria	Muy bien. Siéntate. Me alegro mucho de verte otra vez.
Carmen	Yo también.
Gloria	¿Cómo están tus papás?
Carmen	Están muy bien.

hola	hello
siéntate	sit down (fam)
me alegro mucho de verte	I am very glad to see you (fam)
otra vez	again
también	too, also
tus	your (fam, pl)
los papás / padres	parents

▶3 ¿Dónde está la oficina? *Where is the office?*

Señor Alonso, a Colombian, has come to see señor Martínez, a Mexican businessman, at his office in Mexico City. A key phrase here is **¿dónde está ...?** *where is ...?*

Señor Alonso	Buenas tardes. ¿Dónde está la oficina del señor Martínez, por favor?
Recepcionista	La oficina del señor Martínez está al final del pasillo, a la izquierda.
Señor Alonso	Gracias.
Recepcionista	De nada.

What phrase has been used in the dialogue to say *Señor Martínez's office?*

la oficina	office
al final de	at the end of
el pasillo	corridor
a la izquierda	on the left
de nada	don't mention it

▶4 En la oficina del señor Martínez *In señor Martínez's office*

Señor Martínez greets señor Alonso. Note here the formal greetings **¿Cómo le va? ¿Cómo está?** *How are you?*

Señor Martínez	¡Señor Alonso, buenas tardes!
Señor Alonso	Buenas tardes, señor Martínez.
Señor Martínez	Siéntese, por favor. Me alegro mucho de verlo. ¿Cómo le va?

| Señor Alonso | Bien, gracias. ¿Y usted, cómo está? |
| Señor Martínez | Muy bien, gracias. |

What expression does señor Martínez use to say *How are you?*

| **me alegro mucho de verlo** | *I am very glad to see you* (pol) |

▶ 5 Está a dos cuadras de aquí *It is two blocks from here*

At the hotel Las Américas (n° 2 on the map), a Mexican visitor asks the receptionist if there is an underground station, **una estación de metro**, nearby, **por aquí**. A key word in this dialogue is **hay**, meaning *there is, is there?* or *there are, are there?*

Señorita	Buenas tardes.
Recepcionista	Buenas tardes, señorita. A sus órdenes.
Señorita	¿Hay una estación de metro por aquí?
Recepcionista	Sí, hay una, la estación de Cuauhtemoc. Está a dos cuadras de aquí, a la derecha, cerca del monumento a Cuauhtemoc.
Señorita	Muchas gracias. Muy amable.
Recepcionista	Para servirle. ¡Que le vaya bien!

a sus órdenes.	*may I help you?*
la cuadra	*block*
a la derecha	*on the right*
muy amable	*very kind*
cerca	*near*
para servirle	*don't mention it*
¡que le vaya bien!	*have a nice day!*

Say it in Spanish

How would you say the following in Spanish? Study the dialogue again if necessary.

a Is there a bureau de change (**una casa de cambio**) nearby?
b Is there a bank (**un banco**) nearby?
c It is three blocks from here, on the left.
d It is four blocks from here, on the right.

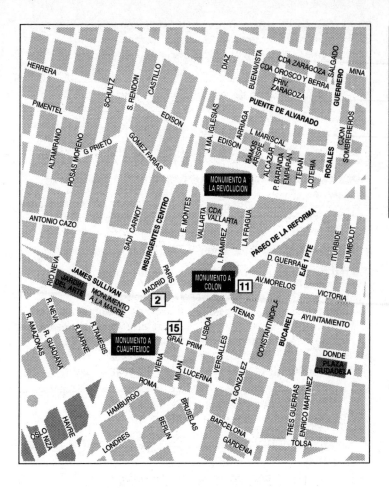

ℹ️ Formality

Notice the use of phrases such as **a sus órdenes** *at your service*, **para servirle** lit. *at your service*, and **¡Que le vaya bien!** *Have a nice day!* Latin Americans, on the whole, and Mexicans in particular, are very polite, and you will encounter many such phrases when meeting Latin American people. Some of these phrases, like those above, are not used in Spain, where speech tends to be rather informal.

Key phrases

Asking and saying where places are

¿Dónde está la oficina / la habitación?	*Where is the office / room?*
Está al final del pasillo.	*It is at the end of the corridor.*
Está en el quinto piso.	*It is on the fifth floor.*
Está a la derecha / izquierda.	*It is on the right/left.*
Está a cinco cuadras / minutos de aquí.	*It is five blocks / minutes from here.*

Asking and answering questions regarding the existence of something

¿Hay una estación/un banco por aquí?	*Is there a station / bank nearby?*
Hay una/uno cerca de aquí.	*There is one near here.*

Asking people how they are and saying how you are

¿Cómo estás/está? (fam/pol)	*How are you?*
¿Cómo te / le va? (fam/pol)	
Estoy (muy) bien.	*I am fine / (very) well.*
¿Cómo están tus papás / padres?	*How are your parents?*
Están (muy) bien.	*They are (very) well.*

Grammar

1 Definite article: *los, las* the (pl), and the plural of nouns

a In Unit 1 you learned the use of **el** and **la** *the* (m / f), with singular nouns. With plural nouns, you use **los** for masculine and **las** for feminine.

el señor	*the gentleman*	**los** señores	*the gentlemen*
la señora	*the lady*	**las** señoras	*the ladies*

b Most nouns form the plural by adding –s.

el nombre	*the name*	**los** nombres	*the names*
la oficina	*the office*	**las** oficinas	*the offices*

c Nouns ending in a consonant add –es.

el hotel	*the hotel*	**los** hoteles	*the hotels*
la habitación	*the room*	**las** habitaciones	*the rooms*

(See **Pronunciation**, p. 226, for notes on **Stress and accentuation**)

d Masculine nouns which refer to people may refer to both sexes in the plural.

el padre	*father*	**los** padres	*parents*
el hermano	*brother*	**los** hermanos	*brothers* or *brothers and sisters*

2 *Del (de + el), al (a + el)*

In the spoken and written language, **de** + **el** becomes **del** and **a** + **el** becomes **al**.

la casa **del** señor García	*señor García's house*
al final del pasillo	*at the end of the corridor*
al museo	*to the museum*

3 *Estar to be*

In Unit 1 you learned the use of **ser** *to be,* to give personal information such as nationality, and place of origin, for example **Soy argentino, soy de Buenos Aires** *I'm Argentinian, I'm from Buenos Aires.* But Spanish has another verb meaning *to be,* which is **estar.** Try learning each use separately to avoid mixing them up. The notes below explain two main uses of **estar.**

a Using **estar** to express location and distance

Location and distance are normally expressed with **estar**

El elevador / ascensor **está** allí.	*The lift is there.*
Está a dos cuadras de aquí.	*It is two blocks from here.*

a Using **estar** to refer to a state or condition

To ask and answer questions about a state or condition, for example someone's health, use **estar.**

¿Cómo estás (tú)/está (usted)?	*How are you?*
Estoy **bien, gracias.**	*I'm fine, thank you.*

4 The present tense of *estar*

The following are the present tense forms of **estar.**

yo estoy	*I am*	nosotros/as estamos	*we are* (m/f)
tú estás	*you are* (fam, sing)	ustedes están	*you are* (pl)
usted está	*you are* (pol, sing)	ellos/as están	*they are* (m/f)
él, ella está	*he, she, it is*		

Consider again the uses of **estar** in the dialogues and look at the examples listed under **Key phrases.**

5 *Hay* there is, there are

To say *there is* or *there are* and to ask questions regarding the existence of something, Spanish uses the single word **hay**, from the auxiliary verb **haber**.

¿**Hay** una estación de metro por aquí?	*Is there an underground station nearby?*
Sí, **hay** una.	*Yes, there is one.*
¿**Hay** habitaciones?	*Are there any rooms?*
No **hay**.	*There aren't any.*

6 Diminutives

Diminutives are very frequently used in Latin America, and you will need to recognize them when you hear them. Their main function is to give a more friendly tone to words or statements. Diminutives are usually formed with **-ito** (m) or **-ita** (f) added to the word, for example:

un rato – un ra**tito**	*a while*
ahora – aho**rita**	*now, straight away*
(very frequent in Mexico and other countries)	

Some words undergo other changes, for example:

un café – un cafe**cito**	*a coffee*
un poco – un po**quito**	*a little*

In some regions of Latin America you will hear the endings **-ico** or **-ica** instead of **-ito** and **-ita**, for example:

un momento – un momen**tico**	*moment*

7 Numbers

50	cincuenta	300	trescientos
60	sesenta	400	cuatrocientos
70	setenta	500	quinientos
80	ochenta	600	seiscientos
90	noventa	700	setecientos
100	cien	800	ochocientos
101	ciento uno	900	novecientos
200	doscientos	1000	mil
210	doscientos diez	1501	mil quinientos uno
		2000	dos mil
1.000.000	un millón		
2.000.000	dos millones		

Numbers which finish in -cientos, e.g. **doscientos, trescientos,** must change according to the gender of the noun which follows.

el peso (Latin Am. currency) doscien**tos** pesos
la libra (pound) doscien**tas** libras
el dólar (dollar) doscien**tos** dólares
Cien (*one hundred*) does not change, e.g. cien pesos.

Note the way in which years are read in Spanish:

1850 mil ochocientos cincuenta
1999 mil novecientos noventa y nueve
2003 dos mil tres

Ordinal numbers (1st to 6th)			
primero/a	**1st**	cuarto/a	**4th**
segundo/a	**2nd**	quinto/a	**5th**
tercero/a	**3rd**	sexto/a	**6th**

Ordinal numbers function as adjectives, therefore they must agree in gender (m/f) and number (s/pl) with the word they refer to, for example **el segundo piso** *the second floor*, **la segunda cuadra** *the second block*, **las primeras cuadras** *the first few blocks*. Before a masculine noun, **primero** changes to **primer**, and **tercero** to **tercer**, for example **el primer / tercer piso** *the first / third floor*.

Practice

1 A visitor has come to see a hotel guest.

Visita ¿Cuál es la habitación del señor Valdés, por favor?
Recepcionista El señor Valdés está en la habitación trescientos diez, en el tercer piso.
Visita Gracias.

Make up similar dialogues using the information below. You will find numbers on pages 19 and 30.

NOMBRE	HABITACIÓN	PISO
Sra. Marta Molina	220	2º
Sr. Cristóbal Salas	430	4º
Srta. Rosa Chandía	550	5º

2 On a visit to Mexico, you meet Carmen, a Mexican friend you have not seen for some time. Complete your part of the conversation with her, using the familiar form.

Ud.	*Say hello to your friend and ask her how she is.*
Carmen	Estoy bien, gracias. Y tú, ¿cómo estás?
Ud.	*Say you are very well. Ask her to sit down and say you are very glad to see her again.*
Carmen	Yo también.
Ud.	*You have met her parents; ask her how they are.*
Carmen	Están muy bien, gracias.

3 Señora Ramírez, a Latin American businesswoman, is visiting your company. She has come to see you in your office. Complete your part of this conversation with her, using the polite form.

Ud.	*Say good morning to her; ask her how she is.*
Sra. Ramírez	Yo estoy muy bien, gracias. Y usted, ¿cómo está?
Ud.	*Say you're fine; thank her. Ask her to sit down and say you are very glad to see her.*

4 Look at this dialogue between a receptionist and a hotel guest in Mexico.

Señor	Disculpe, ¿dónde están los teléfonos, por favor?
Recepcionista	Están al final del pasillo, a la izquierda, al lado del bar.
Señor	Gracias.
Recepcionista	Para servirle.

Now look at the plan of a hotel and make up similar dialogues. Choose appropriate words and phrases from the dialogue and from those listed below.

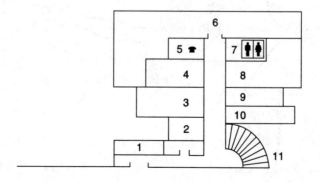

al lado de . . .	next to . . .
a la derecha	on the right
entre . . . y . . .	between . . . and . . .
frente a . . .	opposite . . .
pasado el / la . . .	past the . . .
antes de . . .	before . . .

KEY:
1 La recepción *reception*
2 El elevador *lift*
3 La agencia de viajes *travel agency*
4 El bar *bar*
5 Los teléfonos *telephones*
6 El comedor *dining-room*
7 Los baños *toilets*
8 El café *café*
9 La peluquería *hairdresser's*
10 La tienda de regalos *gift shop*
11 Las escaleras *stairs*

▶ 5 You will need to understand what people say to you when you inquire about a place or ask for directions. Listen to these conversations, then check your understanding by answering the questions.

In the first exchange, a man is seeking help from a young lady. Learn this new phrase, then listen to the conversation and answer the questions.

una casa de cambio (f)   *bureau de change*

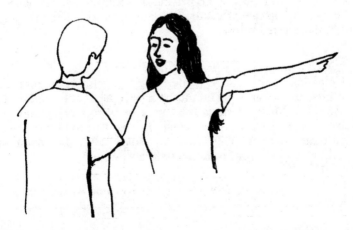

a What is the man looking for?
b Where can he find one?
c How far is it?

In the second exchange, señor Ramos, a Colombian businessman, has come to see señor Silva at his office in Mexico City. Listen to the conversation and answer these questions.

d Where is señor Silva?
e What number is his office?
f On which floor is it?
g Where exactly is it?

6 You are visiting a Latin American city for the first time and you need to find your way around. What questions would you need to ask to get these replies?

a Sí, hay una. La estación de Insurgentes.
b Está a cuatro cuadras de aquí.
c Sí, hay uno. El Hotel Reforma.
d No, está cerca. A cinco minutos de aquí.
e El Banco Nacional está en la plaza.
f La calle Panuco está a cinco cuadras de aquí.

el minuto	*minute*
el banco	*bank*
la calle	*street*

7 Now you are going to hear a conversation between a Colombian and a Chilean tourist who is visiting Bogotá, the capital of Colombia. The tourist is looking for the station (**la estación**). Most streets in the centre of Bogotá carry numbers instead of names: streets going in one direction are called **carreras**, those running across are called **calles**. The questions below will help you to check comprehension.

a pie	*on foot*	**más o menos**	*more or less*

True or false? ¿Verdadero o falso?

a La estación está en la calle dieciséis.
b Está al final de la carrera diecisiete.
c Está a quince minutos a pie, aproximadamente.

▶ **8** You are going to hear part of a conversation with Jorge Vera, a Mexican from Veracruz. Jorge introduces himself as the director of a modern languages centre. Listen to the conversation or, if you are not using the recording, read the transcript on page 232, then answer the questions below. First, familiarize yourself with these key words and then answer the questions below.

el centro de lenguas modernas	*modern languages centre*
localizado	*situated*
media cuadra	*half a block*
una y media cuadra	*one and a half blocks*
es decir	*that is to say*
el parque	*park*

a How far is the modern languages centre from the main street?
b How far is it from the main park?

9 You are planning to travel to Mexico and before you do so you decide to read a little about the country. Below is a description of Mexico City, known also as D.F. (Federal District). The following key words will help you to understand the text. Try to get the gist of it rather than translate it word for word. After you have read the passage answer the questions that follow.

rodeada	*surrounded*
la montaña	*mountain*
el valle	*valley*
goza de	*it enjoys*
se encuentran	*are situated*
como	*such as*
mundialmente	*world* (adj)
la ciudad	*city*
la mezcla	*mixture*
amplia	*wide*
el barrio	*district*
el mercado	*market*
el edificio	*building*
la iglesia	*church*

MÉXICO D.F.

La capital de México, rodeada de montañas, está situada en un valle de 2.240 m de altitud. Goza de una intensa vida cultural y artística, es el centro intelectual de toda Hispanoamérica. Aquí se encuentran lugares históricos como el Zócalo, el Palacio Nacional, la Catedral Metropolitana, la capital azteca de Tenochtitlán o el mundialmente famoso Museo Nacional de Antropología.

Esta ciudad de 21 millones de habitantes es una mezcla del pasado y del presente. Es una ciudad moderna, con amplias avenidas y plazas animadas, barrios elegantes, mercados populares, edificios futuristas, residencias coloniales e iglesias barrocas.

Answer these questions in English:

a Where is the capital of Mexico situated?
b What does the text say about the city's cultural and artistic life?
c How does the text describe the city itself?

03

ocho abren a las ocho

they open at eight

In this unit you will learn
- how to ask and tell the time
- how to talk about opening and closing times
- how to talk about meal times

▶1 ¿Qué hora es? *What time is it?*

Anne Barker, an English visitor who has just arrived in Mexico, wants to set her watch by the local time. She asks the hotel receptionist what time it is. The key phrase here is ¿**Qué hora es?** *What time is it?*

Anne Barker	Buenos días.
Recepcionista	Buenos días, señora.
Anne Barker	¿Qué hora es, por favor?
Recepcionista	Son las ocho y media.
Anne Barker	Gracias.
Recepcionista	De nada.

> **son las ocho y media** *it's half past eight*

Ask and say the time

a 2.30
b 6.30
c 10.30

For other times see Key phrases and paragraph 1 of Grammar.

▶2 ¿Qué hora tiene usted? *What time do you make it?*

Another visitor is asking the time.

Señora	Perdón, ¿qué hora tiene usted?
Recepcionista	Son diez para las nueve.
Señora	Gracias.
Recepcionista	Para servirle.

> **¿qué hora tiene usted?**
> *what time do you have/make it?*
> **son diez para la nueve/las nueve menos diez**
> *it's ten to nine*

▶3 Abren a las ocho *They open at eight*

A hotel guest has come down for breakfast, but the restaurant is closed. Key phrases here are **Está cerrado** *It is closed,* **¿A qué hora abren?** *What time do they open?,* **Dentro de ...** *Within ...*

Señorita	¿Dónde está el restaurante, por favor?
Recepcionista	(pointing) Está ahí, señorita, pero está cerrado.
Señorita	¿A qué hora abren?
Recepcionista	Abren a las ocho. Dentro de cinco minutos.
Señorita	Gracias. Muy amable.

ahí	*there*	**los minutos**	*minutes*
a las (ocho)	*at (eight)*	**¿a qué hora?**	*at what time?*

Ask and say it in Spanish

Example: el bar – 10.00

¿A qué hora abren el bar? Abren a las diez.

a el banco (*bank*) – 9.00
b el museo (*museum*)- 9.30
c la oficina de turismo (*tourist office*) – 10.00

▶4 En la tienda de regalos *In the gift shop*

A visitor needs to buy some presents to take home. He asks the shop assistant in the gift shop what time they close. Key words and phrases here are **¿A qué hora cierran?** *What time do you / they close?* and **cerramos** *we close.*

Cliente	Perdón, ¿a qué hora cierran?
Dependienta	Hoy cerramos a las siete y cuarto.
Cliente	Gracias.

la tienda	*shop*
el regalo	*gift, present*
a las siete y cuarto	*at a quarter past seven*

Ask in Spanish

Example: las tiendas
¿A qué hora cierran las tiendas?

a los bancos
b los museos
c las casas de cambio

▶5 ¿A qué hora es la cena? *What time is dinner?*

Another visitor is inquiring about dinner time.

Recepcionista	Buenas tardes, señorita.
Señorita	¿A qué hora es la cena, por favor?
Recepcionista	Es a las nueve.
Señorita	Y el restaurante, ¿dónde está?
Recepcionista	Está al fondo del pasillo.
Señorita	Muchas gracias.
Recepcionista	Para servirle.

la cena	*dinner*
al fondo	*at the end, at the bottom*

Ask and answer in Spanish

Example: la cena – 9.00
¿A qué hora es la cena? – Es a las nueve.

a el desayuno (*breakfast*) – 7.30
b el almuerzo (*lunch*) – 1.00
c la salida (*departure*) – 8.00

▶6 ¿A qué hora desayunas? *What time do you have breakfast?*

Raúl and Rosa, two Mexicans, talk about their meals. Key words and phrases here are **tomar el desayuno** *to have breakfast*, **almorzar** *to have lunch*, **comer** *to eat*.

Raúl ¿A qué hora tomas el desayuno normalmente?
Rosa A las ocho y media. ¿Y tú?
Raúl Yo tomo el desayuno a las siete.
Rosa ¡Qué temprano! ¿Y a qué hora almuerzas?
Raúl Entre las doce y media y la una.
Rosa Yo almuerzo a las dos.
Raúl ¿Almuerzas en casa?
Rosa Normalmente sí, ¿y tú?
Raúl Yo no, yo como en la universidad.

normalmente	*normally*
¡qué temprano!	*how early!*
en casa	*at home*
la universidad	*university*
tomar (el) desayuno / desayunar	*to have breakfast*

Now, read the the dialogue and answer these question in English

a What time does Rosa normally have breakfast?
b And Raúl?
c What time does Raúl normally have lunch?
d Where does Rosa normally have lunch?

ℹ️ Main meals

Most Latin Americans have a light **desayuno** (*breakfast*), consisting of **café** and **tostadas** or **pan tostado** (*coffee and toast*), not very different from what you might have at home. But in some countries, like Mexico, breakfast is often a more substantial meal. **El almuerzo** (*lunch*) is the main meal in Latin America, and in small towns people usually go home for lunch. In big cities, restaurants normally offer quick, inexpensive meals for working people. If this is what you want, ask for **el menú del día** or **el plato del día** (*the day's menu*), or **la comida corrida** in Mexico. The alternative is to eat **a la carta** (choose from the menu), which will cost you much more. **La cena** (*dinner*) is a light meal, often consisting of **una sopa** (*soup*), **una ensalada** (*salad*), or **un sandwich**.

The names associated with meals vary somewhat from region to region. *To have breakfast* is **desayunar** in some places and **tomar (el) desayuno** in others. The word for *lunch* is **la comida** in certain countries, for example Mexico, where **el almuerzo** is a mid-morning snack. In some regions **la comida** stands for the evening meal, known also as **la cena** or **la merienda**.

Key phrases

Asking and telling the time

¿Qué hora es / tiene?	*What time is it / do you make it?*
Es la una / Son las dos.	*It's one o'clock / two o'clock.*
Son las cinco y cuarto.	*It's a quarter past five.*
Son un cuarto para las seis.	*It's a quarter to six.*
Son las seis menos cuarto.	
Son las ocho y media.	*It's half past eight.*
Son las nueve (y) veinte.	*It's twenty past nine.*
Son diez para las diez.	*It's ten to ten.*
Son las diez menos diez.	

Talking about opening and closing times

¿A qué hora abren / cierran?	*What time do you / they open / close?*
Abrimos / abren a las nueve.	*We / they open at nine.*
Cerramos / cierran a las siete.	*We / they close at seven.*
Está cerrado(a) / abierto(a) (m/f)	*It's open / closed.*

Talking about meal times

¿A qué hora es el desayuno / el almuerzo / la cena?	What time is breakfast / lunch / dinner?
Es a las siete / la una / las ocho.	It's at seven / one / eight o'clock.
¿A qué hora tomas el desayuno / desayunas? (fam)	What time do you have breakfast?
Tomo el desayuno / desayuno a las siete.	I have breakfast at seven.
¿A qué hora almuerzas / cenas? (fam)	What time do you have lunch / dinner?
Almuerzo/ceno a la una / las nueve.	I have lunch/dinner at one / nine.

Grammar

1 Asking and telling the time

To ask and tell the time, use **ser**, *to be.*

¿Qué hora **es**?	*What time is it?*
Es la una / la una y cuarto.	*It's one o'clock / a quarter past one.*
Es la una y media.	*It's half past one.*
Son las dos / tres menos diez.	*It's two o'clock / ten to three.*
Son las cinco / seis y cuarto.	*It's five o'clock / a quarter past six.*

In some countries you will hear the question **¿Qué horas son?** for **¿Qué hora es?** An alternative way of asking the time is to use **tener** *to have,* for example **¿Tiene hora?** *Have you got the time?* Some Latin American countries, among them Mexico and Chile, use phrases such as **Son (un) cuarto para las seis, Son veinte para las dos,** instead of **Son las seis menos cuarto, Son las dos menos veinte** *It's a quarter to six, It's twenty to two.*

2 At what time?

Notice also the use of **ser** in the following examples:

¿A qué hora es el desayuno?	*What time is breakfast?*
Es a las ocho.	*It's at eight o'clock.*

When we inquire about the time a place opens or closes or, more generally, about the time something takes place, the phrase **¿qué** hora? must always be preceded by the preposition **a**: **¿A qué hora . . . ?**

3 The days of the week

Días de la semana	*Days of the week*		
lunes	*Monday*	viernes	*Friday*
martes	*Tuesday*	sábado	*Saturday*
miércoles	*Wednesday*	domingo	*Sunday*
jueves	*Thursday*		

Notice that in Spanish the days of the week are written with small letters. To say *on Monday*, *on Tuesday*, etc., use the word **el** (*the*, m.sing): **el lunes**, **el martes**. To say *Mondays*, *Tuesdays*, etc., use the word **los** (*the*, m/pl): **los lunes**, **los martes**. To say *Today / Tomorrow is Friday / Saturday*, etc., use phrases like these: **Hoy es viernes**, **Mañana es sábado**. To ask what day it is today, say **¿Qué día es hoy?**

4 Three kinds of verbs

According to the ending of the infinitive (or dictionary form of the verb), Spanish verbs may be grouped into three main categories or conjugations: **-ar** (or first conjugation), **-er** (second conjugation) and **-ir** (or third conjugation). For example:

tomar	*to take*
comer	*to eat*
abrir	*to open*

In Spanish, there are regular and irregular verbs. Regular verbs are those that follow a fixed pattern, which varies only according to certain grammatical categories, such as the ending of the infinitive (see above), *person*, for instance **yo** (*I*), **tú** (*you*, fam), **él** (*he*) (see grammar, Unit 1) or *tense*, for example present tense, future tense. Irregular verbs are those that do not follow a fixed pattern in their conjugation, for example **ser** *to be*.

5 The present tense

-ar verbs

In the present tense, all regular **-ar** verbs follow this pattern:

tomar	to take
yo tom**o**	*I take*
tú tom**as**	*you take* (fam, sing)
Ud. tom**a**	*you take* (pol, sing)
él, ella tom**a**	*he, she, it takes*
nosotros/as tom**amos**	*we take*
Uds., ellos, ellas tom**an**	*you take* (pl), *they take*

¿A qué hora tomas el desayuno? *What time do you have breakfast?*

Tomo el desayuno a las ocho. *I have breakfast at eight.*

-er verbs

Regular -er verbs are conjugated in the following way:

comer	to eat
yo com**o**	*I eat*
tú com**es**	*you eat* (fam, sing)
Ud. com**e**	*you eat* (pol, sing)
él, ella com**e**	*he, she, it eats*
nosotros/as com**emos**	*we eat*
Uds., ellos, ellas com**en**	*you eat* (pl), *they eat*

Como en la universidad. *I eat in the university.*

Rosa come en casa. *Rosa eats at home.*

-ir verbs

Regular -ir verbs are conjugated like this:

abrir	to open
yo abr**o**	*I open*
tú abr**es**	*you open* (fam, sing)
Ud. abr**e**	*you open* (pol, sing)
él, ella abr**e**	*he, she, it opens*
nosotros/as abr**imos**	*we open*
Uds., ellos, ellas abr**en**	*you open* (pl), *they open*

¿A qué hora abren? *What time do they open?*

Abrimos a las ocho. *We open at eight.*

Notice that the endings for -er and -ir verbs are the same, except in the first person plural **nosotros**.

6 Stem-changing verbs: *e > ie* and *o > ue*

Certain verbs undergo a change in the stem (the infinitive minus its ending). Stem-changing verbs (also known as radical-changing verbs) have the same endings as regular verbs. **Cerrar** (*to close*) is a stem-changing verb, in which -e changes into -ie. Notice that this change occurs only when the stem is stressed, therefore verb forms corresponding to **nosotros** (*we*) (**cerramos**, *we close*) are not affected by it.

cierro	*I close*
cierras	*you close* (fam, sing)
cierra	*you close* (pol, sing), *he, she, it closes*
cierran	*you close* (pl), *they close*

In later units you will encounter other verbs which change in the same way as **cerrar**.

Almorzar *to have lunch* is also a stem-changing verb, in which -o changes into -ue.

almuerzo	*I have lunch*
almuerzas	*you have lunch* (fam, sing)
almuerza	*you have lunch* (pol, sing), *he, she has lunch*
almuerzan	*you have lunch* (pl), *they have lunch*

In later units you will encounter other verbs which change in the same way as **almorzar**.

Practice

1   Ask and say the time, following the example.

¿Qué hora es? Son las seis y veinte.

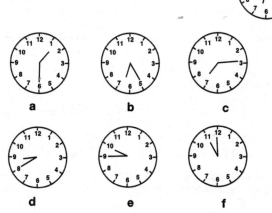

a   b   c

d   e   f

2 You are in Chile on business and want to make several phone calls abroad, so you need to be aware of time differences. Look at the information below and then answer the questions giving the correct time.

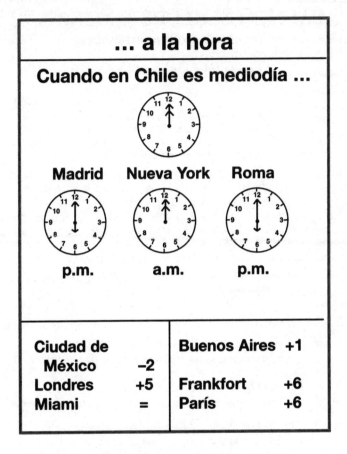

... a la hora

Cuando en Chile es mediodía ...

Madrid   Nueva York   Roma

p.m.   a.m.   p.m.

Ciudad de México	–2	Buenos Aires	+1
Londres	+5	Frankfort	+6
Miami	=	París	+6

En Chile es mediodía (*midday*).

a ¿Qué hora es en la Ciudad de México?
b ¿Qué hora es en Londres?
c ¿Qué hora es en Buenos Aires?
d ¿Qué hora es en París?

3 On your next visit to Mexico, don't miss the **Ballet Folklórico Mexicano**, a well-known group which presents the best of Mexican music and dance. Look at this advertisement for the ballet and the vocabulary which follows. Then answer the questions below.

BALLET FOLKLÓRICO MEXICANO

Dirección: Guillermo González

TEATRO DE LA DANZA

Detrás del Auditorio Nacional

ENERO | Jueves 14 y Viernes 15 / 20:00 hrs.
Sábado 16 / 19:00 hrs Domingo 17 / 12:00 hrs

In advertisements such as the one above, at railway stations, airports, on the radio, and so on, Spanish uses the 24-hour clock. Colloquially, however, people use phrases like the following to distinguish between a.m. and p.m.: **Son las dos de la tarde** *It's two o'clock in the afternoon*, **A las diez de la noche** *At ten o'clock at night*.

el teatro	*theatre*		**enero**	*January*
la danza	*dance*		**detrás**	*behind*

Read the advertisement again and answer these questions in Spanish.

a ¿Dónde está el Teatro de la Danza?
b ¿Cuántas funciones (*performances*) hay el viernes 15 (quince)?
c ¿A qué hora es la función el viernes?
d ¿A qué hora es la función el domingo 17 (diecisiete)?

4 Ask what time these places open and close.

la tienda	*shop*		**el correo**	*post office*
el supermercado	*supermarket*		**el museo**	*museum*

a Ask what time the shops open.
b Ask what time the supermarket opens.
c Ask what time the post office closes.
d Ask what time the museums close.

▶ 5 Jorge Vera from Mexico was asked what time the shops open in Veracruz, his home town. Listen to what he says, then answer the questions. Here are some key words used by Jorge:

la mañana	*morning*	para trabajar	*to work*
entonces	*then*	hasta	*until*
trabajan	*they work*		

Is it true or false? (**¿verdadero o falso?**)

a Las tiendas abren a las ocho y media de la mañana.
b Las tiendas cierran entre una y cuatro.
c En la noche cierran a las siete.

6 You are on holiday in a South American country and you need to change some money. It is 2.30 p.m. and the nearest bureau de change (**casa de cambio**), La Internacional, which is two blocks from your hotel, does not open until 4.00. Use the information to write a dialogue similar to the one below between yourself and a hotel receptionist.

Señorita	Disculpe, ¿qué hora tiene, por favor?
Recepcionista	Es un cuarto para las nueve. / Son las nueve menos cuarto.
Señorita	¿A qué hora abren los bancos?
Recepcionista	Abren a las nueve.
Señorita	¿Hay un banco por aquí?
Recepcionista	Sí, el Banco de la Nación está en la esquina.
Señorita	Muchas gracias. Muy amable.
Recepcionista	Para servirle. ¡Que le vaya bien!

disculpe	*excuse me*	en la esquina	*on the corner*

7 A Spanish-speaking friend is asking you what time you have your meals. Answer his questions.

a ¿A qué hora tomas el desayuno / desayunas normalmente?
b ¿Y a qué hora almuerzas?
c ¿Dónde almuerzas?
d ¿Cenas muy tarde? ¿A qué hora?

cenar	*to have dinner*	muy tarde	*very late*

▶ 8 Jorge Vera and Clotilde Montalvo (Coty) were asked about the main meals and their times in Mexico, their country. Listen to both conversations, and note the differences in the information given by each of them. Then answer the questions below. These key words and phrases will help you to understand:

dime	*tell me*
la comida	*meal*
¿cuál es el horario?	*what are the times?*
cada	*each*
opcionalmente	*alternatively*
podríamos llamarle	*we could call it*
poscena	*after-dinner snack*
que puede ser	*which can be*
si nos acostamos tarde	*if we go to bed late*
la de mediodía	*the midday one*
que varía	*which varies*
en que se toma	*when it is taken*
en adelante	*onwards*
temprano	*early*

Now answer these questions in English:

a What are the times of the three main meals, according to Jorge?

b What time is the optional after-dinner snack?

Complete these sentences with the information given by Coty.

c La comida principal es la de ————— .
d El almuerzo es entre ——— y ————— .
e La cena es ————— .

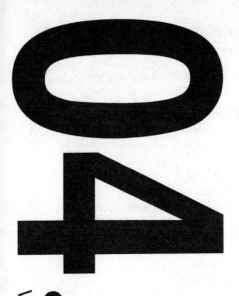

04

¿qué haces?

what do you do?

In this unit you will learn
- how to introduce people
- how to say where you live and what work you do
- how to talk about daily and spare-time activities
- how to ask and answer questions about age

▶ 1 Te presento a mi hermana *Let me introduce you to my sister*

Jorge, a Mexican from Veracruz, introduces his friend Juan, a Chilean, to his sister.

Note the key phrases **Te presento a ...** *Let me introduce you to ...* (fam.), **Vivo en ...** *I live in ...*, **Trabajo en ...** *I work in ...*, **¿Qué haces?** *What do you do?*

Juan	Hola, Jorge.
Jorge	Hola, Juan. Pasa. ¿Cómo te va?
Juan	Bien, gracias, ¿y tú, cómo estás?
Jorge	Pues, un poco cansado. Tengo mucho trabajo. Mira, te presento a mi hermana Luisa, que está aquí de vacaciones. Luisa, éste es Juan, mi amigo chileno.
Luisa	Encantada.
Juan	Mucho gusto.
Luisa	¿De qué parte de Chile eres?
Juan	Soy de Santiago. ¿Y tú no vives en Veracruz?
Luisa	No, vivo en Cancún. Trabajo en una agencia de viajes. Y tú, ¿qué haces?
Juan	Soy arquitecto. Trabajo en una empresa constructora.

pasa	*come in*
pues ...	*well ...*
un poco	*a little*
cansado/a	*tired*
éste / ésta	*this*
mira	*look*
las vacaciones	*holidays*
vivir	*to live*
la agencia de viajes	*travel agency*
la empresa constructora	*construction company*

trabajo en una agencia
de viajes

Say it in Spanish

What phrases are used in the dialogue to express the following?

a How are you? – Well, a bit tired.
b I have a lot of work.
c She is here on holiday.
d This is Juan.
e I work in a travel agency.

▶2 Empiezo a las nueve / start at nine

Juan asks Luisa about her work. First, practise the following key phrases: **¿Estás contenta?** *Are you happy?* (to a woman), **¿Cuál es tu horario de trabajo?** *What are your working hours?*, **Empiezo a las ...** *I start at ...*, **Termino a las ...** *I finish at ...*

Juan ¿Estás contenta de vivir en Cancún?
Luisa Sí, es un lugar muy bonito y tiene un clima muy bueno.
Juan Y tu trabajo, ¿qué tal?
Luisa Es un trabajo interesante, aunque a veces pienso que trabajo demasiado.
Juan ¿Cuál es tu horario de trabajo?
Luisa Empiezo a las nueve de la mañana y termino a las siete de la tarde.
Juan ¿Sin interrupción?
Luisa No, cerramos al mediodía entre las dos y las cuatro.

empezar (e > ie)	*to begin, to start*
el lugar	*place*
bonito/a	*pretty*
tiene	*it has*
bueno/a	*good*
¿Qué tal?	*What is it like?*
aunque	*although*
a veces	*sometimes*
pensar (e > ie)	*to think*
demasiado	*too much*
sin	*without*

Read the dialogue again and answer these questions in English:

a Why does Luisa like Cancún?
b What time does she start and finish work?

▶3 ¿Qué haces los fines de semana? What do you do at weekends?

Luisa asks Juan about his spare-time activities. Note the following key verbs: **me levanto** *I get up*, **salgo** *I go out*, **me quedo** *I stay*, **voy** *I go*, **me acuesto** *I go to bed*, **hago** *I do*, **veo** *I watch*, **leo** *I read*, **escucho** *I listen*.

Luisa	¿Qué haces los fines de semana?
Juan	Por lo general, me levanto bastante tarde. A veces salgo fuera de Santiago, voy a la playa o al campo. Cuando me quedo en Santiago voy al cine o salgo a comer con mis amigos. General-mente me acuesto muy tarde. Y tú, ¿qué haces?
Luisa	No hago nada especial. Normalmente veo la televisión, leo o escucho música.

por lo general	*usually*
bastante tarde	*quite late*
fuera de	*out of*
la playa	*beach*
el campo	*countryside*
cuando	*when*
con	*with*
nada	*nothing, anything*
los fines de semana	*weekends*

Read the dialogue again and answer these questions in English:

a What does Juan do at weekends?
b What does Luisa do?

▶ 4 Tiene doce años *He is twelve years old*

Luisa tells Juan about her family. Note the following questions: **¿Eres casada?** *Are you married?*, **¿Cuántos años tienen?** *How old are they?* Note also how Luisa asks Juan whether he is single: **Tú eres soltero, ¿no?** *You are single, aren't you?*

Juan	¿Eres casada?
Luisa	Sí, soy casada. Tengo dos hijos.
Juan	¿Cuántos años tienen?

Luisa	Mi hijo mayor, José, tiene doce años, y la menor, Cristina, tiene diez. Tú eres soltero, ¿no?
Juan	Sí, soy soltero. Y tu esposo, ¿qué hace?
Luisa	Es maestro.

el hijo	*son*
los hijos	*children*
mayor	*elder*
menor	*younger*
esposo/a	*husband/wife*
maestro/a	*school teacher*

Read the dialogue again and answer these questions in English:

a How many children does Luisa have?
b What are their ages?

ℹ Expressing marital status

To express marital status you can use either **ser** or **estar**, e.g. **soy casado/a** (m/f) or **estoy casado/a** (m/f) *I am married.* The first seems more common in Latin America, while the second is more frequent in Spain. But if reference is to the state of being single or married rather than a definition of someone's marital status, you need to use **estar**:

| Pablo todavía **está** soltero. | *Pablo is still single.* |
| Ya **están** casados. | *They are already married.* |

Key phrases

Introducing people

Éste es Juan.	*This is Juan.*
Ésta es Luisa.	*This is Luisa.*
Te presento a mi hermana / mi hijo *(fam)*	*Let me introduce you to my sister / son.*
Le presento a mi *(pol)* esposo/a	*Let me introduce you to my wife / husband*

Saying where you live and what work you do

| Vivo en ... | *I live in ...* |
| Trabajo en ... | *I work in ...* |

Talking about daily and spare-time activities

| ¿Cuál es tu horario de trabajo? | *What are your working hours?* |

Empiezo / termino a las ocho *I start/finish at eight in the*
de la mañana / noche. *morning / evening.*
¿Qué haces los fines de semana? *What do you do at weekends?*
Por lo general / generalmente *I usually watch television /*
veo la televisión / leo / *read / listen to music /*
escucho música / voy al cine. *go to the cinema.*

Asking and answering questions about age

¿Cuántos años tiene (él / ella) / *How old is he / she / are you?*
tienes (tú)?
Tiene / tengo doce años. *He / she is / I am twelve years old.*

Grammar

1 Possessives: *mi, tu, su ... my, your, his ...*

To say *my*, *your*, *his*, *her*, etc. in Spanish, use the following set of words.

mi	*my*
tu	*your* (fam, sing)
su	*your* (pol, sing), *his, her, its*
nuestro/a	*our* (m/f)
su	*your* (pl), *their*

These words, which are called possessives, agree in number (sing/pl) with the noun that they accompany, but only **nuestro** (*our*) agrees in gender (m/f).

Consider these examples:

Mi hermana se llama Luisa. *My sister is called Luisa.*
Mis hermanas se llaman Luisa *My sisters are called Luisa*
y María. *and María.*
¿Dónde está **nuestro** hotel? *Where is our hotel?*
¿Dónde está **nuestra** habitación? *Where is our room?*

Note that the form **vuestro** (*your*, pl/fam), corresponding to **vosotros** (*you*, pl/fam) used in Spain, is not normally used in Latin America.

2 Demonstratives: *este/a, estos/as this, these*

To say *this* and *these* in Spanish, use the following set of words, which vary for number (sing/pl) and gender (m/f).

este señor (m)	*this gentleman (next to you)*
esta señora (f)	*this lady (next to you)*
estos señores (m)	*these gentlemen (next to you)*
estas señoras (f)	*these ladies (next to you)*

In these examples, **este**, **esta**, etc. have been followed by nouns (e.g. **señor**, **señora**), in which case they are written without an accent. If they are not followed directly by a noun, they are normally written with an accent.

| Ésta es mi hermana. | *This is my sister.* |
| Éste es mi hermano. | *This is my brother.* |

To say *this*, when no gender is specified, use the neuter form **esto**.

| ¿Qué es esto? | *What is this?* |
| ¿Cómo se llama esto? | *What is this called?* |

For *that* and *those*, see Unit 6.

3 Irregular verbs

There are many verbs in Spanish which do not follow a fixed pattern, i.e. they are irregular. In the present tense, some verbs are irregular only in the first person singular. Here are some examples:

hacer	*to do, to make*	**hago**	*I do, I make*
salir	*to go out*	**salgo**	*I go out*
ver	*to watch, to see*	**veo**	*I watch, I see*

For other irregular verbs, see pages 215–18.

No hago nada especial.	*I don't do anything special.*
Salgo a cenar.	*I go out for dinner.*
Veo la televisión.	*I watch television.*

4 *Tener* to have

Tener *to have* is irregular in the first person singular of the present tense. It is also a stem-changing verb, with the **e** of the stem changing into **ie** (see Unit 3).

tengo	*I have*
tienes	*you have* (fam, sing)
tiene	*you have* (pol, sing), *he, she, it has*
tenemos	*we have*
tienen	*you have* (pol/fam), *they have*

Tener has a number of uses, among them the following ones:

a To express age

¿Cuántos años **tienes**?	*How old are you?*
Tengo cuarenta años.	*I'm forty years old.*
Patricia **tiene** treinta y seis.	*Patricia is thirty six.*

b To express possession, including family relationships

Tengo dos hijos / hermanos.	*I have two children / brothers.*
Tiene una casa muy grande.	*He / she has a very large house.*

c To refer to obligations

Tengo mucho trabajo.	*I have a lot of work.*

d To ask the time (see Unit 3)

¿**Tiene** hora?	*Have you got the time?*

e To express availability

¿**Tiene** una habitación?	*Have you got a room?*

5 *Ir to go*

Here are the present tense forms of **ir** (*to go*), a verb which is very irregular.

voy	*I go*
vas	*you go* (fam. sing)
va	*you go* (pol. sing), *he, she, it goes*
vamos	*we go*
van	*you go* (pl), *they go*

Voy a la playa.	*I go to the beach.*
¿Vas al cine?	*Do you go to the cinema?*

6 Reflexive verbs

A reflexive verb is one that has **-se** added to the infinitive, e.g. **levantarse** *to get up*. Normally, **se**, as in this example, is not expressed at all in English, but it sometimes translates into English as *oneself*, for example **mirarse** *to look at oneself*. Many verbs in Spanish are reflexive where their English equivalents are not.

In the examples from dialogue 3 **me levanto** *I get up*, **me acuesto** *I go to bed*, **me quedo** *I stay*, **me** can be said to correspond to the English word *myself*. Words like **se** and **me** are called reflexive pronouns and these precede the conjugated verb. Here is a verb fully conjugated:

levantarse	*to get up*
me levanto	*I get up*
te levantas	*you get up* (fam. sing)
se levanta	*you get up* (pol. sing), *he, she, it gets up*
nos levantamos	*we get up*
se levantan	*you get up* (pl), *they get up*

The plural familiar form **os levantáis** *you get up* has been omitted, as this is not normally used in Latin America.

Remember that in a dictionary, reflexive verbs are listed with -se on the end of the infinitive, for example: **divertirse** *to enjoy oneself*, **quedarse** *to stay*, **acostarse** *to go to bed*.

7 Personal *a*

In the sentence **Te presento a mi hermana** *Let me introduce you to my sister*, **mi hermana**, the person being introduced, is the direct object of the sentence. Before noun direct objects referring to people, Spanish uses the preposition **a**. This is known as the *personal* **a**. Note the use of the personal **a** in the following examples:

Veo **a** Luisa los lunes.   *I see Luisa on Mondays.*
Quiere mucho **a** sus padres.   *He / she loves his / her parents very much.*

But:

Veo la televisión todos   *I watch television everyday.*
  los días.
Quiere mucho su trabajo.   *He/she loves his/her work very much.*

8 Formation of adverbs

Adverbs are used to provide information about verbs, adjectives or other adverbs:

Ceno **normalmente** en casa.   *I usually have dinner at home.*
Es **extremadamente** difícil.   *It's extremely difficult.*
Habla **realmente** bien.   *He / she speaks really well.*

Adverbs can be formed by adding -**mente** to the adjective.

general   *general*
generalmente   *generally, usually*

| normal | *normal* |
| normalmente | *normally* |

| Normalmente escucho música. | *I normally listen to music.* |
| Generalmente voy al teatro. | *I usually go to the theatre.* |

If the adjective ends in **-o**, change the **-o** to **-a** and add **-mente**.

claro	*clear*
claramente	*clearly*
lento	*slow*
lentamente	*slowly*

| Habla claramente. | *He / she speaks clearly.* |
| Progresa lentamente. | *He / she is progressing slowly.* |

In a sentence with two or more adverbs in **-mente**, only the last one takes the ending **-mente**.

| Habla clara y lentamente. | *He / she speaks clearly and slowly.* |

A large number of adverbs are single words or group of words not formed from adjectives, for example **siempre** *always*, **nunca** *never*, **por lo general** *usually*, **a menudo** *often*, **ahora** *now*, **mañana** *tomorrow*, **bien** *well*, **mal** *badly*, and so on.

Practice

1 An informal introduction

Raúl Riveros, from Mexico, is introducing his father to his friend María Elena.

Raúl	Hola, María Elena. ¿Cómo te va?
María Elena	Muy bien, y tú, ¿cómo estás?
Raúl	Bien, gracias. Te presento a mi papá. (*Addressing his father.*) Ésta es María Elena.
Señor Riveros	Encantado.
María Elena	Mucho gusto.

Note that Latin Americans normally use **papá** *father* and **mamá** *mother* in this context. Spaniards would normally use **padre** and **madre** instead.

Raúl is now visiting María Elena, who introduces him to Señora de García, her mother (**su mamá**). Rewrite the dialogue above making the necessary adaptations.

2 A formal introduction

You are on business in Latin America, and after greeting señor Molina, manager of Hispanometal, you introduce your colleague John Evans to him. After exchanging greetings with John Evans, señor Molina offers you a seat. Write a dialogue based on this situation. Then compare your version with the model dialogue in the **Key to the activities**.

> **el gerente de . . .**   *the manager of . . .*
> **mi colega**   *my colleague*
> **siéntense**   *sit down* (pl)

3   Latin Americans tend to be more direct in their questions when they meet people for the first time. For instance, they often ask people about their work, so here is your chance to practise.

a   On a train journey in Latin America you meet Carlos, a student from Uruguay. He uses the familiar form to address you, so you do likewise.

Ud.	*Ask Carlos where he lives.*
Carlos	Vivo en Montevideo. ¿Y tú?
Ud.	*Say where you live and then ask him what work he does.*
Carlos	Soy estudiante. Estudio ingeniería en la Universidad de Montevideo. ¿Y tú?
Ud.	*Say what you do.*

> **estudiar** *to study*   **la ingeniería** *engineering*

b   During an excursion you meet María and her husband José. They use the polite form to address you.

Ud.	*Ask them where they are from.*
María	Somos de Colombia. Y usted, ¿de dónde es?
Ud.	*Say what country you are from and then ask them where they live.*
José	Vivimos en Medellín.
Ud.	*Ask them what work they do.*
María	Mi marido es médico y yo soy periodista.
Ud.	*Don't wait to be asked! Say something about your own work or occupation.*

| **el marido** *husband* | **el/la periodista** *journalist* |
| **el médico** *doctor* | |

▶ 4   Listen to Coty Montalvo, from Mexico, talking about her work. The key words which follow will help you to understand what Coty says, while the questions below will help you check comprehension.

| **regresar** | *to come back* |
| **seguir laborando** | *to continue working* |

Answer true or false (**verdadero o falso**):

   a   Coty empieza a trabajar a las nueve de la mañana.
   b   Sale a almorzar a la una.
   c   Termina de trabajar a las siete.

5   Imagine you are writing in Spanish to someone about your own activities. Use the following guidelines to express these ideas:

   Say what you do.
   Say what days you work or what days you go to school or university.
   Say what time you start and what time you finish.
   Say where you normally have lunch.
   Say what you usually do after work / school.
   Say what you usually do at the weekend.

estudiar	*to study*
ir al colegio / a la universidad	*to go to school / university*
salir de compras	*to go out shopping*
limpiar la casa	*to clean the house*
ir al teatro / a conciertos	*to go to the theatre / concerts*
después de trabajar / de clases	*after work / school*
salir a caminar / correr	*to go out and walk / run*
regar (e > ie) **el jardín**	*to water the garden*
leer el periódico	*to read the newspaper*
cocinar	*to cook*

▶ 6   Coty was asked how she normally spends her holidays. Listen to what she says then answer the questions below. First, look at this new vocabulary:

aprovecho	*I take the opportunity*
los sobrinos	*nephews and nieces*
la frontera	*border*
los Estados Unidos	*United States*
el viaje	*journey*
largo	*long*
hasta allá	*to there*
lo disfruto	*I enjoy it*
veo	*I see*
muy de vez en cuando	*very rarely*

Now answer these questions in English:

a Where does Coty normally go on holiday?
b Why does she enjoy the long journey?

7 Read this information about Luisa Álvarez, then use the information in the box to write a similar passage about Antonio Fernández, his children and his wife (**su mujer** or **esposa**).

Luisa Álvarez es mexicana y trabaja como secretaria en una agencia de viajes. Luisa es casada y tiene dos hijos, José y Cristina. Su hijo José tiene doce años y su hija Cristina tiene diez. El marido de Luisa se llama Pablo. Pablo es maestro.

Nombre:	`Antonio Fernández`
Nacionalidad:	`nicaragüense`
Profesión:	`técnico, empresa textil`
Estado civil:	`casado`
N° de hijos:	`3`
Edades:	`Adela (24 años),` `Mario (21), Domingo (19)`
Casado/a con:	`María Rosa Poblete`
Profesión:	`ama de casa`

nicaragüense	from Nicaragua
el técnico	technician
la empresa textil	textile company
el estado civil	marital status
la edad	age

▶ 8   Coty, whose full name is Clotilde Montalvo Rodríguez, now talks about herself and her family. Listen to what she says, or read the transcript on page 234, and as you do so, fill in the box below with the information given by her. First, look at these key words:

Centro Cultural de Lenguas Modernas	a languages school in Veracruz, Mexico
manejar	to drive
la carretera	highway
el chofer de carretera (m)	coach or lorry driver

Name:	Clotilde Montalvo Rodríguez
Age:	. . . .
Marital Status:	. . . .
Profession:	. . . .
Husband's Profession:	. . . .
N° of children:	. . . .
Age(s):	. . . .

9   During a stay in a Latin American country you meet someone. Like many Latin Americans often do, he/she asks you about yourself and your family. Answer the relevant questions.

a   ¿Es usted casado/a o soltero/a?
b   ¿Tiene hijos? ¿Cuántos?
c   ¿Tiene hermanos? ¿Cuántos?
d   ¿Cuántos años tiene(n) su(s) hijo(s) o hermano(s)?
e   ¿Dónde vive usted?

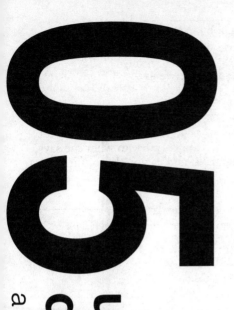

05

una mesa para dos

dos

a table for two

In this unit you will learn
- how to express wants and preferences
- how to order food and drink

▶1 En el avión *On the plane*

James Parker is flying from London to Bogotá with a South American airline. Lunch is now being served and James has to choose from the menu below. Two key words in this dialogue are **prefiero** *I prefer* and **quiero** *I want*.

Almuerzo
ENSALADA MIXTA

Y

BISTEK DE LOMITO
ARVEJAS CON
MANTEQUILLA
ARROZ BLANCO

O

FILETES DE PESCADO
LEGUMBRES MIXTAS
PAPAS FRITAS

🐌

QUESO Y GALLETAS
PASTEL DE DURAZNO
CAFÉ O TÉ

---

la ensalada mixta	*mixed salad*
el bistek de lomito	*fillet steak*
las arvejas con mantequilla	*buttered green peas*
el arroz blanco	*plain rice*
los filetes de pescado	*fish fillets*
las legumbres mixtas	*mixed vegetables*
las papas fritas	*fried potatoes*
el queso	*cheese*
las galletas	*biscuits*
el pastel de durazno	*peach cake*
el café	*coffee*
el té	*tea*

Azafata	¿Qué menú prefiere, señor?
James	Prefiero el filete de lomito.
	(*The stewardess hands James his food tray.*) Gracias.
Azafata	¿Qué va a tomar?
James	Quiero vino tinto, por favor.
	(*The stewardess gives James a small bottle of red wine.*)
	Gracias.
Azafata	De nada.
	(*After lunch, the stewardess comes round with coffee.*)
	¿Va a tomar café?
James	Sí, por favor.

prefiere	*you prefer* (pol)
¿Qué va a tomar?	*What are you going to drink?*
el vino tinto	*red wine*
¿Va a tomar café?	*Are you going to have coffee?*

Say it in Spanish

Use the guidelines below to fill in your part of the conversation with a flight attendant.

Azafata	¿Qué menú prefiere?
Usted	*Say you prefer fish fillets.*
Azafata	¿Y qué va a tomar? Tenemos vino tinto, vino blanco, cerveza, jugo, agua mineral...
Usted	*Say what you want.*
	(*After lunch, the flight attendant comes round with coffee and tea*)
Azafata	¿Va a tomar café o té?
Usted	*Say whether you want coffee or tea.*

ℹ️ Names for fruit and vegetables

Differences in vocabulary between Latin America and Spain and within Latin America itself are common in the area of fruit and vegetables. Here are some examples:

Latin America	Spain	
la papa	la patata	*potato*
el durazno	el melocotón	*peach*
las arvejas / los chícharos (*Mexico and Central America*)	los guisantes	*peas*
los frijoles / los porotos (*Southern Cone countries*)	las judías / las alubias	*beans*

See also Unit 6 and the **Glossary of Latin American** terms at the back.

▶ 2 Una mesa para dos *A table for two*

James Parker and a Colombian associate in Bogotá go to a restaurant for dinner. Key words and phrases here are **pueden** *you can*, **¿Nos trae ...?** *Will you bring us ...?*, **para mí** *for me*.

Mesera	Buenas noches.
Señor Donoso	Buenas noches. ¿Tiene una mesa para dos?
Mesera	(*Pointing to a table*) Sí, pueden sentarse aquí si desean.
Señor Donoso	Sí, está bien. ¿Nos trae la carta, por favor? (*The waitress brings them the menu.*) Gracias.
Mesera	¿Van a tomar un aperitivo?
James	Para mí no, gracias.
Señor Donoso	Para mí tampoco.
Mesera	Bien, ya regreso.

mesero(a) / camarero(a)	*waiter / waitress*
sentarse	*to sit*
si desean	*if you wish*
¿Van a tomar ...?	*Are you going to have ...?*
tampoco	*neither*
Ya regreso	*I'll be right back*
regresar	*to come back*

Say it in Spanish

How would you express the following in Spanish?

a Have you got a table for three?
b I want an apéritif.
c Will you bring us a bottle of (**una botella de**) red wine, please?

▶ 3 ¿Cómo lo quiere? *How do you want it?*

James and señor Donoso order their food. First, try learning these key phrases: **Yo quiero** ... *I want,* **¿Me trae ...?** *Will you bring me ...?,* **Para mí** ... *For me ...,* **Tráiganos** ... *Bring us...*

Mesera	¿Qué van a pedir?
James	Yo quiero una sopa de verduras para empezar.
Mesera	Una sopa de verduras . . . ¿Y qué más?
James	Quiero pollo.
Mesera	El pollo, ¿cómo lo quiere?
James	Lo quiero asado.
Mesera	¿Con qué lo quiere? ¿Con arroz, con puré . . .?
James	Con arroz. Y me trae una ensalada mixta también, por favor.
Mesera	¿Y para usted, señor?
Señor Donoso	Para mí, crema de espárragos, y carne guisada con papas.
Mesera	Las papas, ¿las quiere fritas, doradas . . .?
Señor Donoso	Fritas.
Mesera	¿Y qué van a tomar?
Señor Donoso	Una botella de vino tinto.
Mesera	Tenemos un vino chileno muy bueno.
Señor Donoso	Sí, tráiganos un vino chileno.

una botella de
vino tinto

¿Qué van a pedir?	*What are you going to order?*
la sopa de verduras	*vegetable soup*
para empezar	*to start*
el pollo asado	*roast chicken*
¿Con qué lo quiere?	*What do you want it with?* (pol)
la crema de espárragos	*asparagus soup*
la carne guisada	*stewed meat*
las papas fritas / doradas	*fried / golden potatoes*

Say it in Spanish

You are in a restaurant in a Spanish-speaking country. How would you say the following?

a Will you bring me a vegetable soup?
b I want roast chicken with mashed potatoes.
c Will you bring us a mixed salad?
d Coffee for me, please.

▶ 4 ¿Qué van a comer de postre?
What are you going to have for dessert?

James Parker and señor Donoso order a dessert, **un postre.** Note the expression **yo quisiera** *I would like.*

Mesera	¿Qué van a comer de postre?
Señor Donoso	¿Qué tiene?
Mesera	Tenemos helados, fruta, flan, pastel de queso . . .
James	Yo quiero una ensalada de fruta.
Señor Donoso	Para mí un helado de chocolate.
Mesera	¿Van a tomar café?
James	Yo no, gracias.
Señor Donoso	Sí, yo quisiera un café.

¿Qué van a comer ...?	*What are you going to eat ...?*
el helado	*ice-cream*
la ensalada de fruta	*fruit salad*
el flan	*caramel*
el pastel de queso	*cheesecake*

Say it in Spanish

Use the guidelines below to complete your conversation with the waitress.

Mesera	¿Qué va a comer de postre?
Usted	*Ask whether she has ice-cream.*
Mesera	Sí, tenemos helado de chocolate, de vainilla, de mango y de papaya.
Usted	*Say which one you prefer, and say you would like coffee too.*

▶5 ¿Nos trae la cuenta, por favor?
Will you bring us the bill, please?

Señor Donoso and señor Parker order the bill, **la cuenta**.

Señor Donoso ¿Nos trae la cuenta, por favor?
Mesera Sí, un momento, señor. Enseguida se la traigo.

| **enseguida se la traigo** | *I'll bring it to you straight away* |

Key phrases

Expressing wants and preferences

Quiero/quisiera vino
  blanco / tinto.
Prefiero café / té /
  agua mineral.

*I want/would like
  white / red wine.*
*I prefer coffee / tea /
  mineral water.*

Ordering food and drink

¿Me / nos trae la carta /
  la cuenta?
Tráigame / nos una botella
  de vino, por favor.
Quiero carne/pollo/pescado.
Lo/la quiero asado(a) /
  frito(a) (m/f).
Lo / la prefiero con puré /
  arroz / una ensalada (m/f).
Para mí, una sopa de verduras /
  un helado de vainilla.

*Will you bring me / us the
  menu / bill?*
*Bring me / us a bottle of wine,
  please.*
I want meat / chicken / fish.
I want it roast / fried.

*I prefer it with mashed
  potatoes / rice / a salad.*
*For me, a vegetable soup /
  a vanilla ice-cream.*

Grammar

1 Expressing wants and preferences: *querer* to want, **preferir** to prefer

To say what you want, use **querer** *to want*, and to say what you prefer, use **preferir** *to prefer*. These two verbs are stem-changing, the e of the stem changing into ie (e > ie): yo quiero / prefiero, tú quieres / prefieres, usted / él / ella quiere / prefiere, ustedes / ellos / ellas quieren / prefieren.

¿Qué quieres / prefieres comer / tomar?
What do you want / prefer to eat / drink?

Quiero / prefiero papas fritas / una cerveza.
I want / prefer chips / a beer.

2 *Poder* to be able to, can

Poder is a stem-changing verb in which the o of the stem changes into ue (o > ue): yo puedo, tú puedes, usted / él / ella puede, ustedes / ellos / ellas pueden. **Poder** can be used in requests, as when ordering food and drink, but it has other uses as well.

¿Puede traerme / nos la carta?
Can you bring me / us the menu?

¿Pueden reservarme / nos una mesa?
Can you book me / us a table?

Pueden sentarse aquí.
You can sit here.

3 Direct object pronouns

a *Lo / la, los / las* it, them

To say *it* or *them*, as in *How do you want it / them?*, use **lo** when reference is to a masculine word, and **la** for feminine. In the plural use **los** and **las**.

¿Cómo quiere el pescado?
How do you want the fish?

Lo quiero a la plancha.
I want it grilled.

¿Con qué quiere la carne?
What do you want the meat with?

La quiero con papas.
I want it with potatoes.

¿Cómo quiere las papas?
How do you want the potatoes?

Las quiero fritas.
I want them fried.

These words are known as *direct object pronouns* (see Glossary of grammatical terms) and they normally come before the verb, but in sentences with a finite verb (e.g. **puede** *you / he / she can*) followed by an infinitive (e.g. **traer** *to bring)* or a gerund (e.g. **preparando** *preparing*), the pronoun can either precede the finite verb or be attached to the infinitive or the gerund.

¿Puede traer la carta, por favor?	*Can you bring the menu please?*
¿Puede traer**la**, por favor? *or* ¿**La** puede traer, por favor?	*Can you bring it, please?*
Estoy preparando el almuerzo.	*I'm preparing lunch.*
Estoy preparándo**lo**. *or* **Lo** estoy preparando.	*I'm preparing it.*

(For *gerunds* see Unit 10.)

Object pronouns follow positive imperatives but precede negative one.

Traiga el vino.	*Bring the wine.*
Tráiga**lo**.	*Bring it.*
No **lo** traiga.	*Don't bring it.*

(For *imperatives* see Unit 12)

Lo, la, etc. can also refer to people.

Voy a invitar**lo/la**.	*I'm going to invite him / her.*

b ***me, te, nos*** *me, you* (fam), *us*

Direct object pronouns corresponding to **yo** *I*, **tú** *you* (fam), **nosotros** *we*, are **me, te, nos**, respectively.

Me / te / nos invita.	*He is inviting me / you / us.*
Me / te / nos conocen.	*They know me / you / us.*

Me, te and **nos** can also function as indirect object pronouns. See 4 below.

4 Indirect object pronouns

Me me, to me, nos us, to us...

a To say *me, to me, us, to us*, etc., as in *Will you bring me a salad?*, *Will you bring us the menu?*, use the following set of words, which are called *indirect object pronouns* (see Glossary of grammatical terms). In requests such as the above, these are followed by a verb in the present tense.

me	me, to me, for me
te	you, to you, for you (fam, sing)
le	you, to you, for you (pol, sing)
le	him, to him, for him
le	her, to her, for her
nos	us, to us, for us
les	you, to you, for you (pl)
les	them, to them, for them

¿**Me** pasa la sal?	*Will you pass me the salt?*
¿**Te** preparo un café?	*Shall I prepare a coffee for you?*
Ahora **le / les** traigo el postre.	*I'll bring you the dessert right now.*
¿**Nos** reserva una mesa?	*Will you reserve a table for us?*

Note that **le** and **les** are used for both masculine and feminine.

b In sentences with two object pronouns, one direct and the other indirect, the indirect object pronoun comes first.

| ¿**Me** trae la ensalada? | *Will you bring me the salad?* |
| ¿**Me la** trae? | *Will you bring it to me?* |

c Le and les become **se** before **lo / la, los / las**.

| Enseguida **le** doy la cuenta. | *I'll give you the bill right away.* |
| Enseguida **se la** doy. | *I'll give it to you right away.* |

5 *Para*

a Para mí, para usted … *for me, for you …*

To say *for me, for you, for him*, etc. use **para** followed by **mí** *me* and **ti** *you* (fam) for the first and second person singular, and **usted, él, ella, nosotros/as, ustedes, ellos/as** with all other persons.

Para mí, pescado con papas fritas.	*For me, fish and chips.*
¿Y para ti?	*And for you?* (fam)
¿Y para usted, señor?	*And for you, sir?* (pol)

With the exception of **con** *with* (see Grammar, Unit 11), other prepositions (words like *from, in, without, to*, etc.) follow the same rule as **para**.

Él va sin mí.   *He is going without me.*
Ellos vienen sin ella.   *They are coming without her.*

b   Notice the use of **para** in these sentences:

¿Tiene una mesa para dos?   *Have you got a table for two?*
Quiero una sopa para empezar.   *I want a soup to start with.*

6 Agreement of adjectives

In Spanish, adjectives (words like *big, small, long*) must agree in gender (masc/fem) and number (sing/pl) with the word they refer to. Here are some examples taken from this unit.

una ensalada mixta   *a mixed salad*
legumbres mixtas   *mixed vegetables*
un pollo asado   *a roast chicken*
pollos asados   *roast chickens*

Practice

1   You are on business in Bogotá, and today you are having lunch with a Colombian colleague at Casa Brava, so you decide to telephone the restaurant to make a reservation. Complete your part of the conversation, overleaf, with the restaurant manager.

CASA BRAVA

Km. 4.5 Vía a la Calera
Tel: 6124106

Está decorado con buen gusto, originalidad, sencillez. La calidad de su cocina es excelente y el servicio es especialmente amable.

En la noche el ambiente es alegre de fiesta. Pero durante el día es apacible y acogedor. Ideal para un almuerzo de negocios.

Jefe   (*Al teléfono*) Restaurante Casa Brava, buenos días.

Ud.   *Answer the greeting and say you would like to book a table for two.*

Jefe	Para hoy, ¿verdad?
Ud.	*Yes, for today.*
Jefe	¿Y para qué hora?
Ud.	*For half past one.*
Jefe	¿A nombre de quién?
Ud.	*Say in what name you want the reservation.*

> **¿A nombre de quién?**   *In whose name?*

2   You arrive at Restaurante Casa Brava with your colleague and you are met by the head waiter.

Mesero	Buenas tardes.
Ud.	*Answer the greeting and say you have a reservation for half past one.*
Mesero	¿Cómo se llama usted?
Ud.	*Give your name.*
Mesero	Sí, su mesa es ésa, la que está junto a la ventana.

> **junto a** *next to*   **la ventana** *window*

3   You are ready to order now. First, study the menu opposite, then write a dialogue between you and your companion and the **mesera**, using some of the phrases in the box on page 78 and those you learned in dialogue 3. You can then compare what you have done with the model dialogue in the **Key to the activities**.

los camarones	*shrimps*
el aguacate relleno	*stuffed avocado*
la empanada	*turnover, pie*
la sopa de zapallo	*pumpkin soup*
la chuleta	*chop*
la ternera	*veal*
a la plancha	*grilled*
los duraznos en almíbar	*peaches with syrup*
la fresa	*strawberry*
la crema	*cream*
el pastel	*cake*

<u>Restaurante</u>
<u>Casa Brava</u>

PARA EMPEZAR
Cocktail de camarones
Aguacate relleno
Empanadas

SOPAS Y CREMAS
Sopa de verduras
Sopa de tomate
Crema de espárragos
Crema de zapallo
Sopa o crema del día

CARNES Y PESCADOS
Chuletas de ternera
Chuletas de cerdo
Carne asada
Pollo asado
Filete de pescado
  a la plancha
Pescado frito

POSTRES
Duraznos o mangos
  en almíbar
Flan de vainilla
Fresas con crema
Pastel de fresas
Helados

¿Qué desean comer?
Para empezar tenemos ...
Tambien tenemos sopas y cremas.
¿Y qué más?
¿Con qué lo / la quiere?
¿Y para usted señor/a?
¿Algo más?
¿Qué van a tomar?
¿Qué desean de postre?
¿Van a tomar café?

▶ 4   At a table next to you, a Colombian is ordering food.
What food has she ordered? Listen to her conversation with the
waiter then complete the order below, as the waiter might have
done. First, look at these new words.

los champiñones	*mushrooms*
pollo en salsa de mostaza	*chicken in mustard sauce*
el soufflé de calabaza	*pumpkin soufflé* (a baked dish containing squash, beaten eggs and seafood, served with sauce)
no queda	*we don't have any left*
el jugo	*juice*

Mesa –

_____
_____
_____
_____

_____
_____
_____

_____
_____
_____
_____

5 You are going out for a meal with an English-speaking colleague who is travelling in Latin America with you. Your colleague has spotted the advertisement below for a restaurant and would like to know more about it. Look at the key words before you read the advertisement, then answer your colleague's questions.

el sabor	*taste*
la atención	*service*
el precio	*price*
acogedor	*warm, welcoming*
sabrá	*you will know*
a cuerpo de rey	*like a king*
ser atendido	*to be served*
como un príncipe	*like a prince*
pagar	*to pay*
el plebeyo	*plebeian*

LA COMBINACIÓN PERFECTA…!

¡Sí! Ahora **Sebastián** tiene la combinación perfecta para convertirse en su restaurante favorito. Los mejores pescados, mariscos y deliciosas carnes en un acogedor ambiente. Visítenos y sabrá lo que es comer a cuerpo de rey, ser atendido como un príncipe y pagar precios de plebeyo.

LA COCINA DE SEBASTIÁN

José Domingo Cañas 1675
(Esq. M. Eyzaguirre –
Nuñoa)
Reservas: 2091565

Now answer these questions in English:

a Why is Sebastián the 'perfect combination'?
b What sort of food do they serve?

6 The passage below looks at the contribution of the *New World* – el **Nuevo Mundo** – to the European diet. As you read the text, try answering the following questions with the help of the key words below:

a Which two main products came to Europe from the Americas?
b According to the text, what is difficult to imagine?

La contribución del Nuevo Mundo a la dieta europea

Algunos productos que hoy en día son esenciales en la dieta europea, son en realidad originarios de las Américas. Los más importantes son la papa y el tomate. Pero hay muchos otros, entre ellos los frijoles, las habas, el chile, los aguacates, los cacahuetes, los damascos, las papayas, el chocolate, etcétera. Es difícil imaginar la cocina europea sin algunos de estos productos, especialmente la papa y el tomate.

algunos	*some*
hoy en día	*nowadays*
son originarios de	*they come from*
el frijol	*bean*
el haba	*broad bean*
el aguacate	*avocado*
el cacahuete	*peanut*
el damasco	*apricot*

7 The passage which follows deals with Latin American food. Look at the key words before you read the text, then check your comprehension by answering the questions which follow the passage.

variada	*varied*	**el plato**	*dish*
el pan de maíz	*maize bread*	**como en**	*as in*
la base	*basis*	**el mar**	*sea*
a base de carne	*based on*	**la carne de vaca**	*beef*

La cocina hispanoamericana es inmensamente variada y está basada fundamentalmente en los productos típicos de cada país o región. La dieta de los mexicanos, por ejemplo, es muy diferente a la de los colombianos o a la de los argentinos. Lo más típico de México, quizás, son las tortillas, una especie de pan de maíz, que constituye la base de muchos platos mexicanos. Otro ingrediente básico en la dieta mexicana es el chile. México es un país muy grande y existen platos típicos de cada región, muchos de ellos a base de carne. En la costa se come mucho pescado y mariscos.

En los países centroamericanos, como en la mayoría de los países de la región, se comen muchos platos a base de maíz. El arroz con pollo es un plato típico en muchos países del Caribe y de América del Sur, entre ellos Colombia. Pero en Colombia, como en otros países sudamericanos, la cocina es muy variada y los restaurantes presentan una gran variedad de platos nacionales e internacionales. En el Perú y Chile, por ejemplo, se comen muchos productos del mar. En la Argentina y el Uruguay se come preferentemente carne de vaca.

Answer these questions in English:

a What is the most typical food in Mexico?
b What is the staple food in Central America?
c Name a typical dish in many Caribbean and South American countries.
d What do Argentinians and Uruguayans prefer to eat?

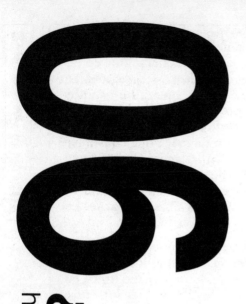

06

¿cuánto vale?

how much does it cost?

In this unit you will learn
- about shopping
- how to describe things
- how to express comparisons
- how to express likes and dislikes

▶1 ¿Cuánto vale? *How much does it cost?*

Mario, a Colombian, is buying a briefcase, **un maletín**. Try learning these key phrases first: **Quisiera ver ...** *I would like to see ...*, **Me gusta** *I like it*, **¿Cuánto vale?** *How much does it cost?*, **Es un poco caro** *It is a little expensive*.

Mario	Buenos días. Quisiera ver ese maletín que está en la vitrina.
Vendedora	¿Éste?
Mario	Sí, ése, el negro.
	(*Mario examines the briefcase.*)
Vendedora	Es un maletín muy bonito y muy elegante.
Mario	¿Es de cuero?
Vendedora	Sí, todos los artículos que vendemos son de cuero.
Mario	Me gusta mucho. ¿Cuánto vale?
Vendedora	Doscientos cincuenta mil pesos.
Mario	Es un poco caro. ¿No tiene otro más barato?
Vendedora	Sí, ése de color café es más barato. Vale ciento veinte mil pesos.
Mario	Ése no me gusta mucho.
Vendedora	No tenemos otro.
Mario	Bueno, voy a llevar el negro. ¿Puedo pagar con tarjeta de crédito?
Vendedora	Claro que sí.

la vitrina / el escaparate	shop window
bonito	nice, pretty
el cuero	leather
el artículo	article
vender	to sell
el peso	Colombian currency
otro/a	another (one), other
más barato	cheaper
café	brown
llevar	to take
pagar	to pay
la tarjeta de crédito	credit card
claro que sí	certainly

Say it in Spanish

You go into a shop to buy a suitcase, **una maleta**. How would you express the following in Spanish?

a I would like to see that (**esa**) suitcase.
b It is a little expensive. Have you got a cheaper one?
c I don't like that (suitcase) very much.
d I'm going to take the black one.
e May I pay with traveller's cheques (**cheques de viaje**)?

🛈 Latin American currency

The currency used in Colombia is **el peso**. **Pesos** are also used in Bolivia, Chile, Cuba, Dominican Republic, Mexico and Uruguay. The rate of exchange, **el cambio**, of the peso in relation to the dollar, the euro, the pound and other currencies is not the same in all countries which use this currency. The unit of currency in Argentina is **el austral**, in Paraguay **el guaraní**, in Peru **el sol**, and in Venezuela **el bolívar**. Costa Rica and El Salvador use **el colón**, Nicaragua **el córdoba**, Guatemala **el quetzal**, Honduras **la lempira** and Panama **el balboa**. Ecuador and Puerto Rico use American dollars, **el dólar**.

The standard word for money is **el dinero**, but in many Latin American countries you will hear the more informal word **la plata** (literally *silver*), for example **No tengo plata** *I have no money*, **Es mucha plata** *It's a lot of money*.

▶2 Me lo puedo probar *May I try it on?*

Clara, a Colombian, is buying a sweater, **un suéter.** First, try learning these key phrases: **¿Me lo puedo probar?** *May I try it on?*, **Me queda un poco pequeño** *It is a bit small for me,* **¿Tiene uno más grande?** *Have you got a larger one?*

Vendedor	A la orden.
Clara	(*Pointing to some sweaters*) Quisiera ver esos suéteres, por favor.
Vendedor	¿Qué talla tiene usted?
Clara	Talla ocho.
Vendedor	Bueno, tenemos en blanco, azul, verde, rojo y amarillo.
Clara	El verde me gusta más. Es muy bonito. ¿Me lo puedo probar?
Vendedor	Claro que sí.
	(*Clara tries the sweater on.*)
Clara	Éste me queda un poco pequeño. ¿Tiene uno más grande?
Vendedor	Sí, aquí tiene uno en la talla diez, en el mismo color.
	(*Clara tries on the other sweater*).
Clara	Sí, éste me queda bien. ¿Cuánto vale?
Vendedor	Cuarenta mil pesos.
Clara	Sí, lo voy a llevar.
Vendedor	¿Va a pagar en efectivo?
Clara	Sí, en efectivo.

a la orden	*can I help you?*
la talla	*size*
más	*more*
más grande	*bigger*
mismo/a	*same*
me queda	*it fits me*
pagar en efectivo	*to pay cash*

Los colores *colours*

amarillo/a	*yellow*	**naranja**	*orange*
azul	*blue*	**negro**	*black*
blanco/a	*white*	**rojo/a**	*red*
gris	*grey*	**rosa**	*pink*
café / marrón	*brown*	**verde**	*green*

Say it in Spanish

During a holiday in a Spanish-speaking country you decide to buy some trousers, **unos pantalones**. Fill in your part of the conversation with the shop-assistant.

Vendedor	Buenas tardes. ¿Qué desea?
Ud.	*Say you would like to see the trousers which are in the shop window.*
Vendedor	¿Ésos?
Ud.	*Yes, those ones.*
Vendedor	¿Qué talla tiene usted?
Ud.	*Say what size you wear.*
Vendedor	Los tenemos en negro, gris, café y blanco.
Ud.	*Say what colour you want them in.*
Vendedor	Aquí tiene usted.
Ud.	*Ask if you can try them on.*
Vendedor	Sí, sí, pase por aquí, por favor.

▶3 En el mercado *In the market*

Silvia, a Colombian, is buying some vegetables in the market. Colombians use **libras** *pounds,* instead of **kilos.** First, try learning these key phrases: **deme** *give me,* **¿Qué precio tienen?** *How much are they? / What is the price?,* **Eso es todo** *That's all,* **¿Cuánto es?** *How much is it?*

Vendedor	A la orden, señora.
Silvia	¿Cuánto valen las papas?
Vendedor	Doscientos cincuenta pesos la libra.
Silvia	Deme tres libras.
	(The stallholder weighs the potatoes and puts them in a bag.)
Vendedor	¿Algo más?
Silvia	Sí, ¿qué precio tienen las lechugas?
Vendedor	Treinta pesos cada una.
Silvia	Quiero dos. Y los tomates, ¿cuánto valen?
Vendedor	Doscientos cincuenta pesos la libra.
Silvia	Deme libra y media.
Vendedor	¿Algo más?
Silvia	No, eso es todo. ¿Cuánto es?
Vendedor	Son mil ciento ochenta y cinco pesos.
Silvia	Hasta luego, gracias.
Vendedor	Hasta luego.

¿algo más?	anything else?
cado uno/una	each one
medio/a	half
hasta luego	goodbye

Say it in Spanish

You are in a market buying some fruit and vegetables. How would you express the following in Spanish?

a How much are the tomatoes?
b What's the price of the mangoes (**los mangos**)?
c Give me two pounds / kilos.
d I want one and a half kilos.

🔢 Libras y kilos *pounds and kilos*

Most Latin American countries use kilos, but a few, for example Colombia, use libras, *pounds*: **un kilo** *one kilo*, **medio kilo** *half a kilo*, **un kilo y medio** *one and a half kilos*, **una libra** *one pound*, **media libra** *half a pound*, **una libra y media** *one and a half pound*.

▶ 4 En la oficina de correos *In the post office*

Silvia is sending a postcard, **una postal**. Key words here are **mandar** *to send*, **la estampilla** *stamp*, **el buzón** *postbox*, and **afuera** *outside*.

Silvia	¿Cuánto vale mandar una postal a Inglaterra?
Empleado	Mil doscientos pesos.
Silvia	Quiero dos estampillas de mil doscientos y cinco de seiscientos pesos.
	(*The clerk gives Silvia the stamps and she pays for them.*)
	Gracias. ¿Dónde está el buzón?
Empleado	Está afuera.

Say it in Spanish

You are travelling in Latin America and you want to send some letters home. How would you say the following in Spanish?

a Where is the post office?
b How much does it cost to send a letter (**una carta**) to ...?
c I'd like three eight hundred *peso*-stamps.

Key phrases

Shopping

Quisiera ver esa maleta / ese suéter.	*I'd like to see that suitcase / sweater.*
Quiero dos kilos / libras.	*I want two kilos / pounds.*
Deme un kilo y medio / uno / una.	*Give me one and a half kilos / one.*
¿Tiene otro/a?	*Have you got another one?*
¿Cuánto vale/n?	*How much is it / are they?*
¿Cuánto cuesta/n?	
¿Qué precio tiene/n?	
¿Cuánto es?	*How much is it (all)?*
¿Puedo pagar con tarjeta de crédito / cheques de viaje?	*May I pay with a credit card / traveller's cheques?*
Voy a pagar en efectivo.	*I'll pay cash.*

Describing things

Es un poco caro(a) / pequeño(a) / grande.	*It is a bit expensive / small / big.*
Es / son (muy) bonito/s.	*It is/they are (very) nice / pretty.*
¿Es / son de cuero?	*Is it / are they made of leather?*

Expressing comparisons

Ése / ésa es más grande / pequeño(a).	*That is bigger / smaller.*
¿Tiene algo más barato / uno(a) más barato(a)?	*Have you got something cheaper / a cheaper one?*

Expressing likes and dislikes

Me gusta/n (mucho)	*I like it / them (very much)*
No me gusta/n.	*I don't like it / them.*

Grammar

1 Demonstratives: *ese/a, esos/as* that, those

To say *that* and *those* in Spanish we use the following set of words:

that	**those**
ese (m)	esos (m)
esa (f)	esas (f)

Quisiera ver ese maletín.	*I would like to see that briefcase.*
Quisiera ver esos suéteres.	*I would like to see those sweaters.*

When **ese, esa,** etc. are used instead of a noun, they are normally written with an accent.

Ése de color negro.	*That black one. (masc)*
Me gusta ésa.	*I like that one. (fem)*

To say *that*, as in *That is all, What is that?*, we use the word **eso**, which is neuter:

Eso es todo.	*That is all.*
¿Qué es eso?	*What is that?*

2 *Me gustar* I like (it)

To express likes and dislikes in Spanish, we use the verb **gustar** (literally *to please*), preceded by an object pronoun (words like *me, you, him, her*) (see Unit 5).

me gusta	*I like (it)*
te gusta	*you like (it) (fam, sing)*
le gusta	*you like (it) (pol, sing)*
	he, she likes (it)
nos gusta	*we like (it)*
les gusta	*you like (it) (pl)*
	they like (it)

These phrases translate literally into English as *it pleases me, it pleases you, it pleases him,* etc. Therefore the verb remains in the third person singular. To say *I like them, you like them, he likes them,* use the third person plural of the verb (**gustan**):

me gustan	*I like them*
te gustan	*you like them*
le gustan	*you like, he, she, likes them*

To say what you like to do, use the appropriate form of **gustar** followed by the infinitive. Look at these examples:

Me gusta viajar.	*I like to travel.*
Nos gusta jugar al tenis.	*We like playing tennis.*

3 Comparisons

To express comparisons in Spanish (e.g. cheaper, bigger), we simply place the word **más** (*more*) before the adjective. Here are some examples:

Ése es más barato.	*That is cheaper.*
Ésos son más caros.	*Those are more expensive.*
Esos suéteres son más grandes.	*Those sweaters are bigger.*

4 *Ser* to describe things

To describe things, we normally use the verb **ser** *to be*:

Es un maletín muy bonito.	*It's a very nice briefcase.*
Es muy elegante.	*It is very elegant.*
Son bonitos.	*They are nice.*
Es de cuero / fibra sintética.	*It is made of leather / synthetic fibre.*

este suéter es demasiado grande

5 *Todo* all, whole

Todo agrees in number (sing / pl) and gender (m / f) with the noun it refers to.

Todo el día	*The whole day*
Todos los días	*Every / each day.*
Toda la gente	*All the people*
Todas las tiendas	*All the shops*

6 *Otro* another (one), other

Like **todo** above, **otro** agrees in number and gender with the noun it refers to.

Otro color	*Another colour*
Otros pantalones	*Other trousers*
Otra falda	*Another skirt*
Otras camisas	*Other shirts*
Deme otro	*Give me another one*

Practice

1 You are on holiday in Bogotá and before going back home you decide to buy a present for someone. Choose one of these articles and then play your part in this conversation with a shop assistant.

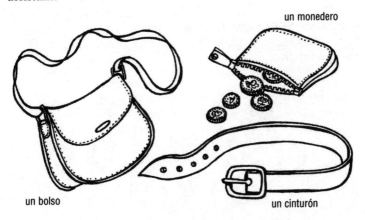

un monedero

un bolso

un cinturón

Ud.	*Tell the shop assistant which article you would like to see from the shop window.*
Vendedora	¿Cuál? ¿Éste?
Ud.	*That one, the brown one.*
Vendedora	Aquí tiene usted.
Ud.	*Say it is very nice and ask if it is made of leather.*

Vendedora	Sí, es de cuero. Sólo vendemos artículos de cuero.
Ud.	*Ask how much it costs. The price given by the shop assistant seems a bit high, so ask if they have a cheaper one.*
Vendedora	No, éste es el más barato que tenemos. Es muy fino. Es un cuero de muy buena calidad.
Ud.	*Say you like it very much.*
Vendedora	Sí, es precioso.
Ud.	*Say you are going to take it and ask if you can pay with a credit card.*
Vendedora	Sí, por supuesto. ¿Lo quiere para regalo?
Ud.	Yes, it is for a present.

sólo	*only*
el más barato	*the cheapest one*
fino/a	*good quality*
la calidad	*quality*
precioso	*very nice*
por supuesto	*certainly, of course*
el regalo	*present*

2 Clothes seem to be cheaper in Colombia than back home, so you decide to buy something for yourself. Choose from one of these items and then play your part in the conversation with the shop assistant.

una blusa

una falda

una chaqueta

una camisa

| **la blusa** | blouse | **la falda** | skirt |
| **la camisa** | shirt | **la chaqueta** | jacket |

Ud.	Tell the shop assistant what you would like to see.
Vendedor	¿Qué talla tiene usted?
Ud.	Say what size you are.
Vendedor	¿En qué color la prefiere?
Ud.	Ask what colours they have.
Vendedor	Las tenemos en negro, gris, blanco, beige y naranja.
Ud.	Say you prefer it in white.
Vendedor	Aquí tiene usted una blanca.
Ud.	Say you don't like the style (**el modelo**) very much. Ask if they have others.
Vendedor	(Showing you other items) Sí, éstas son diferentes. ¿Le gustan?
Ud.	Yes, you like those more.
Vendedor	Aquí tiene una en blanco.
Ud.	Ask if you can try it on.
Vendedor	(Pointing to the fitting room) Sí, allí está el probador.
Ud.	Say it fits very well and ask how much it costs.
Vendedor	Ésa cuesta treinta y cinco mil pesos.
Ud.	Yes, you are going to take it.
Vendedor	¿Cómo va a pagar?
Ud.	Say you are going to pay cash (with ready money).

| **¿En qué colores...?** | What colours...? |

▶ 3   You go out shopping again. This time you buy several things, and while waiting to have them wrapped, you overhear a conversation between a Colombian customer buying shoes (**unos zapatos**) and a shop assistant. Listen to the conversation, and as you do so, complete the box overleaf with details of the purchase. First look at these new words:

¿Podría decirme . . .?	Could you tell me . . .?
¿cuáles?	which ones?
el descuento	discount
el número	size (of shoes)

artículo	precio	precio con descuento	color	número
zapatos				

▶ 4 'Next time you want to buy men's clothes, why don't you try Almacenes García. They have big discounts for you.' Listen to this radio advertisement, and try to understand what discounts are being offered and on what articles of clothing. First look at these key words, then answer the questions below.

los almacenes	*department store*
por fin de temporada	*for end of season*
la manga larga	*long sleeve*
la manga corta	*short sleeve*
el caballero	*gentleman*
los pantalones	*trousers*
las promociones	*special offers*

Now answer these questions in English:

a   What sort of shirts are on offer?
b   What discounts are they giving on men's trousers?
c   What phrases have been used in the advertising to express the following: *all men's trousers* and *special offers are not included*?

5   You are in a market buying some fruit and vegetables. Study these key words first and then do the exercise opposite.

los aguacates	*avocados*	**las zanahorias**	*carrots*
los mangos	*mangoes*	**las lechugas**	*lettuces*
los duraznos	*peaches*	**los repollos**	*cabbages*

How would you express the following in Spanish?

a How much are the avocados?
b Have you got mangoes?
c What is the price of the peaches?
d I would like a kilo of carrots.
e Give me one lettuce.
f I want two cabbages.
g That is all.
h How much is it?

6 Here is an incomplete dialogue between a Colombian post-office clerk and a customer who is sending a letter (**una carta**) to the United States. Fill in the missing words.

Cliente	¿Cuánto cuesta _____ una carta _____ los Estados Unidos?
Empleado	Mil _____
Cliente	Deme una _____ de mil y cuatro _____ seiscientos.
Empleado	¿Algo más?
Cliente	_____ es todo. ¿Cuánto _____?
Empleado	Son _____ pesos.
Cliente	¿Dónde está el _____?
Empleado	Está afuera, _____ la derecha.

▶ **7** Understanding figures in Spanish may not be easy at first, so here is a chance to practise. First, look at the advertisement for furniture, overleaf, and try reading each of the prices a few times until you feel sure that you can say them fluently. Luis Nuñez, from Bogotá bought several pieces of furniture from the shop, and now the shop assistant is adding up the price. As you listen to the figures, make a list of the items bought by Luis and write down the total amount he paid. First, look at this new vocabulary:

el saldo	*sale, bargain*
la feria	*trade fair*
la oferta	*special offer*
el sofacama	*sofabed*
juvenil	*for young people*
la nevera	*refrigerator*
la lavadora	*washing machine*
el equipo de sonido	*stereo equipment*
la cama	*bed*

07

planes de vacaciones
holiday plans

In this unit you will learn
- how to talk about the future
- how to express intentions
- how to describe places
- how to talk about the weather

▶ 1 Vamos a ir en tren *We're going by train*

Elisa and Antonio, from Chile, talk about their holiday plans. Note the following future forms in this dialogue: **ya saldrás de vacaciones** *you will soon go on holiday,* **podrás descansar** *you will be able to rest,* **iré** *I will go,* **tomaré** *I will take.* Note also forms like **pensamos** *we are thinking of,* **piensas** *you are thinking of,* **voy / vamos a ...** *I am/we are going to ...*

Elisa	Hola, ¿qué tal?
Antonio	Hola, ¿cómo te va?
Elisa	No muy bien. Estoy muy cansada. ¡Tengo mucho trabajo!
Antonio	Bueno, ya saldrás de vacaciones y podrás descansar. ¿Tienes algún plan para este verano?
Elisa	Bueno sí, iré con Alfonso al sur por un par de semanas. Pensamos llegar hasta Chiloé. Es la primera vez que voy. Yo no conozco nada del sur.
Antonio	Te va a gustar mucho. Chiloé es precioso. ¿Van en auto?
Elisa	No, vamos a ir en tren y pensamos volver en bus. Y tú, ¿qué piensas hacer?
Antonio	Bueno, yo tomaré mis vacaciones en febrero. Voy a ir a México y Ecuador.
Elisa	¡Estupendo! ¿Vas solo?
Antonio	No, voy con dos amigos de la oficina.
Elisa	¿Y por cuánto tiempo van?
Antonio	Bueno, es un tour, vamos a estar ocho días en México y cuatro días en Quito.
Elisa	¡Te felicito! Dicen que México es un país muy lindo. Espero que lo pases muy bien.
Antonio	Gracias. Tú también.
Elisa	Adiós.
Antonio	Chao.

Vamos a ir en tren y pensamos volver en bus

cansado/a	*tired*
llegar hasta	*to go all the way to*
la primera vez	*first time*
no conozco nada del sur	*I don't know the south at all*
solo/a	*on my/your own*
¿por cuánto tiempo ...?	*How long ... for?*
¡te felicito!	*congratulations!*
espero que lo pases muy bien	*I hope you have a very good time*

🛈 Means of transport

Some of the words associated with transport vary within Latin America. While the more general word for a local *bus*, **el autobús**, will probably be understood almost everywhere, other words are used alongside or instead of this: **el camión**, in Mexico and Central America, **el colectivo**, in Argentina and Venezuela, **el ómnibus**, in Perú and Uruguay, **la micro**, in Chile, **la guagua**, in Cuba.

The words **el coche** and **el automóvil**, for a *car*, will be familiar to most Latin Americans, but some regions will use other terms: **el carro** is the standard word in a number of places, but not in the Southern Cone countries (Argentina,Uruguay, Chile), where the most commonly used term is **el auto**.

🛈 **¡Adiós!** *goodbye*, and **hasta luego**, *see you (later)*, are standard terms and are used in all Latin American countries. **¡Chao!**, or **¡Chau!** in some places, is strictly familiar and is common in many Latin American countries. Diminutives of these expressions, like **adiosito**, **hasta lueguito**, **chaíto**, are more colloquial.

---

los meses *the months*

enero *January*	**julio** *July*
febrero *February*	**agosto** *August*
marzo *March*	**septiembre** *September*
abril *April*	**octubre** *October*
mayo *May*	**noviembre** *November*
junio *June*	**diciembre** *December*

Note that in Spanish, months are written with small initial letters.

---

las estaciones *the seasons*

el otoño *autumn*	**la primavera** *spring*
el invierno *winter*	**el verano** *summer*

Say it in Spanish

Ricardo, a Spanish-speaking friend, asks you about your holiday plans. Use the guidelines to answer his questions.

Ricardo ¿Tienes algún plan para este verano?
Ud. *Say you will go to Cuba with a friend.*
Ricardo Te va a gustar mucho Cuba. Es un país muy interesante. ¿Y por cuánto tiempo van?
Ud. *Say you are going to be four days in Havana and three days in Santiago de Cuba. Ask your friend what he is thinking of doing.*
Ricardo Voy a ir a Guatemala.
Ud. *Say it is a very nice country and add that you hope he has a very good time.*
Ricardo Gracias. Tú también.

▶2 No hace frío *It isn't cold*

Alfonso tells Elisa about the weather in Chiloé. First, try learning these expressions: **¿Qué tal el tiempo?** *What's the weather like?* **(No) hace frío** *It is (not) cold,* **Llueve mucho** *It rains a lot.*

Elisa ¿Qué tal el tiempo en Chiloé? ¿Crees que hará frío?
Alfonso No, en esta época del año no hace frío, pero sí puede llover. En el sur llueve mucho, especialmente en Chiloé.
Elisa Tendremos que llevar algo para la lluvia, por si acaso.
Alfonso Sí, creo que sí.

¿crees que hará frío?	*do you think it will be cold?*
la época	*time*
tendremos que	*we will have to*
llevar	*to take, carry*
algo	*something*
la lluvia	*rain*
por si acaso	*just in case*
creo que sí	*I think so*

Now answer these questions in English:

a Does Alfonso think it may be cold in Chiloé?
b What does Elisa propose to take with them?

Key phrases

Talking about the future

Iré / iremos a ...	*I / we will go to ...*
Tomaré / tomaremos mis / nuestras vacaciones.	*I / we will take my / our holidays.*
Voy / vamos a ir / estar ...	*I am / we are going to go / be ...*

Expressing intentions

Pienso / pensamos ir a ...	*I am / we are thinking of going to ...*
¿Qué piensas hacer?	*What are you thinking of doing?*

Describing places

Es un país / una ciudad muy lindo(a) / bonito(a).	*It's a very beautiful country / city.*
Es precioso(a).	*It's gorgeous / lovely.*

Talking about the weather

¿Qué tal el tiempo?	*What's the weather like?*
Hace frío / calor.	*It is cold / hot.*
Llueve (mucho).	*It rains (a lot).*

Grammar

1 Talking about the future and expressing intentions

To refer to the future you can use:

a The future tense:

Iré con Alfonso al sur.	*I am going to the south with Alfonso.*
¿Hará frío?	*Will it be cold?*

b The construction **ir a** with an infinitive:

Voy a ir a México.	*I am going to Mexico.*
Vamos a estar diez días en México.	*We are going to be in Mexico for ten days.*

c The present tense, particularly with verbs which indicate movement:

¿Van en auto?	*Are you going by car?*
¿Por cuánto tiempo van?	*How long are you going for?*

d The verb **pensar** to *think, to intend, to plan,* followed by the infinitive, another common way of expressing intentions.

¿Qué piensas hacer este verano?	*What are you planning to do this summer?*
Pienso ir a Costa Rica.	*I'm thinking of going to Costa Rica.*

Of these four ways of referring to the future, the future tense is the least common, particularly in Latin America, where ir a + the infinitive is far more frequently used, especially in colloquial speech. However, you will hear the future tense in some contexts and with certain verbs, for instance when there is an implication of inevitability, e.g. **Tendremos que llevar algo para la lluvia** *We'll have to take something for the rain,* or when there is uncertainty, e.g. **¿Crees que hará frío?** *Do you think it will be cold?,* or simply for reasons of economy, e.g. **iré con él** instead of **voy a ir con él.** In formal spoken language, the future tense is more frequent (e.g. a tourist guide outlining plans for an excursion: **Saldremos del hotel a las 7.00** *We'll leave the hotel at 7.00*). In the press, the future tense is the standard form used to refer to future events.

2 The future tense

To form the future tense, you use the infinitive followed by the appropriate ending, which is the same for the three conjugations (-**ar**, -**ir**, and -**er**). Here is an example of a fully conjugated regular verb.

tomar to take	
tom**aré**	*I will take*
tom**arás**	*you will take* (fam, sing)
tom**ará**	*you will take* (pol, sing), *he, she, it will take*
tom**aremos**	*we will take*
tom**arán**	*you will take* (pl), *they will take*

Here are some more examples of the use of the future tense:

Tomaremos una semana de vacaciones.	*We will take a week's holiday.*
Veremos qué podemos hacer.	*We'll see what we can do.*
¿Adónde irás este verano?	*Where will you go this summer?*

Irregular future forms

Some verbs have an irregular stem in the future tense but the endings are the same as for regular verbs. Here is a list of the most important.

decir	to say, to tell	diré, dirás, dirá, diremos, dirán
hacer	to do, to make	haré, harás, hará, haremos, harán
poder	can, to be able to	podré, podrás, podrá, podremos, podrán
salir	to go out	saldré, saldrás, saldrá, saldremos, saldrán
tener	to have	tendré, tendrás, tendrá, tendremos, tendrán
venir	to come	vendré, vendrás, vendrá, vendremos, vendrán

Here are some examples of the future tense with irregular verbs:

El avión saldrá a las 7.00 de la mañana.	*The plane will leave at 7.00 in the morning.*
Tendrán que estar en el aeropuerto dos horas antes.	*You'll have to be at the airport two hours earlier.*
El autobús vendrá a las 4.30.	*The bus will come at 4.30.*

For other irregular future forms see pages 215–18.

3 Time expressions associated with the future

The following expressions of time are normally associated with the future.

mañana	*tomorrow*
pasado mañana	*the day after tomorrow*
la próxima semana	*next week*
el próximo mes / año	*next month / year*
la semana / el mes / año que viene	*next / the coming week / month / year*
dentro de dos días / una semana	*within two days / a week*

4 Describing places: *ser* to be and *tener* to have

To describe places, Spanish normally uses **ser** *to be* or **tener** *to have*. To say where a place is, use **estar** *to be* (see Unit 2). To say what you can find in a place use **hay** *there is / are*.

Es un lugar/ sitio muy lindo / *It is a very beautiful place.*
  bonito.
Tiene playas muy buenas.   *It has very good beaches.*
Está en el sur/norte.   *It is in the south/north.*
Hay museos excelentes.   *There are excellent museums.*

5 Describing the weather

To describe the weather, Spanish normally uses the verb **hacer** *to
do, make.*

Hace / hará (mucho) frío/calor. *It is/will be (very) cold / hot.*
Hace / hará sol/viento.   *It is/will be sunny/windy.*
Hace / hará buen/mal tiempo. *The weather is / will be good /
                                    bad.*

Other weather expressions require different verbs:

Llueve.   *It rains. It is raining.*
Está lloviendo.   *It is raining.*
Nieva.   *It snows.*
Está nevando.   *It is snowing.*
Está nublado / despejado. *It is overcast / clear.*

6 *Conocer* and *saber* to know

In dialogue 1 above you encountered the verb **conocer** *to know*
or *to be acquainted with something, a person or a place.* **Saber**,
above, also translates into English as *to know*, but it is used to
refer to knowledge of a fact or the ability to do something. Like
conocer, the first person singular of **saber** in the present tense is
irregular: **sé** *I know.* Compare the following:

Conozco México.   *I know Mexico.*
Conozco a Isabel.   *I know Isabel.*
No sé dónde está Quito. *I don't know where Quito is.*
No sé manejar.   *I don't know how to drive.*

Practice

1 You have been posted by your company to Chile, and
during your first holiday there you decide to visit other parts of
Latin America with a local friend. The following holiday
advertisement in a Chilean newspaper catches your attention,
and one of the destinations – Quito, Mexico – seems to be what
you want. The following day in your office you talk about it
with a Chilean colleague.

MEXICO–CANCUN RIO–ACAPULCO

ESPECTACULARES TOURS 03/04

MEXICO-RIO $999 CU
(14 días, 2 personas)

CANCUN-MEXICO-RIO $1.290 CU
(12 días, 2 personas)

MEXICO-TAXCO ACAPULCO-QUITO $1.089 CU
(12 días, 2 personas)

MIAMI-MEXICO $1.199 CU
(13 días, 2 personas)

MEXICO-QUITO $949 CU
(12 días, 2 personas)

MIAMI-ORLANDO $849 CU
(8 días, auto, 4 personas)

CUBA $990 CU
(7 días, 2 personas, media pensión)

PRECIOS INCLUYEN:
• Pasaje Aéreo • Hotelería • Excursiones • Traslados

Avda. Providence 1941
Fonos: 233442829 2331774
2316676 • 2318608 • Fax: 2334428

Economy Tour

Colega	¿Qué piensas hacer este verano?
Ud.	*Say you are thinking of going to Mexico and Quito.*
Colega	¡Qué interesante! México es un país muy lindo y Quito también me gusta mucho. ¿Vas por mucho tiempo?
Ud.	*No, you are going to be there 12 days in all (en total).*
Colega	¿Es un tour?
Ud.	*Yes, it is a tour and it's not very expensive. It costs 949 dollars.*
Colega	No está caro. ¿Incluye el pasaje aéreo?
Ud.	*Yes, it includes the flight, 4-star hotels, excursions and transfers.*
Colega	Me parece muy barato. ¿Vas a ir solo/a?
Ud.	*No, you are going to travel with a friend. Ask your colleague what he is going to do in the summer.*
Colega	Voy a ir a la playa con mi familia. Pensamos ir a Viña del Mar.

el pasaje aéreo	plane ticket, flight
la estrella	star
el traslado	transfer
c/u (cada uno)	each one

2 You decide to take the tour advertised on page 105, but before you travel you e-mail a Mexican acquaintance to tell him of your visit to Mexico. In his reply, your Mexican friend suggests some places to visit together during your stay in Mexico City. Read what he says, then check your understanding by answering the questions which follow. First study these key words and phrases.

me alegro mucho de	I am glad ...
que vengas	... you are coming
aunque	although
estoy seguro	I am sure
como tendrás	as you will have
el lugar	place
el barrio	district
así que	so
juntos	together
si te interesa	if it interests you

Me alegro mucho de que vengas a México. Aunque la ciudad es enorme, estoy seguro de que te gustará. Como tendrás algunos días libres, te llevaré en el coche a conocer algunos de los lugares más interesantes de la ciudad. Podremos ir a Coyoacán, que es un barrio típico, con buenos restaurantes y algunos monumentos importantes. Allí está el Museo de Frida Khalo. Yo no lo conozco, así que lo visitaremos juntos.

Si te interesa, podremos ir a Cuernavaca y Taxco, dos ciudades coloniales que no están muy lejos de México ...

The word **México** in the passage refers to Mexico City. That is the word most Mexicans use to refer to the capital city.

Answer these questions in English:

a   What is Coyoacán?
b   What museum will you be able to visit there?
c   What cities will your friend take you to?
d   Are they far from Mexico City?

3   In his reply, your Mexican acquaintance also gives you information about the weather in Mexico City. Read it through, then check your understanding by answering the questions below.

En general, el clima es bastante agradable, aunque en invierno a veces hace un poco de frío, especialmente entre diciembre y enero, que es cuando tú vendrás. Pero en esta época del año no llueve mucho. El invierno este año ha sido muy suave, con mucho sol y algunos días de bastante calor. En todo caso, tendrás que traer un suéter para las mañanas y para la noche...

Answer these questions in English:

a   What is the weather generally like in Mexico City?
b   Is it cold in winter?
c   Does it rain in December and January?
d   What does your acquaintance suggest you bring?

4   In Mexico you are going to stay at the Hotel Ana Luisa, a 4-star hotel. In this description of the hotel, all the verbs are missing. Complete the passage with the appropriate verb, then check your answers in the **Key to the activities.**

El hotel Ana Luisa es un hotel de 4 estrellas que ___ situado frente al Monumento de la Revolución, a pocos pasos del Paseo de la Reforma. Este elegante hotel ___ 250 habitaciones, todas con baño privado, TV a color, teléfono y mini-bar. En el hotel Ana Luisa ___ dos restaurantes de comida internacional, dos bares y una cafetería. Para su confort durante los meses de verano, el hotel ___ aire acondicionado.

a pocos pasos de	*a few steps away from*
el baño privado	*private bath*
los meses de verano	*summer months*
el aire acondicionado	*air conditioning*

▶ 5 While in Mexico, you might have a chance to visit Veracruz. A friend back home went on holiday there and he liked it very much. He has recommended somewhere to stay: **Motel Miraflores**. Listen to this advertisement from Mexican radio, and pay special attention to the facilities they announce at **Motel Miraflores**. Then make a list of them in English. The vocabulary which follows includes some new words you will hear in the advertisement. You should be able to guess the meanings of other new words.

el paraíso	*paradise*
para que usted disfrute	*so that you may enjoy*
cómodamente	*comfortably*
la estancia	*stay*
antena parabólica	*satellite dish*
la cama	*bed*
la alberca	*swimming pool* (Mex)
siempre deseará volver	*you will always want to come back*
sin número	*without number*

▶ 6 In Quito, Ecuador, you will stay at the Hotel Quito. Listen to how someone from Quito describes the hotel, then answer the questions below. First study these new words and phrases:

la piscina	*swimming pool*
en la parte trasera	*at the back*
el espacio verde	*green area*
bien grandes	*very large*
Techo del Mundo	*roof of the world*
los salones	*room, hall*
se hacen	*are held*
las convenciones	*conferences*
aparte	*besides*

Answer these quesions in English:

a   How many rooms has the hotel got?
b   How many restaurants does it have?
c   What other facilities does it have?

7   It is your last day in the office before your departure for Mexico and you are very busy. A colleague is trying to set up an urgent meeting with you. Answer his questions by looking at the diary notes below.

VIERNES 31

10.00 *Entrevista con el Sr. Valdés*

11.00 *Ir al banco y comprar cheques de viaje.*

12.00 *12.30 - Reunión con el director de*

13.00 *producción. Almuerzo con el gerente.*

14.00 —

15.00 *Llamar a la agencia de viaje para reconfirmar hora del vuelo.*

Answer these quesions in Spanish:

a   ¿Qué vas a hacer a las 11.00?
b   ¿Y a las 12.30?
c   ¿Vas a almorzar solo/a?
d   ¿Estarás libre en la tarde? ¿A qué hora?

▶ 8   You are already thinking about your next holiday, which may be in Panama or Peru. They sound like good places to escape to in winter. Listen first to what Elizabeth from Panama City says about the weather in her country. Then listen to Karina Tomas, a Peruvian, describing Lima, the capital of Peru. First, look at the new vocabulary overleaf, then check your comprehension by answering the questions.

el clima	climate
la temperatura promedio	average temperature
todo el año	the whole year
netamente	essentially
lluviosa	rainy
seca	dry

Are these questions true or false (**verdadero o falso**)?

a   La temperatura promedio en Panamá es de dieciocho grados centígrados.

b   En invierno llueve mucho.

c   En verano no llueve.

aún	still
se conservan	they are retained
la época colonial	colonial times
el zoológico	zoo
en cuanto a	as regards
cálido	warm
las lluvias	rains

Answer these questions in English:

d   How does Karina describe Lima?

e   What does Lima have to offer, according to her?

f   What is the weather like?

9   The people you will meet in Mexico and Ecuador will probably ask you about your own city. How would you answer the following questions:

a   ¿Cómo es la ciudad?

b   ¿Cuántos habitantes tiene?

c   ¿Cómo es el clima?

10 On the seat next to you on the plane you find a newspaper giving information on the weather in different capital cities, including Mexico, your destination. Study the table opposite and then answer these questions in Spanish:

a   ¿Hace sol en México?

b   ¿Cómo está el tiempo en Londres?

c   ¿Está lloviendo en París?

d   ¿Cómo está el tiempo en Madrid?

El tiempo en el mundo

Ciudades	Mín	Máx	Estado
Amsterdam	9	25	despejado
Asunción	18	30	despejado
Atenas	17	25	despejado
Berlín	13	18	nublado
Bruselas	18	27	despejado
Buenos Aires	12	20	lluvioso
Caracas	18	28	despejado
Ginebra	8	23	despejado
La Habana	19	30	despejado
La Paz	2	19	despejado
Lima	17	23	variable
Londres	16	23	despejado
Los Ángeles	16	26	nublado
Madrid	12	22	lluvioso
México	12	26	nublado
Miami	22	29	despejado
Montevideo	14	20	lluvioso
Moscú	12	15	nublado
Nueva York	17	25	nublado
París	12	25	despejado
Pekín	16	28	despejado
Río de Janeiro	20	26	despejado
Roma	11	23	despejado
San José	15	26	nublado
Seúl	14	24	despejado
Tokio	18	22	nublado
Varsovia	17	22	despejado
Viena	10	16	despejado
Washington	16	27	nublado

08

de viaje

travelling

In this unit you will learn
- how to ask and give travel information
- how to book in at a hotel
- how to say how long you have been doing something

▶ 1 Sale a las dieciocho treinta
It leaves at 6.30 p.m.

Elisa and her husband Alfonso are travelling to Puerto Montt, in southern Chile, and from there to the island of Chiloé. Elisa is buying train tickets. Key words and phrases here are **el tren** *train,* **sale** *it leaves,* **llega** *it arrives,* **el boleto** *ticket,* **de ida** *single,* **de ida y vuelta** *return.*

Elisa	Buenos días. ¿A qué hora hay trenes a Puerto Montt?
Empleado	Tiene el rápido, que sale a las dieciocho treinta, y el expreso, que sale a las veintiuna treinta.
Elisa	¿A qué hora llega el rápido?
Empleado	A las catorce horas del día siguiente.
Elisa	¿Y el expreso?
Empleado	El expreso llega a las diecinueve diez del día siguiente. El rápido demora diecinueve horas y media y el expreso veintiuna horas con cuarenta minutos.
Elisa	Bueno, en ese caso prefiero el rápido. Lleva coche dormitorio, ¿verdad?
Empleado	Sí, lleva departamentos sencillos, para dos personas, y departamentos grandes, para cuatro.
Elisa	¿Cuánto cuesta el departamento sencillo?
Empleado	El sencillo vale cuarenta y cinco mil pesos ida y vuelta.
Elisa	Quiero de ida solamente.
Empleado	De ida le sale a veinticinco mil pesos.
Elisa	¿Por persona?
Empleado	No, ése es el precio del departamento.
Elisa	Muy bien, deme dos boletos para el sábado 15 de febrero.
Empleado	Aquí tiene. Son veinticinco mil pesos.
Elisa	Gracias.

rápido	*fast*
el día siguiente	*following day*
demora	*it takes*
llevar	*to carry, to have*
el coche-dormitorio / cama	*sleeping car*
el departamento /	
compartimento / compartimiento	*compartment*
sencillo	*single*
le sale a ... pesos	*it will cost you/ comes to ... pesos*
solamente / sólo	*only*

Ask in Spanish

You are buying train tickets for a long distance journey in a South American country.

a Ask what time the train leaves.

b Ask what time it arrives.

c Ask how much a return ticket costs.

d Ask whether they have tickets for Friday 12th. You want two.

▶2 Una habitación para dos *A room for two*

Alfonso is booking a hotel room for him and Elisa. First, try learning these key phrases: **¿tiene una habitación?** *have you got a room?*, **con / sin desayuno** *with/without breakfast*, **nos vamos** *we are leaving*, **¿cómo se escribe?** *how do you spell it?*

Alfonso	Buenas tardes.
Recepcionista	Buenas tardes.
Alfonso	¿Tiene una habitación para dos personas?
Recepcionista	Sí, sí tenemos.
Alfonso	¿Cuánto cuesta?
Recepcionista	Dieciocho mil pesos.
Alfonso	¿Con desayuno?
Recepcionista	No, sin desayuno. El desayuno es aparte.
Alfonso	Bueno, está bien.
Recepcionista	¿Cuántos días van a quedarse?
Alfonso	Dos días solamente. Nos vamos el martes.
Recepcionista	De acuerdo. Me da su nombre, por favor.
Alfonso	Alfonso Abucadís.

Recepcionista	¿Cómo se escribe el apellido?
Alfonso	A-b-u-c-a-d-i-s. Abucadís.
Recepcionista	¿Y la dirección?
Alfonso	Calle Las Acacias 731, departamento D, Santiago.
Recepcionista	Bien, aquí tienen la llave. Es la pieza veinticuatro, en el segundo piso, al final del pasillo. Allí está la escalera.
Alfonso	Gracias.

aparte	*separate*
quedarse	*to stay*
de acuerdo	*fine*
¿me da su nombre?	*will you give me your name?*
la llave	*key*
la pieza	*room*
el pasillo	*corridor*
la escalera	*stairs*

How was the following expressed in the dialogue?

a Breakfast is not included.
b How many days are you going to stay?
c Two days only.
d We are leaving on Tuesday.

ℹ️ Spelling names

Many Latin Americans have non-Spanish surnames or names which are fairly uncommon and which need to be spelled. **¿Cómo se escribe?** *How do you spell it?* (lit. *How do you write it?*) is the standard phrase to use. A less frequent phrase is **¿Puede / podría deletrearlo?** (*Can / could you spell it?*). The verb here is deletrear (*to spell*). For the Spanish alphabet, see page 230.

ℹ️ ¿Cómo se pronuncia? *How do you pronounce it?*

To ask somebody how to pronounce a name or any other word simply say:

¿Cómo se pronuncia su nombre / apellido?	*How do you pronounce your name / surname?*
¿Cómo se pronuncia esta palabra?	*How do you pronounce this word?*

ℹ️ Asking somebody to repeat a word or phrase

If you have not heard properly, you may say **¿Cómo?** or **¿Perdón?** (*Pardon? Sorry?*) or **¿Puede / podría repetir, por favor?** (*Can / could you repeat, please?*). In some parts of Latin America, for example Mexico and Ecuador, you will hear the word **¿mande?** for *pardon?*

ℹ️ Asking somebody to speak more slowly

If the speaker is talking too fast for you, simply say: **Más despacio, por favor** (*More slowly, please*) or **¿Podría hablar más despacio, por favor?** (*Could you speak more slowly, please?*).

ℹ️ Apologizing for your Spanish!

If you are not too confident about your Spanish, use one or more of these phrases:

Disculpe, pero no hablo muy bien español.	*I am sorry, but I don't speak Spanish very well.*
Hablo muy poquito español.	*I speak only a little Spanish.*
Disculpe, pero no entiendo.	*I am sorry, but I don't understand.*
¿Qué significa . . .?	*What does . . . mean?*

In an emergency, you might want to add:

¿Habla usted inglés?	*Do you speak English?*
¿Alguién habla inglés?	*Does anybody speak English?*

▶ 3 ¿Tiene agua caliente? *Does it have hot water?*

A tourist from Venezuela arrives at a hotel in Puerto Montt. Note the word she uses for *room*, **un cuarto**. Note also the following key phrases: **con baño** *with a bathroom*, **con baño compartido** *with a shared bathroom*, **¿sirven desayuno?** *do you serve breakfast?*, **se paga aparte** *it's paid separately*.

Turista	Buenos días.
Recepcionista	Buenos días.
Turista	¿Tiene un cuarto individual?
Recepcionista	Sí, sí tenemos.
Turista	¿Cuánto vale?
Recepcionista	Doce mil pesos.

Turista	¿Tiene baño?
Recepcionista	No, es con baño compartido, pero también hay una habitación con baño. Ésa cuesta quince mil pesos.
Turista	¿Sabe?, yo prefiero una con baño. ¿Tiene agua caliente?
Recepcionista	Sí, sí, tiene agua caliente, sí.
Turista	¿Y ustedes sirven desayuno?
Recepcionista	No, no señora. El desayuno se paga aparte.
Turista	Bueno, bueno.
Recepcionista	Bien, por favor, ¿puede escribir su nombre y dirección aquí? Y su firma también.
Turista	De acuerdo.

¿puede escribir ...?	*can you write ...?*
la firma	*signature*

Ask in Spanish

You arrive in a hotel in a Latin American country.

a Ask whether they have a single room (use the word **habitación**)
b Ask whether the room has a bathroom.
c Ask whether it has hot water.
d Ask whether they serve breakfast.

▶ 4 ¿Cuánto tiempo llevan aquí? *How long have you been here?*

Elisa meets a colleague of hers in Puerto Montt. Two key phrases here are **¿cuánto tiempo hace que están aquí?** and **¿cuánto tiempo llevan aquí?**, which are two alternative ways of saying *how long have you been here?* Note also the words for *why?* **¿por qué?** and *because* **porque**.

Elisa	Andrés, ¡qué sorpresa! ¿Qué haces aquí?
Andrés	Estoy aquí de vacaciones con mi señora y los niños. Ellos están en el hotel ahora.
Elisa	Te presento a Alfonso, mi marido. (*addressing Alfonso*) Éste es Andrés, un compañero de trabajo.
Alfonso	Mucho gusto.
Andrés	Hola, encantado.
Elisa	¿Cuánto tiempo hace que están aquí?
Andrés	Hace una semana, pero nos vamos pasado mañana.

Elisa	¿Por qué se van tan pronto?
Andrés	Porque Carmen tiene que volver al trabajo.
Elisa	¡Qué lástima!
Andrés	Y ustedes, ¿cuánto tiempo llevan aquí?
Elisa	Llevamos dos días solamente, pero pensamos estar dos semanas. Vamos a ir a Chiloé.

¡qué sorpresa!	what a surprise!
mi marido (or esposo)	my husband
mi señora (or esposa / mujer)	my wife
compañero/a de trabajo	colleague
pasado mañana	the day after tomorrow
tan pronto	so soon
¡qué lástima!	what a pity!

Say it in Spanish

What expressions were used in the dialogue to say the following?

a What are you doing here?
b I'm here on holiday.
c We are leaving the day after tomorrow.
d We've been here two days only.

Key phrases

Asking and giving travel information

¿A qué hora hay trenes / autobuses a ...?	What time are there trains / buses to...?
¿A qué hora sale / llega?	What time does it leave / arrive?
Llega / sale a las ...	It leaves / arrives at ...

Booking in at a hotel

¿Tiene una habitación individual (or sencilla) / doble?	Have you got a single / double room?
¿Tiene una habitación para dos / tres?	Have you got a room for two / three?
Quiero / prefiero / quisiera una habitación con baño.	I want / prefer / would like a room with a bathroom.
¿Tiene agua caliente?	Does it have hot water?

¿Sirven desayuno?	*Do you serve breakfast?*
con / sin desayuno	*with/without breakfast*

Saying how long you have been doing something

¿Cuánto tiempo hace que estás / vives aquí?	*How long have you been / lived here?*
Hace un año que estoy / vivo aquí.	*I've been / lived here for a year.*
¿Cuánto tiempo llevas trabajando / esperando?	*How long have you been working / waiting?*
Llevo una semana trabajando / esperando.	*I've been working / waiting for a week.*

Grammar

1 Impersonal sentences

Notice the use of **se** in impersonal sentences such as the following:

¿Cómo se escribe?	*How do you spell it?*
¿Cómo se pronuncia?	*How do you pronounce it?*
¿Cómo se dice?	*How do you say it?*

2 Saying how long you have been doing something

a *Hace* + time phrase + *que* + present tense

To refer to an action or a state which began in the past and is still in progress, use this construction with the present tense.

¿Cuánto tiempo hace que estás aquí?	*How long have you been here?*
Hace dos semanas que estoy aquí.	*I've been here for two weeks.*
¿Cuánto tiempo hace que trabajas en Chile?	*How long have you been working in Chile?*
Hace un año que trabajo en Chile.	*I've been working in Chile for a year.*

b Present tense + *desde hace* + time phrase

An alternative to the construction above, with exactly the same meaning, is this one in which the verb is highlighted by being placed in initial position.

Estoy aquí desde hace dos semanas.
Trabajo en Chile desde hace un año.

c *Llevar* + time phrase

Another way of referring to an action or state which began in the past and is still in progress, is to use this construction with **llevar** in the present tense.

¿Cuánto tiempo llevan aquí?	*How long have you been here?*
Llevamos (aquí) dos días solamente.	*We've been here for two days only.*
¿Cuánto tiempo llevas con Rodrigo?	*How long have you been with Rodrigo?*
Llevo un año con él.	*I've been with him for a year.*

3 *Para / por*

Observe the uses of **para** and **por** in the following examples:

Para el sábado 15 de febrero.	*For Saturday, 15th February.*
Una pieza para dos.	*A room for two.*
Cinco mil pesos por persona.	*Five thousand pesos per person.*

Practice

1   You are in Chile, and you want to travel from Santiago to Concepción, one of the largest cities in Chile, in the region of BíoBío, about 500 km south of Santiago. You go to the railway station to get information about trains. Follow the model (dialogue 1) to ask the questions, then use the information below to fill in the answers.

RÁPIDO DEL BÍOBÍO: Sale a las 22:30 horas para llegar a las 7:30 horas a Concepción (sólo se detiene en San Rosendo para conectar con Los Ángeles).

Departamento gran dormitorio: 44.200 pesos (ida y vuelta)
Departamendo sencillo: 37.900 pesos (ida y vuelta)
Cama baja: 23.500 pesos (ida y vuelta)
Cama alta: 19.900 pesos (ida y vuelta)
Salón: 6.900 pesos (ida)
Económica: 5.150 pesos (ida)
Primera: 4.350 (ida)
No tiene segunda

se detiene	*it stops*
detenerse	*to stop*
cama baja	*bottom berth*
cama alta	*upper berth*

Ud.	*Ask what time there is a train to Concepción.*
Empleado	— .
Ud.	*Ask what time it arrives in Concepción.*
Empleado	— .
Ud.	*Ask if it has a sleeping car.*
Empleado	— .
Ud.	*You are travelling on your own, so ask how much a berth is.*
Empleado	— .
Ud.	*Ask if that is the single or return price.*
Empleado	— .
Ud.	*Say it is all right, and ask for a return ticket for Monday, 20th July. Say you prefer a bottom berth.*
Empleado	Aquí tiene. Son veintitrés mil quinientos pesos.

2 You are telling a Chilean friend about your planned journey to Concepción.

Ud.	*Say you are going to travel to Concepción.*
Amigo	¿Cuándo piensas viajar?
Ud.	*Say you are leaving on July 20th.*
Amigo	¡Qué bien! Concepción es una ciudad muy bonita. Te va a gustar. Hace mucho tiempo que no voy allí. ¿Vas en bus?
Ud.	*No, you are going to travel by train.*
Amigo	Pero el tren demora bastante, ¿no?
Ud.	*It takes nine hours.*
Amigo	¿Va directo?
Ud.	*No, it stops in San Rosendo.*
Amigo	Sí, conozco muy bien San Rosendo. Tengo una amiga allí a quien no veo desde hace mucho tiempo. Se llama Carmela. Estudiamos juntos en la universidad.

a quien	*whom*
estudiamos juntos	*we studied together*
¡qué bien!	*great!*
demora bastante	*it takes a long time*

3 Someone has recommended the Hotel Arauco in Concepción to you, and you decide to get a room there. Write the conversation you might have with the hotel receptionist, using dialogue 2 as a model and some of the words and phrases listed under **Key phrases**. In the **Key to the activities** you will find another model dialogue to compare with your own version.

dos noches	*two nights*
cinco días	*five days*
una semana	*a week*
¿cuánto cuesta / vale?	*how much does it cost?*
¿está incluido el desayuno?	*is breakfast included?*

4 While reading a newspaper in Concepción you notice the advertisement opposite for an adventure holiday down the rapids of the river BíoBío which, in spite of protests in Chile and abroad, is going to be turned into a dam to provide electricity for the region. This is the sort of holiday that might interest one of your friends back home. Make sure you understand what they are offering so that you can tell your friend later on. Here are some key words:

la balsa	*raft*
a punto de	*about*
ser represado	*to be turned into a dam*
partiendo	*departing*
a primera hora	*early*
regresando	*returning*
ha sido pensado	*it has been planned*
la carpa / tienda (de campaña)	*tent*
Stgo.	*Short for Santiago*
$	*pesos (Chilean currency)*

BÍO-BÍO para Ejecutivos(as)

DESCENSO EN BALSA

A punto de ser represado, ésta puede ser la última oportunidad para conocer el río BíoBío. Tres días de excitante aventura en los rápidos más extraordinarios del mundo. Partiendo en avión el viernes a primera hora y regresando el domingo por la noche, este programa ha sido pensado para usted, que sabe aprovechar su tiempo libre.

En CASCADA tomamos su diversión en serio.

Valor (*): $250.000/persona enero, febrero, marzo.

Incluye: Pasaje aéreo Stgo-Concepción-Stgo, transporte terrestre, comidas, alojamiento en carpas, equipos y guías profesionales.

(*) Descuentos a grupos sobre 8 personas.

CASCADA

NATURE EXPEDITIONS

Now answer these questions in English:

- a   How long does this adventure holiday last?
- b   When does the plane leave Santiago?
- c   When does it return to Santiago?
- d   What does the holiday include?
- e   Are there any special discounts?

5   Your friend is flying to Chile from Sao Paulo, Brazil, where he had to do some business. He has asked you to meet him at the airport, so you want to make sure you are there on time. Check the flight details in the box below.

LLEGAN: HOY

PROCEDENCIAS	VUELO	COMPAÑÍA	LLEGA
GUAYAQUIL	041	ECUATORIANA	15.30
MENDOZA	201	LADECO	17.30
MONTEVIDEO-BUENOS AIRES	140	LAN CHILE	19.15
MONTEVIDEO-BUENOS AIRES	350	LADECO	19.30
MIAMI-BOGOTÁ-GUAYAQUIL	301	LADECO	21.30
SAO PAULO	173	LAN CHILE	21.55

Now answer these questions in Spanish:

a ¿En qué vuelo llega su amigo?
b ¿En qué compañía viaja?
c ¿A qué hora llega?

▶ 6 Guillermo, someone you met in Santiago, would like to go to Mendoza in Argentina, across the Andes from Chile. He is not sure how best to travel there, so he asks advice from his friend Carlos. Listen to their conversation, then answer the questions below. These key words will help you:

me gustaría	*I would like*
si en bus o...	*whether by bus or ...*
mira	*look*
muchísimo más	*very much more*
demora	*it takes (time)*
veces	*times*
el pasaje	*fare*
te puedo recomendar	*I can recommend to you*
te los puedo dar	*I can give them to you*

Are these statements true or false (**verdadero o falso**)?

a Carlos recomienda el bus porque el viaje es más barato.
b El bus demora dieciséis horas.
c El pasaje en bus no es caro.
d El hotel Plaza está en la calle principal.

7 The passage which follows deals with long-distance transport in Latin America. Study the key words before you read the text, then answer the questions opposite.

los países de habla hispana	*Spanish-speaking countries*
varía	*it varies*
suele ser	*it usually is*
soler (o > ue)	*(verb to express often)*
por ferrocarril	*by railway*
la red ferroviaria	*rail network*
la razón	*reason*
los viajes de larga distancia	*long-distance journeys*
llevan	*they have*
el tiempo de vacaciones	*holiday time*
por lo que	*so*
con antelación / por adelantado	*in advance*
llamado/a	*called*

América es un gran continente, y el transporte en los países de habla hispana varía entre lo más primitivo y lo más moderno y sofisticado. En general, predomina el transporte por carretera, que suele ser más rápido y más eficiente que el transporte por ferrocarril. La mayoría de los países hispanoamericanos no tiene una red ferroviaria importante. Argentina es una excepción. En otros países, en México y Chile por ejemplo, la red ferroviaria es mucho más reducida y presenta grandes deficiencias. Por esta razón, en los viajes de larga distancia, la mayoría de la gente prefiere utilizar el autobús o el avión.

En algunos países, entre ellos México, Chile, Argentina, existe un excelente servicio de autobuses de larga distancia, a precios bastante económicos. En México, por ejemplo, hay un servicio de autobuses (llamados también **camiones**) de primera clase que llevan aire acondicionado y baño (llamado también **lavabo** o **sanitario**). Este servicio, con asientos reservados, es mucho más cómodo que el servicio de segunda clase. En tiempo de vacaciones, mucha gente viaja en autobús, por lo que es necesario reservar los asientos con antelación.

Answer these questions in English:

a How do most people travel in Latin America?
b What does the text say about first-class long-distance buses in Mexico?
c What do you need to do during holiday time if you want to travel by bus? Why?

09 un recado
a message

In this unit you will learn
- how to talk about the past
- how to say how long ago something happened
- how to use the phone

▶ 1 ¿Cuándo hizo la reserva? *When did you make the reservation?*

Dennis Clerk arrives in a hotel in Santiago, Chile, where a room has been booked for him. Note how the following is expressed: **tengo una habitación reservada** *I have a room booked*, **una amiga reservó la habitación** *a friend booked the room*, **hace una semana** *a week ago*.

Dennis Clerk	Buenas tardes. Mi nombre es Dennis Clerk. Tengo una habitación reservada.
Recepcionista	Perdone, ¿puede repetir su nombre, por favor?
Dennis Clerk	Dennis Clerk. C-l-e-r-k. Clerk.
Recepcionista	Un momentito, por favor. ¿Cuándo hizo la reserva?
Dennis Clerk	Bueno, no la hice yo. Una amiga, la señorita Barbara Butler, reservó la habitación por teléfono, hace una semana más o menos.
Recepcionista	Ah sí, aquí está. Tiene la habitación ochenta y cinco. ¿Podría llenar esta ficha, si es tan amable?
Dennis Clerk	Sí, cómo no.

¿cuándo hizo ...?	*when did you make ...?*
por teléfono	*over the telephone*
más o menos	*more or less*
¿Podría llenar ...?	*Could you fill in ...?*
la ficha	*registration form*
si es tan amable	*if you would be so kind*
llenar / rellenar	*to fill in*
cómo no	*certainly*

Say it in Spanish

How is the following expressed in the dialogue?

a Can you repeat your name?
b When did you make the reservation?
c I didn't do it myself.

▶2 ¿Quiere dejar algún recado?
Would you like to leave a message?

Dennis Clerk telephones señora Patricia Miranda, a Chilean businesswoman, to make an appointment to see her. Note how the following is expressed: **quisiera hablar con ...** *I'd like to speak to ...,* **dígale que llamó ...** *tell her/him that ... called,* **salió** *he / she went out,* **llegué ayer** *I arrived yesterday.*

Recepcionista	Seguros Ibero-américa, buenos días.
Dennis Clerk	Buenos días. Quiero el anexo dos cinco cero, por favor.
Recepcionista	Un momentito. (*The receptionist puts him through to extension 250.*)
Secretaria	¿Aló?
Dennis Clerk	Buenos días, quisiera hablar con la señora Patricia Miranda, por favor.
Secretaria	La señora Miranda salió a almorzar con un cliente. Va a volver a las cuatro. ¿Quiere dejar algún recado?
Dennis Clerk	Sí, por favor dígale que llamó Dennis Clerk. Llegué ayer a Santiago y estoy en el hotel Santiago Park Plaza. La voy a llamar a las cuatro y media.
Secretaria	Muy bien, señor Clerk. Le daré su recado.

el seguro	*insurance*
el anexo (Chile) / **la extensión**	*extension*
almorzar	*to have lunch*
llamar	*to call*
dígale	*tell her / him*
le daré	*I'll give her / him*
llegar	*to arrive*
¿quiere dejar ...?	*do you want to leave ...?*
el recado	*message*

Answer these questions in English:

a What word in Spanish does the secretary use on the phone to say *hello*?
b Where is señora Miranda?
c What message does Dennis Clerk leave for her?

ℹ Reading telephone numbers

Telephone numbers in Spanish are read out as pairs of figures or as single figures, for example: **extensión** (or **anexo**, in Chile) **dos-cincuenta** or **dos-cinco-cero** (250), **teléfono seis-tres-nueve-seis-cinco-cero-siete** or **seis-treinta y nueve-sesenta y cinco-cero-siete** (639 6507).

▶ 3 Ya volvió *She has come back already*

Dennis Clerk telephones señora Miranda again. Note how the following is expressed: **¿podría decirme ...?** *could you tell me ...?*, **¿de parte de quién?** *who is calling?*, **volvió** *she/he came/has come back*.

Secretaria	¿Aló?
Dennis Clerk	Buenas tardes. ¿Podría decirme si volvió la señora Miranda?
Secretaria	Sí, ya volvió. ¿De parte de quién?
Dennis Clerk	De parte de Dennis Clerk.
Secretaria	Ah sí, un momentito señor Clerk.

si	*if*	**de parte de ...**	*this is ..., from ...*
ya	*already*		

Say it in Spanish

You have been trying to get your friend Alfonso on the phone. Use the guidelines below to complete your part of the conversation with señora Díaz, his mother.

Señora Díaz	¿Aló?
Ud.	*Say good evening and ask whether Alfonso has come back.*

Señora Díaz	Sí, volvió hace un momento. ¿De parte de quién?
Ud.	*Say who is calling.*
Señora Díaz	Un momentito, por favor.

▶ 4 Fue muy agradable *It was very pleasant*

Dennis Clerk meets señora Miranda and they talk about his journey. Note the following past tense forms: **llegó** *you arrived,* **llegué** *I arrived,* **fue** *It was,* **estuve aquí** *I was here,* **me gustó** *I liked it.*

Señora Miranda	Encantada de conocerlo, señor Clerk. Bienvenido a Chile.
Dennis Clerk	Muchas gracias.
Señora Miranda	¿Cuándo llegó?
Dennis Clerk	Llegué el miércoles en la noche.
Señora Miranda	¿Y qué tal el viaje?
Dennis Clerk	Fue muy agradable, aunque un poco largo.
Señora Miranda	¿Es la primera vez que viene a Santiago?
Dennis Clerk	No, estuve aquí hace cinco años y me gustó mucho.
Señora Miranda	Me alegro.

¿y qué tal el viaje?	*and how was the journey?*
hace cinco años	*five years ago*
agradable	*pleasant*
aunque	*although*
largo/a	*long*
la primera vez	*the first time*
me alegro (alegrarse)	*I'm glad (to be glad)*

Say it in Spanish

On a visit to Santiago you talk about your journey with a Chilean. Use the guidelines below to complete your part of the conversation.

Chileno	¿Es la primera vez que visita Santiago?
Ud.	*Say you were in Santiago two years ago. Say you liked it very much.*
Chileno	Me alegro mucho. ¿Y cuándo llegó?
Ud.	*Say you arrived on Saturday morning.*
Chileno	¿Y qué tal el viaje?
Ud.	*Say it was a bit long.*

ℹ️ Exchanging greetings with people you meet

Greetings used with people you meet for the first time, such as *pleased to meet you*, vary depending on the degree of formality (formal or familiar) but also on the gender of those involved (masculine or feminine). The exceptions are **mucho gusto**, which is invariable and may be used in formal and informal situations, and **hola**, which is informal.

- Formal or informal: **encantado** (if you are a man), **encantada** (if you are a woman)
- Formal: **encantado(a) de conocerlo/a** (to a man / woman)
- Informal: **encantado(a) de conocerte** (to a man or woman)

Key phrases

Talking about the past

¿Cuándo hizo la reserva / llegó?	*When did you make the reservation / arrive?*
Volvió / llegó / salió.	*He/she came back / arrived / went out.*
Me gustó (mucho).	*I liked it (very much).*

Saying how long ago something happened

Reservó la habitación hace una semana.	*He / she booked the room a week ago.*
Estuve aquí hace cinco años.	*I was here five years ago.*

Using the phone (see also Unit 11)

¿Aló? ¿Sí? (South Am), ¿Bueno? (México), ¿Holá? (River Plate)	*Hello?*
Quiero la extensión / el anexo (Chile) / el interno (River Plate) ...	*I want extension ...*
Quisiera hablar con ...	*I'd like to speak to ...*
¿Podría hablar con ...?	*Could I speak to ...?*
¿De parte de quién?	*Who is speaking? / Who shall I say?*
De parte de ...	*This/it is (name).*
¿Quiere dejar un recado/	*Would you like to leave a message?*
Dígale que ...	*Tell him / her that ...*

Grammar

1 Looking back: the preterite tense

Usage

To refer to events which happened and were completed in the past, as in *She went out for lunch*, English uses the simple past, which corresponds to the preterite tense in Spanish, **Salió a almorzar**. Here are some further examples:

Una amiga reservó la habitación.	*A friend booked the room.*
Llegué el lunes.	*I arrived on Monday.*
Fue muy difícil.	*It was very difficult.*
Estuvo aquí el año pasado.	*He / she was here last year.*
¿Qué hiciste ayer?	*What did you do yesterday?*
Salí con Antonia.	*I went out with Antonia.*

Events which happened in the recent past are normally expressed by Latin Americans with the preterite tense.

Ya almorcé.	*I've already had lunch.*
Hoy trabajamos mucho.	*We worked a lot today.*
Esta mañana vi a Isabel.	*I saw Isabel this morning.*

An alternative way of referring to recent past events is to use the perfect tense (see Unit 12), which is generally infrequent in Latin America in such contexts.

Ya he almorzado.	*I've already had lunch.*
Hoy hemos trabajado mucho.	*We've worked a lot today.*
Esta mañana he visto a Isabel.	*I've seen Isabel this morning.*

Formation

There are two sets of endings for the preterite tense, one for **-ar** verbs and another one for verbs in **-er** and **-ir**.

reservar	*to book*
reserv**é**	*I booked*
reserv**aste**	*you booked* (fam, sing)
reserv**ó**	*you booked* (pol, sing), *he, she booked*
reserv**amos**	*we booked*
reserv**aron**	*you booked* (pl), *they booked*

Note that the first person plural, **reservamos** *we booked*, is the same as for the present tense (see Unit 3).

volver	to return
volv**í**	I returned
volv**iste**	you returned (fam, sing)
volv**ió**	you returned (pol, sing), he, she returned
volv**imos**	we returned
volv**ieron**	you returned (pl), they returned

Here are some further examples of the use of the preterite tense with regular verbs.

¿Hablaste con él? — *Did you speak to him?*
Hablé con él el sábado. — *I spoke to him on Saturday.*
Nos quedamos una semana allí. — *We stayed there for a week.*
Bebió demasiado. — *He / she drank too much.*
No entendí nada. — *I didn't understand anything.*
Vivieron aquí muchos años. — *They lived here for many years.*
Subió a su habitación. — *He / she went up to his / her room.*

Irregular forms

Some verbs form the preterite tense in an irregular way. Here is a list of the main ones. Note the similarity among some of the forms.

andar *to walk*	anduve, anduviste, anduvo, anduvimos, anduvieron
estar *to be*	estuve, estuviste, estuvo, estuvimos, estuvieron
tener *to have*	tuve, tuviste, tuvo, tuvimos, tuvieron
poder *to be able, can*	pude, pudiste, pudo, pudimos, pudieron
poner *to put*	puse, pusiste, puso, pusimos, pusieron
saber *to know*	supe, supiste, supo, supimos, supieron
hacer *to do, make*	hice, hiciste, hizo, hicimos, hicieron
querer *to want, love*	quise, quisiste, quiso, quisimos, quisieron
venir *to come*	vine, viniste, vino, vinimos, vinieron
decir *to say*	dije, dijiste, dijo, dijimos, dijeron
traer *to bring*	traje, trajiste, trajo, trajimos, trajeron
dar *to give*	di, diste, dio, dimos, dieron
oír *to hear*	oí, oíste, oyó, oímos, oyeron
ver *to see*	vi, viste, vio, vimos, vieron
ir *to go*	fui, fuiste, fue, fuimos, fueron
ser *to be*	fui, fuiste, fue, fuimos, fueron

Here are some examples of the use of the preterite with irregular verbs.

¿Hizo usted la reserva?	*Did you make the reservation?*
No pude hacerla.	*I couldn't do it.*
No quiso venir con nosotros, vinimos solos.	*He / she didn't want to come with us, we came on our own.*
Fui a la fiesta de María, que estuvo muy buena.	*I went to María's party, which was very good.*
Fue el sábado.	*It was on Saturday.*
Le dije que lo necesitaba, pero no lo trajo.	*I told him / her that I needed it, but he / she didn't bring it.*

For other irregular preterite forms, see pages 215–18.

2 Time phrases associated with the past

To talk about the past, use time phrases like the following:

ayer	*yesterday*
ayer en la mañana / tarde / noche	*yesterday morning / afternoon / evening*
anteayer / antes de ayer / antier (México, Colombia, etc.)	*the day before yesterday*
la semana pasada	*last week*
el mes / año pasado	*last month/ year*
el lunes / martes pasado	*last Monday / Tuesday*
anoche	*last night*
en 1999	*in 1999*
hace mucho / poco tiempo	*a long/short time ago*

3 Saying how long ago something happened:

Hace + time phrase + preterite tense

To say how long ago something happened, use **hace** in this construction with a time phrase and a verb in the preterite tense.

¿Cuánto tiempo hace que llegó?	*How long ago did you / he / she arrive?*
Llegué hace una semana.	*I arrived a week ago.*
Hace un año que llegó.	*He / she arrived a year ago.*

Practice

1 Write a dialogue based on this situation, using dialogue 1 as a model.

- You arrive in a hotel in a Latin American country. At the reception desk you identify yourself and say that you have a reservation.
- The receptionist asks you to repeat your name. You do so and spell your surname for him.
- He wants to know when you made the reservation. Explain that this was not made by yourself, but by your secretary who phoned directly from your home town (give the name of the town) about five days ago.
- The receptionist finally finds the reservation. He's given you room 50 on the fifth floor. Before giving you the key, he asks you to fill in the registration form.

mi secretaria	*my secretary*
directamente	*directly*
desde	*from*
más o menos	*about, more or less*

2 What would you say, in Spanish, in these situations?

a You are in a hotel in Santiago, Chile, and the telephone rings in your room. You lift up the receiver and say ...?

b You telephone Viña San Sebastián in Chile, a company you are doing business with, and ask for **extension 2552.**

c The secretary on extension 2552 answers the phone. Ask to speak to señor Juan Miguel García.

d The secretary asks who is speaking. Identify yourself.

e You meet señor Juan Miguel García for the first time. Say how pleased you are to meet him.

f Back at your hotel, you telephone señorita Elena Alonso, an acquaintance of yours. She is not at home at the moment, and the person who answers the phone asks if you want to leave a message. Ask them to tell señorita Alonso that you phoned and to inform her that you arrived in Santiago two days ago. Say which hotel you are staying at (**Hotel Plaza**) and give the room number (**habitación 50**).

▶ 3 At the office of señor Solís, a businessman from Santiago, Chile, the receptionist has taken two messages for him. The first is from señora Carmen Puig, from Venezuela and the second from señorita Marilú Pérez, a Chilean. Listen to the two messages then note down each message in English. First, look at these key words:

el mensaje	message	urgentemente	urgently
el recado	message	vino	he / she came
la reunión	meeting		

4 Back in his country, Dennis Clerk receives a postcard from someone he met in Chile. Unfortunately, it got a bit smudged. Here are the words you need to fill in. Put them in the right order in the gaps below.

a	estuvimos	e	gustó
b	levanté	f	fue
c	fui	g	tomé
d	senté	h	entramos

Querido Dennis:

Me alegro mucho de haberte conocido y espero que vuelvas a Chile el año próximo, como me prometiste. Tengo recuerdos muy bonitos de tu estadía en Chile. Para mí _____ muy especial.

Ayer en la tarde _____ con Mónica al café donde nos conocimos. Allí _____ hasta las cinco de la tarde. Después Mónica y yo _____ a un cine a ver una película inglesa que nos _____ mucho. Hoy me _____ muy tarde, _____ un café y después me _____ frente a mi escritorio a escribirte esta tarjeta.

Te abraza

María Soledad

querido/a	dear
de haberte conocido	to have met you
espero que vuelvas	I hope you come back
prometiste	you promised
los recuerdos	memories
la estadía	stay (in Spain, **la estancia**)
nos conocimos	we met
la película	film
después	afterwards
el escritorio	desk
la tarjeta	postcard
te abraza (abrazar)	love (to embrace)

5 What questions would you need to ask to get the following replies?

a Llegué ayer en la tarde.
b El viaje fue bastante tranquilo.
c Sí, la señorita Alonso ya volvió.
d No, no es la primera vez que vengo. Estuve en Santiago hace un año y medio.
e Sí, me gustó mucho Chile.
f Sí, ya cené.

▶ 6 Marilú, a Chilean, was asked about her last holiday. Listen to what she says, then answer the questions below. First, look at this new vocabulary:

la costa	*coast*
disfrutamos	*we enjoyed it*
ya que	*as*
maravillosas	*wonderful*
el aire	*air*
tan puro	*so clean (pure)*
harto	*a lot*
nadar	*to swim*
llenos de energía	*full of energy*
deportes	*sports*

Answer these questions in English:

a   Where did Marilú go during the holidays?
b   Where did they stay?
c   How does she describe the place?
d   How does she express the following: *we went out a lot, we sunbathed, we swam, we played some sports?*

7 A Latin American friend asks you about your last holiday. Answer his questions using real or imaginary information.

a   ¿Dónde fuiste de vacaciones?
b   ¿Fuiste solo/a o acompañado/a?
c   ¿Dónde te quedaste?
d   ¿Cuánto tiempo estuviste allí?
e   ¿Qué hiciste durante tus vacaciones?

10

vivía en España

I used to live in Spain

In this unit you will learn
- how to say what you used to
  do or were doing
- how to describe places and
  people you knew
- how to say what you are
  doing now

▶ 1 ¿Qué hacías en Barcelona?
What were you doing in Barcelona?

Marta and José Luis, both Argentinian, talk about Barcelona, where Marta used to live. Key words and phrases here are **vivía/s** *I/you used to live,* **hacías** *you used to do,* **trabajaba** *I used to work,* **estoy buscando ...** *I'm looking for ...* Note also the use of **vos** instead of **tú**, and the change in the accentuation of verbs in the second person singular of the present tense, a feature which is characteristic of Argentinian Spanish.

José Luis	Hola, ¿cómo te llamás?
Marta	Me llamo Marta, ¿y vos?
José Luis	Yo me llamo José Luis. ¿Sos de Buenos Aires?
Marta	Sí, soy de acá, pero recién volví. Vivía en España. Estuve allá varios años.
José Luis	¡No me digas! Yo estuve en España hace un par de años y me gustó mucho. ¿Dónde vivías vos?
Marta	En Barcelona. ¿Conocés Barcelona?
José Luis	Sí, pasé una semana allá. Es una ciudad muy linda. Y vos, ¿qué hacías en Barcelona?
Marta	Trabajaba con un colega argentino. Yo soy psicóloga. ¿Y vos, qué hacés?
José Luis	Recién terminé mis estudios en la universidad. Estudié arquitectura y ahora estoy buscando trabajo.
Marta	¡Qué tengas suerte!
José Luis	Gracias.

sos	*you are* (fam., Argentina)
acá / allá	*here / there*
recién volví / terminé	*I have just returned / finished*
varios/as	*several*
¡no me digas!	*you don't say!*
pasé (pasar)	*I spent (to spend)*
¡que tengas suerte!	*good luck!*

Match each question with an appropriate answer

a ¿Qué hacías?

b ¿Qué estudiabas?

c ¿Dónde trabajabas?

d ¿Dónde vivías?

1 Medicina.

2 En un apartamento / departamento

3 Estudiaba en la universidad.

4 En un banco

▶2 Estaba frente a la playa
It was opposite the beach

Marta describes the place where she used to live. Key words here are **era** *it was*, **estaba** *it was* (position), **tenía** *it had*. Note also how she says what she used to do: **viajaba** *I used to travel*, **compartía** *I used to share*, **pasaba** *I used to spend* (time).

José Luis	¿En qué parte de Barcelona vivías?
Marta	Bueno, yo no vivía en la ciudad misma. Vivía en Sitges, un lugar muy lindo que está a media hora de Barcelona. Viajaba a Barcelona en tren los días de semana. Los fines de semana los pasaba en Sitges. Compartía un departamento con una amiga catalana. Era una chica bastante joven, y era muy simpática. Nos llevábamos muy bien.
José Luis	¿No extrañás todo eso?
Marta	Bueno, la verdad es que estoy contenta de estar otra vez en Buenos Aires, pero sí, a veces extraño la vida allá. Teníamos un departamento muy agradable. No era muy grande, pero estaba frente a la playa y tenía una vista maravillosa.
José Luis	Y ahora, ¿dónde vivís?
Marta	Estoy viviendo en la casa de mis padres en Villa Devoto, pero pienso alquilar un departamento más cerca del centro.
José Luis	¡Ojalá que tengas suerte!
Marta	Gracias.

mismo/a	*itself*
los días de semana	*weekdays*
catalán / catalana	*Catalan, Catalonian*
chico/a	*boy / girl*
nos llevábamos muy bien	*we got on very well*
extrañar	*to miss*
la verdad es que ...	*the truth is that ...*
otra vez	*again*
teníamos	*we had*
la vista	*view*
maravilloso/a	*wonderful*
alquilar	*to rent, hire*
el departamento / apartamento	*apartment, flat*
ojalá que ...	*let's hope that ...*

Fill in the blanks

In a letter to a friend Ricardo described the house where he used to live, and the friends he used to share it with. Fill in the blanks below with a suitable verb from the list: **tenía, trabajaba, era, estudiaba, estaba, compartía.**

La casa en que vivía _____ muy linda y _____ a pocos minutos del centro de la ciudad. No _____ muy grande, pero _____ bastante cómoda, y _____ tres habitaciones. Yo _____ la casa con Javier y Ana. Javier _____ arquitectura y _____ un excelente amigo. Ana _____ en un hospital. Ella _____ enfermera *(nurse)*.

Key phrases

Saying what you used to do or were doing

¿Qué hacías?	*What did you do / were you doing ...?*
(Yo) vivía / compartía / trabajaba ...	*I used to live / share / work ...*

Describing places and people you knew

Era grande / bonito(a).	*It was big / pretty.*
Estaba frente a la playa / cerca del centro de la ciudad.	*It was opposite the beach / near the city centre.*
Tenía tres habitaciones / una vista maravillosa.	*It had three rooms / a wonderful view.*
Era joven / simpático(a).	*He / she was young / nice.*
Era alto(a) / delgado(a).	*He / she was tall / slim.*
Tenía cabello largo y ojos oscuros.	*He / she had long hair and dark eyes*

Saying what you are doing now

Estoy buscando trabajo / viviendo con mis padres.	*I'm looking for work / living with my parents.*

Grammar

1 The imperfect tense

Usage

The imperfect tense is used to say what you used to do or were doing and to describe people, places and things you knew in the past.

Unlike the preterite tense, which you studied in Unit 9, it denotes actions which were incomplete or whose beginning or end is not specified. Compare for instance:

(preterite tense)
Viví allí durante un año.   *I lived there for a year.*
(imperfect tense)
En 1992 yo **vivía** allí.   *In 1992 I was living there.*

The first sentence refers to an event which lasted over a definite period of time and ended in the past, therefore the preterite tense is used. The second sentence focuses on the action itself, *I was living.* We don't know when the action was completed, therefore the imperfect tense is used.

In descriptive language in general, for instance *she was nice, the apartment was pleasant,* there is no concern for time (except to show that a past experience is being referred to, e.g. **era simpática** as opposed to **es simpática**), so the imperfect tense is used.

Note, however, that this difference between the two tenses in Spanish is not always expressed in English, as English often uses the simple past where Spanish would use the imperfect tense, for example:

Yo trabajaba con un colega.   *I worked / used to work /*
                              was working with a colleague.
El apartamento era agradable. *The apartment was nice.*

Formation

There are two sets of endings for the imperfect tense, one for **-ar** verbs and another for **-er** and **-ir** verbs.

trabajar *to work*	
trabaj**aba**	*I worked / used to work / was working*
trabaj**abas**	*you worked / used to work / were working* (fam, sing)
trabaj**aba**	*you worked / used to work / were working* (pol, sing)
	he, she worked / used to work / was working
trabaj**ábamos**	*we worked / used to work / were working*
trabaj**aban**	*you worked / used to work / were working* (pl)
	they worked / used to work / were working

Note that the first and third person singular share the same endings.

tener *to have*	
ten**ía**	*I had / used to have*
ten**ías**	*you had / used to have* (fam, sing)
ten**ía**	*you had / used to have* (pol, sing)
	he, she had / used to have
ten**íamos**	*we had / used to have*
ten**ían**	*you had / used to have* (pl)
	they had / used to have

Note that the first and third person singular share the same endings. Note also that -**ir** verbs, e.g. **vivir** *to live*, have the same endings as -**er** verbs: **vivía, vivías, vivía**, etc. Here is another example demonstrating the use of the imperfect tense:

Vivíamos en un departamento muy agradable que **estaba** frente al mar. Los fines de semana **nos levantábamos** muy tarde, **desayunábamos** y después **bajábamos** a la playa. En la playa **había** siempre mucha gente que **venía** de Barcelona a pasar el fin de semana, especialmente durante el verano. A partir de octubre, Sitges **era** un lugar muy tranquilo.

bajar	*to go down*	**a partir de**	*starting in*
había	*there were*	**tranquilo**	*quiet*
la gente	*people*		

Irregular imperfect forms

There are only three irregular verbs in the imperfect tense:

ir *to go*	iba, ibas, iba, íbamos, iban
ser *to be*	era, eras, era, éramos, eran
ver *to see*	veía, veías, veía, veíamos, veían

Here is an example demonstrating the use of the imperfect tense with irregular verbs:

Yo **veía** a Carmen todos los días. Carmen **era** alta, delgada, de pelo muy negro y ojos cafés. Carmen y yo **íbamos** a la playa a tomar el sol y nadar. Carmen **era** muy linda e inteligente.

| **tomar el sol**   *to sunbathe* | **nadar**   *to swim* |

Notice that before an **i**, **y** changes to **e**: **e inteligente**.

2 *Estar* + gerund

To refer to events which are taking place at the moment of speaking, you can use the simple present tense, e.g. **¿Qué haces?** *What are you doing?* or the present continuous, which is formed with the verb **estar** followed by a gerund (words like **buscando** *looking for* and **viviendo** *living*).

| Estoy buscando trabajo. | *I am looking for work.* |
| Estoy viviendo en la casa de mis padres. | *I am living in my parents' house.* |

There are two endings for the gerund in Spanish, one for **-ar** verbs and one for **-er** and **-ir** verbs.

-ar verbs form the gerund with **-ando**:
   (trabajar)   Estoy trabaj**ando**.   *I am working.*

-er and **-ir** verbs form the gerund with **-iendo**:
   (comer)   Estamos com**iendo**.   *We are eating.*
   (escribir)   Ellos están escrib**iendo**.   *They are writing.*

3 The use of *vos* for *tú*

In certain regions of Latin America, **tú** is replaced by **vos**. This is the standard form in the River Plate area (Argentina, Uruguay). Verb endings corresponding to **vos** are generally the same as for **tú**, except in the present tense, the present subjunctive (Unit 13) and the imperative (Units 12 and 13). The following examples illustrate the use of **vos** with present tense verbs:

Standard	Argentinian
¿Cómo te llamas (tú)?	¿Cómo te llamás (vos)?
	What's your name?
¿Qué haces (tú)?	¿Qué hacés (vos)?
	What do you do?

¿Dónde vives (tú)?   ¿Dónde vivís (vos)?
                       Where do you live?

Note that stem-changes do not apply to **vos**:
¿Cuándo vuelves (tú)? ¿Cuándo volvés (vos)?
                       When are you coming back?

¿Qué dices (tú)?   ¿Qué decís (vos)?
                       What are you saying?

¿Qué quieres (tú)?   ¿Qué querés (vos)?
                       What do you want?

Eres, from **ser** *to be*, changes in Argentina to **sos**:
¿(Tú) eres de aquí?   ¿(Vos) sos de aquí?
                       Are you from here?

4 *Recién (just)* + preterite tense

To refer to an action which has just taken place, use the word
recién *just*, followed by a verb in the past:

Recién terminé.   *I have just finished.*
Recién volví.   *I have just returned.*
Recién salió.   *He / she has just gone out.*

This usage is Latin American. In Spain, **recién** is only used
before past participles, e.g. **El pan está recién hecho** *The bread
has just been made.* Peninsular Spanish normally uses a
construction with **acabar de** followed by the infinitive, e.g.
Acaba de llegar *He/she has just arrived.* This construction is also
used by Latin Americans, though perhaps less frequently (see
Unit 13)

Practice

1 In the passage below, which is based on dialogues 1 and 2,
all the verbs are missing. Try to complete it with the verbs from
the list, without looking at the dialogues.

a	pasaba	**g**	se llamaba
b	estaba	**h**	tenía
c	compartía	**i**	era
d	vivían	**j**	vivía
e	trabajaba	**k**	gustaba
f	había	**l**	viajaba

En 1990, Marta _____ en Sitges y _____ con un colega argentino en Barcelona. Marta _____ a Barcelona en tren los días de semana. Los fines de semana los _____ en Sitges donde _____ un departamento con una amiga catalana. Su amiga _____ Montserrat. El departamento donde ellas _____ no _____ muy grande, pero_____ una vista maravillosa, ya que _____ frente a la playa. A Marta le _____ mucho Sitges, especialmente a partir de octubre, cuando _____ poca gente en el lugar.

2 Below is an extract from a letter written by María Inés, an Argentinian, to a correspondent. María Inés writes about her life in Bariloche, in southern Argentina, before she came to live in Buenos Aires. Read it through, then check your understanding by answering the questions below. Here are some key words:

preguntar	*to ask*
acerca de	*about*
la vida	*life*
antes de	*before*
te conté (contar)	*I told you (to tell)*
el lago	*lake*
ganaba (ganar)	*I used to earn (to earn)*
la plata	*money*
la temporada	*season*
a pesar de que	*although*
así fue como . . .	*this was how . . .*
hice mis valijas	*I packed my suitcases*
el paisaje	*landscape*
el aire puro	*pure air*

Querido Paul:

En tu última carta me preguntás acerca de mi vida antes de venir a Buenos Aires. Bueno, ya te conté que llegué aquí hace cinco años. Antes vivía en Bariloche, una ciudad muy linda que está a unos 1.700 kilómetros de Buenos Aires.

Bariloche es un lugar de mucho turismo y yo trabajaba como guía en una agencia de viajes. Vivía en un departamento muy agradable, frente al lago. Durante el verano estaba siempre muy ocupada y ganaba bastante plata, pero a partir de marzo, cuando terminaba la temporada de vacaciones, la vida era muy tranquila y a veces un poco monótona.

Mi familia vivía en Buenos Aires y los extrañaba, a pesar de que en Bariloche tenía algunos amigos. Así fue como un día hice mis valijas y decidí volver a la capital. Estoy contenta de estar aquí otra vez, aunque a veces extraño el paisaje y el aire puro de Bariloche ...

---

me preguntás (Arg.)	*you ask me*
la valija (Arg.)	*suitcase*

Answer these questions in Spanish:

a ¿Dónde vivía María Inés?
b ¿En qué trabajaba?
c ¿Cómo era su departamento?
d ¿Dónde estaba su departamento?
e ¿Cómo era la vida a partir de marzo?
f ¿Por qué decidió volver a Buenos Aires?

3 Look at this plan of the flat where María Inés used to live and then answer the questions which follow.

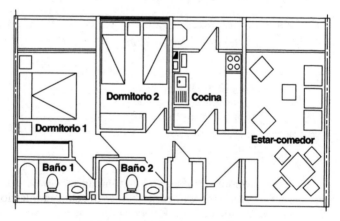

a ¿Cuántos dormitorios tenía el departamento?
b ¿Cuántos baños tenía?
c ¿Dónde estaba la cocina?
d ¿Cuántas camas había en el dormitorio uno?

el estar *sitting room*	**la cocina** *kitchen*

▶ **4**   Now listen to Carlos García, an Argentinian who used to live in São Paulo, Brazil. He talks about his life in that city. Look at the key words, then answer the questions.

¿Siempre has vivido . . .?	*Have you always lived . . .?*
daba clases de pintura	*I used to teach painting*
el barrio	*district, area*
arborizados	*with many trees*
la vegetación	*vegetation*
los vecinos	*neighbours*
¿Qué tal eran?	*What were they like?*
como todos los brasileros	*like all Brazilians*
todavía	*still*

Are these statements true or false (**verdadero o falso**)?

a   Carlos era profesor de pintura.
b   El barrio de Vila Mariana tenía poca vegetación.
c   El departamento de Carlos era grande.
d   Carlos tenía buenos vecinos.
e   Carlos volvió a Buenos Aires porque no le gustaba San Pablo.

5   Imagine you are asked by a Latin American friend about your life five or ten years ago. Answer these questions giving real or imaginary information.

a   ¿Dónde vivías tú hace cinco / diez años?
b   ¿Estabas soltero/a o casado/a?
c   ¿Con quién vivías?
d   ¿Qué hacías? ¿Estudiabas / trabajabas?
e   ¿Dónde estudiabas / trabajabas?
f   ¿Te gustaba tu trabajo?
g   ¿Cómo era tu casa?

6   At a party you meet Pedro, an Ecuadorean who now lives in your country. Follow the guidelines below to ask him questions, using the familiar form.

a   Ask where he lived before.
b   Ask in what part of Ecuador he lived.
c   Ask what he used to do there.
d   Ask what he is doing here.

▶ 7 Carlos García, from Argentina, describes his native Buenos Aires. Listen to the description, then answer the questions below. First, look at these key words:

¿Cómo describirías . . .?	How would you describe . . .?
los rincones	corners
la unidad común	common unity
el movimiento cultural	cultural life (movement)
el alma	soul
la vida nocturna	nightlife
expresarse	to express oneself
la tendencia	tendency
los porteños	name given to the inhabitants of Buenos Aires
entristecer	to become sad
la melancolía	melancholy

Now answer these questions in English:

a How does Carlos describe Buenos Aires?
b What does he like most about the city?
c What doesn't he like about the city?

8 During a holiday in a Latin American country, you meet someone you like very much. When you get back home that evening you describe that person to your Spanish-speaking friend.

Use this description as a guideline, and add further information if you wish.

• He / she was very good-looking, dark, tall and slim.
• He / she had black hair and green eyes.
• He / she was about your age.
• He / she was very nice.

9 Write a brief passage recounting a period in your life, including information about a place and someone you used to know. Try using some of the words and phrases from earlier parts of the unit and, with a help of a dictionary, add others of your own.

11

me gustaría alquilar un coche

I would like to hire a car

In this unit you will learn
- how to hire a car
- how to offer to do something
- how to make requests
- how to make a telephone call

▶1 Allá alquilan coches
There they rent cars

Gonzalo, an Argentinian, asks his friend Lucía to recommend a car rental agency. First, try learning these key phrases: **Me gustaría alquilar un coche** *I'd like to hire a car,* **¿Me podrías recomendar alguna agencia?** *Could you recommend an agency?*

Gonzalo	Hola Lucía, buen día.
Lucía	Buen día, Gonzalo.
Gonzalo	¿Qué vas a hacer hoy?
Lucía	Voy a ir a nadar. ¿Querés venir conmigo?
Gonzalo	No, gracias. Me gustaría alquilar un coche para salir con Silvia y los chicos. ¿Me podrías recomendar alguna agencia?
Lucía	Sí, sí, a media cuadra del Centro Cívico está la agencia Nahuelhuapi. Allá alquilan coches.
Gonzalo	¿Cerca del Centro Cívico dijiste?
Lucía	Sí, dos cuadras más abajo, a la derecha.

buen día (Arg.)	*good morning*
hoy	*today*
alquilar / arrendar	*to hire, rent*
conmigo	*with me*
los chicos / niños	*children*
¿podrías ...? (poder)	*could you...? (can)*
a media cuadra	*half a block away*
¿... dijiste?	*...did you say? (fam)*
más abajo	*further down*

Say it in Spanish

How would you express the following in Spanish?

a We'd like to hire a car.
b Could you (formal) recommend us an agency?
c It's half a block from here.
d It's four blocks further down, on the left.

▶2 Alquilando un coche *Hiring a car*

Gonzalo hires a car. First, try learning these key phrases: **¿Qué me recomienda?** *What do you recommend?*, **Le recomiendo ...** *I recommend ...,* **¿Cuánto cuesta el alquiler?** *How much is the rental?*

Empleada	Buen día. ¿Qué desea?
Gonzalo	Buen día. Quisiera alquilar un coche ¿Qué me recomienda?
Empleada	Bueno, tenemos varios modelos. ¿Quiere un coche chico?
Gonzalo	No demasiado chico. Somos cuatro personas.
Empleada	Bueno, en ese caso le recomiendo el Ford Fiesta, que tiene capacidad para cuatro personas. Es un coche bastante cómodo y económico.
Gonzalo	¿Cuánto cuesta el alquiler?
Empleada	Si es por uno o dos días, cuesta noventa dólares diarios, con kilometraje ilimitado. Por semana, vale cuatrocientos dólares. El impuesto y el seguro están incluidos.
Gonzalo	Bueno, lo quiero por dos días solamente, sábado y domingo.
Empleada	Muy bien. ¿Quiere reservarlo ahora?
Gonzalo	Sí, prefiero reservarlo ahora mismo.
Empleada	Pase por aquí, por favor.

chico/a	*small*
la capacidad	*room*
cómodo/a	*comfortable*
el kilometraje ilimitado	*unlimited mileage*
ahora mismo	*right now*
pase por aquí	*come this way*
el impuesto	*tax*
el seguro	*insurance*

Answer these questions in English

a How does the employee describe the car she recommends?
b How much is the rental per day?
c What does the rental price include?
d How long does Gonzalo want the car for?

▶ 3 En la estación de servicio
At the petrol station

Gonzalo stops at a petrol station (**estación de servicio**) to fill up. Practise saying these key sentences first: **¿Se lo lleno?** *Shall I fill it up for you?*, **Llénelo** *Fill it up*, **¿Me revisa la presión de las** ruedas? *Will you check the tyre pressure for me?*, ¿Le miro el aceite? *Shall I look at the oil for you?*

Empleado	¿Se lo lleno?
Gonzalo	Sí, llénelo. Y me revisa la presión de las ruedas también.
Empleado	¿Le miro el aceite?
Gonzalo	No, el aceite está bien.
Empleado	Listo señor.
Gonzalo	¿Cuánto es?
Empleado	Son quince pesos.
Gonzalo	Gracias. ¿Me podría decir si falta mucho para llegar a Esquel?
Empleado	Veinte kilómetros más o menos.
Gonzalo	Gracias.

llenar	*to fill up*
revisar	*to check*
la rueda	*wheel*
el aceite	*oil*
la gasolina	*petrol*
listo/a	*ready*
¿Falta mucho?	*Is it a long way off?*

Answer these questions in English:

a What services does Gonzalo request at the service station?
b What expression does he use to say *Could you tell me ...?*

▶ 4 Una rueda pinchada *A puncture*

Gonzalo has a puncture, and he drives to the nearest garage to have the tyre repaired. Note the use of the word **la goma**, Argentinian Spanish for *tyre*, known as **la llanta** or **el neumático** in other Latin American countries.

Gonzalo	Buenas tardes. ¿Podrían repararme esta goma?
Mecánico	¿Para cuándo la quiere?
Gonzalo	Para esta misma tarde. Tenemos que volver a Bariloche.
Mecánico	A las tres y media se la puedo tener lista.
Gonzalo	Sí, está bien. Vuelvo a esa hora.

pinchada	*punctured*
reparar	*to repair*
esta misma tarde	*this afternoon*
a esa hora	*at that time*

Say it in Spanish

What expressions are used in the dialogue to say the following?

a Could you repair ... for me?
b When do you want it for?
c I can have it ready for you.

▶5 Una llamada telefónica
A telephone call

Back at his hotel, Gonzalo makes an international telephone call through the hotel switchboard. First, try learning these key sentences: **Quiero llamar a Londres** *I want to call London,* **Es una llamada de persona a persona** *It's a personal call,* **¿Hay mucha demora?** *Is there a long delay?*

Telefonista	¿Hola?
Gonzalo	Hola, telefonista. Llamo desde la habitación trescientos diez. ¿Sería posible hacer una llamada internacional desde mi habitación? Quiero llamar a Londres.

Telefonista	Sí, sí se puede. ¿A qué número de Londres desea llamar?
Gonzalo	Al 81-601 1326.
Telefonista	81-601 1326.
Gonzalo	Es una llamada de persona a persona.
Telefonista	¿Su nombre, por favor?
Gonzalo	Gonzalo Lira.
Telefonista	¿Y el nombre de la persona con quien desea hablar?
Gonzalo	Robert Major. M-a-j-o-r, Major. ¿Hay mucha demora?
Telefonista	No, en este momento no. Cuelgue por favor. Yo lo llamaré.
Gonzalo	Gracias.

llamo (llamar) desde	I am calling (to call) from
¿sería posible ...?	would it be possible ...?
la llamada	telephone call
se puede	it is possible
cuelgue (colgar)	hang up (to hang up)

Say it in Spanish

While travelling in a Latin American country you telephone your family back home.

Use the guidelines below to talk to the operator at your hotel.

a Say you are calling from room twenty-five.
b Ask if it would be possible to phone (name the country) from your room.
c Say it is a personal call, and give the telephone number and the name of the person you want to call.

Key phrases

Hiring a car

Me gustaría / Quisiera alquilar / arrendar un coche / carro.	I would like to hire a car.
¿Cuánto cuesta / vale el alquiler?	How much is the rental?
Cuesta ... diarios / por día / semana.	It costs ... per day / week.
Quiero un coche / carro chico (or pequeño) / grande / mediano.	I want a small / big / medium size car.

| Lo quiero por dos días / una semana. | *I want it for two days / a week.* |
| ¿Está incluido el impuesto / iva / seguro? | *Is tax / vat / insurance included?* |

Offering to do something

| ¿Se lo lleno? | *Shall I fill it up?* |
| ¿Le reviso/miro ...? | *Shall I check / have a look at ...?* |

Making requests

¿Me revisa la presión de las ruedas / el aceite?	*Will you check the air pressure in the wheels / the oil?*
¿Podría(n) repararme el coche / carro / este neumático?	*Could you repair my car / this tyre?*
Lo / la quiero para hoy / esta tarde.	*I want it for today / this afternoon.*

Making a telephone call (see also Unit 9)

Quiero / quisiera llamar a Londres / Nueva York.	*I want / would like to call London / New York.*
¿Sería posible hacer una llamada internacional / de larga distancia / de persona a persona?	*Would it be possible to make an international / long distance / personal call?*
Quiero hacer una llamada con cobro revertido / por cobrar.	*I want to reverse the charges.*
¿Hay mucha demora?	*Is there a long delay?*

Grammar

1 The conditional tense

To say what you would like, as in *I would like to hire a car*, and to ask whether something is possible, e.g. *Could you repair this tyre?* or *Would it be possible to make an international phone call from my room?*, you can use the conditional tense.

Formation

Like the future tense (see Unit 8), the conditional is formed with the infinitive, to which the appropriate ending is added. The endings are the same for **-ar**, **-er** and **-ir** verbs. Here is the conditional tense of a regular verb:

ser	to be	
ser**ía**		*I would be*
ser**ías**		*you would be* (fam, sing)
ser**ía**		*you would be* (pol, sing)
		he, she, it would be
ser**íamos**		*we would be*
ser**ían**		*you would be* (pl)
		they would be

Notice that the first and third person singular are the same and that all forms carry an accent.

Here are some examples of the use of the conditional tense with regular verbs:

Me gustaría ir a la Argentina.	*I would like to go to Argentina.*
¿Qué te gustaría hacer?	*What would you like to do?*
Preferiría un coche chico.	*I would prefer a small car.*
¿Cuándo irían a Sudamérica?	*When would you / they go to South America?*

Remember that **gustar**, *to like*, takes the third person of the verb (see Unit 6): **me gustaría** *I would like*, **te gustaría** *you would like* (fam), **le gustaría** *you* (pol) / *he / she would like*, **nos gustaría** *we would like*, **les gustaría** *you / they would like*.

Irregular conditional forms

Verbs with irregular stems in the future tense (see Unit 8) also have them in the conditional. The endings are the same as those of regular verbs. Here are some of the most common:

decir	*to say, to tell*	diría, dirías, diría, diríamos, dirían
hacer	*to do, to make*	haría, harías, haría, haríamos, harían
poder	*can, to be able*	podría, podrías, podría, podríamos, podrían
salir	*to go out, to leave*	saldría, saldrías, saldría, saldríamos, saldrían
tener	*to have*	tendría, tendrías, tendría, tendríamos, tendrían
venir	*to come*	vendría, vendrías, vendría, vendríamos, vendrían

¿Qué diría él?	*What would he say?*
Yo no lo haría.	*I wouldn't do it.*
¿Podrían repararlo?	*Could you repair it?*

For other irregular conditional forms, see the table starting on page 215.

2 Conmigo, contigo ... *with me, with you ...*

With me translates into Spanish as **conmigo**. *With you* (fam) becomes **contigo**.

¿Quieres venir conmigo?	*Do you want to come with me?*
No puedo ir contigo.	*I can't go with you.* (fam)

With other persons, use **usted** (pol), **él, ella, nosotros, nosotras, ustedes, ellos,** ellas

Iré con usted.	*I will go with you.* (pol)
Iremos con él.	*We will go with him.*

Remember that, in the first and second person singular, other prepositions (words like *for, without, to*) are followed by **mí** and **ti** (see Unit 5).

Para mí un café.	*Coffee for me.*
¿Y para ti?	*And for you?*

3 Offering to do something: the present tense

To offer to do something Spanish speakers normally uses the present tense, usually preceded by one or two object pronouns (see **Grammar**, Unit 5).

¿Le limpio el coche / carro?	*Shall I clean the car for you?* (pol)
¿Se lo limpio / reviso?	*Shall I clean it / check it for you?* (pol)
¿Le hago la habitación?	*Shall I make the room for you?* (pol)
¿Te ayudo?	*Shall I help you?* (fam)

4 Making requests

a The present tense

To make simple requests Spanish speakers normally use a construction with the present tense, usually preceded by one or two object pronouns, as above.

¿Me permite usar su teléfono?	*Will you let me use your telephone?*
¿Me lo llena, por favor?	*Will you fill it up for me?*

b ¿Podría...? *Could you...?*

To make more polite requests, use **poder** in the conditional tense.

Por favor, ¿podría ayudarme? *Could you help me, please?*
¿Me podrías recomendar algo *Could you recommend*
                                   something (to me)?
¿Podría reparármelo/la? *Could you repair it for me?*

Practice

1 You are in a Latin American city, staying at a hotel in **calle Mac Iver** (marked on the map). You would like to hire a car and you ask the hotel receptionist to recommend a car rental firm. He recommends one, which is on **calle Agustinas,** opposite **cerro** (*hill*) **Santa Lucía**, two blocks down **calle Moneda**, then left at **Santa Lucía** and left again at **calle Agustinas,** as shown on the map. Use dialogue 1 as a model to write the conversation between you and the hotel receptionist. You can then compare your own version of the dialogue with the one in the **Key to the activities.**

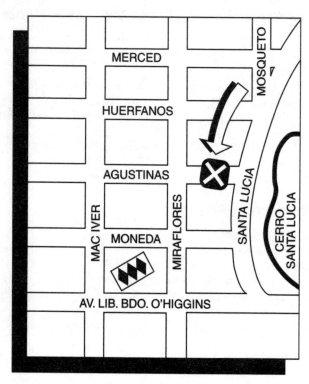

2 At the car rental agency you speak to the person in charge

TARIFAS

	MODELO	DÍA	SEMANA
A	Económico	$ 27.300	$ 175.000
B	Mediano	$ 34.300	$ 224.000
C	Todo Equipado	$ 45.500	$ 294.000
F	Lujo	$ 66.500	$ 413.000
D	Van	$ 77.000	$ 455.000
E	Doble cabina 4 x 4	$ 77.000	$ 455.000

Empleado Buenos días. ¿Qué desea?

Ud. *Say you would like to hire a car. Ask him what he recommends.*

Empleado Bueno, tenemos varios modelos. ¿Qué tipo de auto busca usted?

Ud. *Say you want a small car, not too expensive.*

Empleado El más económico que tenemos es éste. Es un coche pequeño y muy bueno.

Ud. *Ask what the rental is per day.*

Empleado Por día cuesta veintisiete mil trescientos pesos. Es un precio bastante conveniente.

Ud. *And per week?*

Empleado Ciento setenta y cinco mil pesos.

Ud. *Ask if that is with unlimited mileage.*

Empleado Sí, no hay recargo por kilómetro.

Ud. *Ask if VAT and insurance are included.*

Empleado Sí, están incluidos en el precio.

Ud. *Say that is fine. You'll take it.*

Empleado ¿Tiene su licencia de conducir al día?

Ud. *Yes, here it is.*

Empleado Gracias.

Ud. *Ask if it would be possible to leave the car in another city. You want to travel south and leave the car there. You prefer to come back by train.*

Empleado No, no se puede. Tendría que devolver el coche aquí mismo.

el recargo	*surcharge*
la licencia de conducir	*driving licence*
al día	*valid, up to date*
devolver	*to return (something)*

3 You may have difficulties with your car, so be prepared! What would you say in Spanish in these situations? If necessary, revise dialogue 3 and **Key phrases**.

  a Your car is running out of petrol. You stop a passer-by and ask if there is a service station nearby.

  b At the service station you ask the attendant to fill it up for you.

  c You need the oil and the tyre pressure checked.

  d The windscreen is dirty (el parabrisas está sucio), so you ask the attendant to clean it for you.

  e Fifty miles down the road you have a puncture. You change the wheel, then stop at a garage where you ask the mechanic to mend the tyre for you.

  f Before continuing your journey, you ask the mechanic if Santa Isabel is a long way off.

4 While on holiday, you telephone your manager Andrew Bronson at your office back home. It is company business, so you decide to reverse the charges. Use dialogue 5 as a model, and the relevant expressions under **Key phrases**, to write a conversation between you and the hotel operator. You can then compare your own version of the dialogue with the model in the **Key to the activities**.

▶ **5** Carlos García, from Buenos Aires, Argentina, was asked where he would like to spend his next holiday. Listen to what he says, then answer the questions. First, look at these key words:

pasar	to spend
próximo/a	next
la imagen	image
quedó profundamente grabada	remained deeply imprinted
solo o acompañado	alone or accompanied
recorrería	I would visit / tour
la naturaleza	nature
la vida frívola	frivolous life

Now answer these questions in English:

a Why would Carlos like to spend his next holiday in Bariloche?

b Who would he go with and for how long?

▶ **6** Carlos García was then asked what sort of car he would like to have. Listen to his reply, then complete the sentences below. First, look at these key words:

la marca	make
el auto	car
el coche deportivo	sports car
salir a pasear	to go for a ride
los lugares cercanos	nearby places
donde abunde la naturaleza	where I can be in contact with nature (lit. where there is plenty of nature)

Complete these sentences:

a Carlos preferiría un coche _____ . (*size*)

b Él preferiría un coche _____ . (*type*)

c Él compraría un coche _____ . (*colour*)

d Él usaría el coche para _____ y _____ . (*use*).

12

¿ha estado en el Cuzco?

have you been to Cuzco?

In this unit you will learn
- how to talk about what you have done
- how to express obligation and need
- how to give instructions and commands

▶ 1 Tengo que estar a las siete en el aeropuerto *I have to be at the airport at seven*

Roberto, from Argentina, is in Lima, Peru. At a party, Roberto talks to Pilar, a Peruvian. Key phrases here are **He estado** *I have been*, **¿Ha ido alguna vez ...?** *Have you ever been ...?*, **No he tenido ...** *I haven't had ...*, **Me han dicho** *I've been told*, **Ya he tomado demasiado** *I've had too much to drink*.

Pilar	¿Es la primera vez que viene a Lima?
Roberto	No, he estado aquí varias veces. Vengo aquí por negocios y, además, el Perú me gusta mucho. ¿Usted es de Lima?
Pilar	No, yo soy de Arequipa, pero vengo mucho a Lima. Tengo parientes aquí. ¿Ha ido alguna vez a Arequipa?
Roberto	No, no he estado nunca allá. No he tenido tiempo. Me han dicho que es una ciudad muy linda. Me gustaría mucho ir.
Pilar	Sí, no deje de ir. Le va a gustar. Es muy diferente a Lima. Si va a Arequipa, llámeme. Le daré mi número de teléfono. Yo misma le enseñaré la ciudad.
Roberto	Muchas gracias.
Pilar	¿Se sirve otro pisco sour?
Roberto	No, gracias. Ya he tomado demasiado y tengo que irme pronto. Mañana tengo que estar a las siete en el aeropuerto.

la primera vez	*first time*
varias veces	*several times*
el negocio	*business*
además	*besides*
los parientes	*relatives*
no deje de ir	*don't fail to go*
llámeme	*call me*
yo mismo/a	*I myself*
enseñar / mostrar	*to show*
¿se sirve ...?	*will you have ...?* (food or drink)

True or false? (¿Verdadero o falso?)

a Roberto no ha estado en Lima antes.
b Está en Lima de vacaciones.
c No conoce Arequipa.

▶2 Lléveme al Hotel Continental
Take me to the Hotel Continental

Roberto takes a taxi to his hotel.

Roberto	¡Taxi!
	(*The taxi stops and Roberto gets in*.)
Taxista	Buenas noches, señor.
Roberto	Buenas noches, lléveme al Hotel Continental en la calle Puno, por favor.
Taxista	Muy bien, señor.

taxista	*taxi driver*	**lléveme**	*take me*

Say it in Spanish

How would you say the following in Spanish?

a Take me to the airport, please.
b Take us to calle San Martín, please.

▶3 Deme la cuenta *Give me the bill*

Roberto asks the hotel receptionist to prepare the bill for him and to wake him up in the morning. Note the following key words and phrases: **deme** *give me*, **¿me despierta?** *will you wake me up?*, **envíemelo** *send it to me*.

Roberto	Buenas noches.
Recepcionista	Buenas noches, señor.
Roberto	Por favor, deme la cuenta de la habitación doscientos treinta. Me voy mañana temprano.
Recepcionista	Sí, señor. Se la daré enseguida.
Roberto	Ah, y me despierta a las seis de la mañana, por favor. Tengo que salir del hotel a las seis y media.

Recepcionista	¿Quiere tomar el desayuno en la habitación o prefiere bajar al comedor?
Roberto	Envíemelo a la habitación, por favor.
Recepcionista	Muy bien, señor.
Roberto	Gracias.

me voy (irse)	*I am leaving (to leave)*
temprano	*early*
se la daré	*I will give it to you*
enseguida / en seguida	*right away*
despertar	*to wake up*
bajar	*to go down*
enviar	*to send*

Say it in Spanish

Use the guidelines below to express the following:

a Ask the hotel receptionist for the bill for room 150. Say you are leaving tomorrow morning.

b Ask to be woken up at 7.30. You've got to be at the airport at 9.00.

▶ 4 En el aeropuerto *At the airport*

Roberto goes to the airline desk and hands in his ticket. Key phrases here are **¿Me da ...?** *Will you give me ...?*, **Tiene que pagar / embarcar ...** *You have to pay / board*, **Pase por ...** *Go through ...*

Empleada	Me da su pasaporte, por favor. (*Roberto hands in his passport.*) Gracias. ¿Cuál es su equipaje?
Roberto	Tengo esta valija solamente.
Empleada	¿Tiene equipaje de mano?
Roberto	Este bolso.
Empleada	Bien. ¿Fumador o no fumador?
Roberto	No fumador. Y prefiero un asiento junto al pasillo, por favor.
Empleada	Sí, cómo no . . . Aquí está su pasaje, su pasaporte y su tarjeta de embarque. Primero tiene que pagar su impuesto de aeropuerto y después pase por policía internacional. Tiene que embarcar a las nueve y media por la puerta número seis.
Roberto	¿Está retrasado el vuelo?
Empleada	Sí, hay media hora de retraso.

el equipaje de mano	*hand luggage*
la valija (River Plate) / **maleta**	*suitcase*
el bolso	bag
(no) **fumador**	(non) *smoker*
junto al pasillo	*on the aisle*
el pasaje	*ticket* (for transport)
la tarjeta de embarque	*boarding card*
embarcar / abordar	*to board*
retrasado/a	*delayed*
el retraso	*delay*

Say it in Spanish

You are at a small airport in a Latin American country, where you and your travelling companion need to communicate in Spanish. Use the guidelines in English to fill in your part of the conversation:

Empleada	¿Tienen equipaje?
Ud.	*Yes, we have two suitcases* (use the word **maleta**)
Empleada	¿Tienen equipaje de mano?
Ud.	*Yes, we have two small rucksacks* (**mochilas**)
Empleada	¿Fumador o no fumador?
Ud.	*Non-smoker, and you prefer a seat next to the window* (**la ventanilla**)

Key phrases

Talking about what you have done

¿Ha estado alguna vez en / ido alguna vez a Sudamérica?	*Have you ever been to South America?*
No he estado / ido nunca allá.	*I have never been there.*
He estado aquí una vez / dos veces / varias veces.	*I have been here once / twice / several times.*

Expressing obligation and need

Tengo que estar allá / salir a las seis y media.	*I have to be there / leave at half past six.*
Tiene que embarcar / pagar su impuesto.	*You have to board / to pay your tax.*

Giving instructions and commands

Deme la cuenta.	*Give me the bill.*
Lléveme/nos al aeropuerto / a la terminal.	*Take me / us to the airport / terminal.*
Envíemelo/la a la habitación.	*Send it to my room.*

Grammar

1 The perfect tense

Usage

The perfect tense is used to say what you or others have done. It is much less frequent in Latin America than in Spain. To refer to recent past events, e.g. *I have worked too much today*, Latin Americans will normally use the preterite tense, **Hoy trabajé demasiado**, while most Spaniards will use the perfect tense, **Hoy he trabajado demasiado**. However, with certain phrases, such as **alguna vez** *ever*, **una vez / dos veces** *once / twice*, **varias veces** *several times*, **nunca** *never* and **todavía** *still*, which bear some relationship with the present tense (the idea of *so far, up till now*), the perfect tense is fairly frequently used in Latin America. Look at the following examples.

He estado aquí varias veces.	*I have been here several times.*
¿Ha ido alguna vez a Arequipa?	*Have you ever been to Arequipa?*
No he ido nunca.	*I have never been.*

Formation

To form the perfect tense, you need to use the present tense of **haber** (auxiliary verb *to have*) followed by a past participle (the Spanish equivalent of forms like *drunk*, *gone*), which is invariable. To form the past participle of -**ar** verbs, add -**ado** to the stem, e.g. **estar** *to be* – **estado** *been*; to form the past participle of -**er** and -**ir** verbs, add -**ido** to the stem: **tener** *to have* – **tenido** *had*, **ir** *to go* – **ido** *gone*. Here are two examples, one showing an -**ar** verb, the other showing an -**er** verb.

estar	*to be*
he estado	*I have been*
has estado	*you have been* (fam, sing)
ha estado	*you have been* (pol, sing) / *he, she, it has been*
hemos estado	*we have been*
han estado	*you have been* (pl)
	they have been

tener	*to have*
he tenido	*I have had*
has tenido	*you have had* (fam, sing)
ha tenido	*you have had* (pol, sing), *he, she, it has had*
hemos tenido	*we have had*
han tenido	*you have had* (pl)
	they have had

Here are some examples of the use of the perfect tense:

Todavía / Aún no hemos terminado.	*We haven't finished yet.*
Nunca he viajado a Sudamérica.	*I have never travelled to South America.*
He ido muchas veces al Perú.	*I have been to Peru many times.*

Irregular past participles

Some verbs form the past participle in an irregular way. Here are the most common:

abrir *to open*	**abierto** *opened*
decir *to say, to tell*	**dicho** *said, told*
escribir *to write*	**escrito** *written*
hacer *to do, to make*	**hecho** *done, made*
ver *to see*	**visto** *seen*
volver *to come back*	**vuelto** *come back*

Me han dicho que es una   *I have been told it's a very*
ciudad muy bonita.   *nice city.*

Aún / Todavía no le he escrito. *I still haven't written to*
him / her.

Los he visto varias veces.   *I have seen them several times.*

For other irregular past participles, see the table starting on page 215.

2 Expressing obligation and need

a *Tener que* + infinitive

Obligation and need are usually expressed with the construction **tener que** *to have to*, followed by the infinitive.

¿Qué tienes que hacer?   *What do you have to do?*
Tengo que trabajar / estudiar. *I have to work / study.*
Tenemos que volver pronto.   *We have to come back soon.*
Tuvimos que hacerlo.   *We had to do it.*

b *Haber que* + infinitive

Obligation and need is also expressed with the impersonal form **haber que** followed by the infinitive. In the present, use **hay que** *one has to, you / we have to*; in the past, use **había** or **hubo que** *one had to, you / we had to*, and for future reference **habrá que** *one will have to, you / we will have to*. This construction is very common in the spoken language.

Hay que tener visa.   *You need to have a visa.*
Hay que reservar una   *You need to book a room.*
habitación.
Había/hubo que decírselo.   *We had to tell him/her/them.*

c *Deber* + infinitive

A less frequent alternative is the construction with **deber** *must* followed by the infinitive. This is normally used to express stronger obligation or need.

No debes hacerlo.   *You mustn't do it.*
Debes traerlo.   *You must bring it.*

3 The imperative or command form

Usage

To give instructions and commands, and to make suggestions, e.g. *call me, please take me to the hotel*, you can use the imperative form, which is normally followed or preceded by the phrase **por favor** to soften the command:

Si va a Arequipa, llámeme.   *If you go to Arequipa, call me.*
Lléveme al hotel Continental,   *Please take me to the hotel*
    por favor.   *Continental.*

Formation

In Spanish there are different imperative forms depending on who you are talking to (polite or familiar) and whether you are speaking to one or more than one person (singular or plural). To form the polite imperative you need the stem of the first person singular of the present tense followed by the appropriate ending, one for **-ar** verbs, another for **-er** and **-ir** verbs. Here are two examples:

Infinitive	Present (1st person)	Imperative
llev**ar** (*to take*)	llev**o**	lleve**(n)** (sing/pl)
sub**ir** (*to go up, to take up*)	sub**o**	sub**a(n)** (sing/pl)

Notice that the polite imperative is formed by adding -e to the stem of -**ar** verbs and -**a** to the stem of -**er** and -**ir** verbs. The negative imperative is formed by placing **no** before the verb: **no lleve** *don't take*, **no suba** *don't go up / take up*.

Examples:

Lleve esta maleta a la habitación   *Please take this suitcase*
    número veinte, por favor.   *to room twenty.*
Suba mi equipaje a la   *Take my luggage to my*
    habitación, por favor.   *room please.*

Familiar imperatives have different positive and negative forms, and are not given here. If you wish to learn their forms, consult your grammar book.

Irregular imperatives

As the imperative is formed from the first person singular of the present tense, verbs which are irregular or stem-changing in the first person singular of the present tense are also irregular (though not always in the same way) or stem-changing in the imperative. Here are some examples:

Infinitive	Present (1st person)	Imperative
dar *to give*	doy	dé/den
decir *to say*	digo	diga(n)
hacer *to do, to make*	hago	haga(n)
oír *to hear, to listen*	oigo	oiga(n)
traer *to bring*	traigo	traiga(n)
venir *to come*	vengo	venga(n)

Haga el favor de venir.	*Please come.*
¿Diga?	*Can I help you?* (lit. *Say?*)
Traiga un café, por favor.	*Bring a coffee, please.*

For other irregular imperatives, see the table starting on page 215.

Pronouns with imperatives

Pronouns go at the end of a positive form but before a negative one. Positive imperatives which carry a pronoun may need an accent. Here are some examples:

Llámeme.	*Call me.*
No me llame.	*Don't call me.*
Envíemelo a la habitación.	*Send it to my room.*
	(lit. *Send it to me to the room.*)
No me lo envíe a la habitación.	*Don't send it to my room.*

4 The present tense as a substitute for the imperative

The present tense is often used in place of the imperative to soften the command, instruction or suggestion. Consider the following examples:

Por favor, ¿me **lleva** al aeropuerto?	*Will you take me to the airport, please?*
Lléveme al aeropuerto, por favor.	*Take me to the airport, please.*
¿Me **llama** a las seis?	*Will you call me at six?*
Llámeme a las seis.	*Call me at six.*

(See Making requests, Unit 11.)

Practice

1 You are visiting Peru, and at a party given by some Peruvian friends you meet someone. Use the guidelines in English to complete the conversation.

Conocido/a	¿Es la primera vez que viene al Perú?
Ud.	*Yes, it is the first time. You like it very much. It is a nice country, although you haven't seen very much yet.*
Conocido/a	¿Ha estado en el Cuzco?
Ud.	*No, you haven't been to Cuzco yet, but you hope to go next week. You are going to visit Machu Picchu too. You've been told it is very interesting. Now, ask if he / she has ever been to Europe.*
Conocido/a	No, no he estado nunca en Europa, pero me encantaría ir. Tengo parientes en España y me han invitado. ¿Usted conoce España?
Ud.	*Yes, you have been there several times. You like Spain a lot, especially the south.*
Conocido/a	Usted habla muy bien español. ¿Dónde lo aprendió?
Ud.	*Thank him / her and say you studied Spanish at school. Ask if he / she speaks English.*
Conocido/a	He estudiado inglés varios años, pero todavía no lo hablo muy bien. Lo encuentro muy difícil. Prefiero que hablemos español.
Ud.	*Say that's all right.*
Conocido/a	¿Se sirve otro pisco sour?
Ud.	*Say no, thank you. You've already had two. It is enough. And, besides, tomorrow you have to get up early so you must go back to your hotel soon.*
Conocido/a	No se preocupe usted, yo lo / la llevaré en mi carro.

aunque	*although*
me encantaría	*I would love*
aprender	*to learn*
estudiar	*to study*
suficiente	*enough*
además	*besides*
así que . . .	*so . . .*
el carro (Peru)	*car*
pronto	*soon*

2 Your Peruvian acquaintances do not seem to realize you have only been in the country a few days. They keep asking you what places you have visited. Look at the examples, then answer their questions below.

- ¿Ha visto la catedral?
- Sí, ya la vi.
- ¿Ha ido al Museo Nacional de Arte?
- No, todavía no he ido.

a ¿Ha estado en el Museo de Cultura Peruana? (sí)
b ¿Ha visitado el Palacio de Gobierno? (no)
c ¿Ha visto el Palacio de Torre Tagle? (sí)
d ¿Ha conocido el barrio de Miraflores? (no)

▶ **3** Karina Tomas from Peru was asked whether she had ever been to Cuzco. Listen to her answer and to what she says about travelling to this old Inca city and the ancient Inca ruins of Machu Picchu. The key words which follow will help you to understand and the questions that follow will help you to check your comprehension.

conserva	*it retains*
la cultura incaica	*Inca culture*
mediante	*by*
no sé a cuánto tiempo está	*I don't know how long it takes*
la única forma	*the only way*

Answer these questions in English:

a When was Karina in Cuzco?
b What does she say about the city?
c How can you travel from Lima to Cuzco?
d How can you travel from Cuzco to Machu Picchu?

4 Use an appropriate verb from the list to express polite instructions and commands with the polite form of the imperative.

hacer, subir, darme, llamarme, escribir, cerrar, decirnos

a _____ la cuenta, por favor.
b _____ su nombre aquí, por favor.
c _____ el favor de llamarme a las 8.00.
d _____ dónde está.
e Si va a Buenos Aires, _____ por teléfono.
f _____ este equipaje a la habitación número 510, por favor.
g Por favor, _____ la puerta.

5 Match each question on the left with the corresponding answer on the right.

a ¿Dónde está el mostrador de Aerolatina?

b ¿Fumador o no fumador?

c ¿Cuál es su equipaje?

d ¿Tiene equipaje de mano?

e ¿Va a salir a la hora el avión?

f ¿Cuál es la puerta de embarque?

1 Esta mochila y una maleta.

2 No, hay una hora y media de retraso.

3 Fumador.

4 Número doce.

5 Este bolso solamente.

6 Al fondo del pasillo, frente al mostrador de Aeroperú.

---

el mostrador *desk*   **a la hora** *on time*

---

6 At a tourist office in a Latin American country you are given a leaflet giving advice on what to do and what not to do whilst visiting the country. Read it through and see how much you can understand, then translate the leaflet for a travelling companion who does not understand Spanish.

Recomendaciones para los turistas

Para su propia seguridad, el Servicio Nacional de Turismo de nuestro país le hace las siguientes sugerencias:

◆ Cambie su dinero y cheques de viaje sólo en los bancos o casas de cambio autorizadas.

◆ No cambie dinero en las calles.

◆ Deje sus objetos de valor en la caja de seguridad de su hotel.

◆ No salga con grandes sumas de dinero.

◆ Al tomar un taxi, observe lo que marca el taxímetro, ésa es la cantidad que deberá pagar. En nuestro país no hay recargos adicionales.

◆ En lo posible, utilice los servicios de taxi de su propio hotel.

autorizados/as	*authorized*
los objetos de valor	*valuables*
la caja de seguridad	*safe deposit box*
la suma	*sum*
marcar	*to indicate, to show*
el taxímetro	*taxi meter*
la cantidad	*amount*
el recargo	*surcharge*

13

siga derecho
go straight on

In this unit you will learn
- how to express hope
- how to express certainty, uncertainty and possibility
- how to make complaints
- how to ask for and give directions
- how to describe minor ailments

▶1 Mi maleta no ha llegado
My suitcase hasn't arrived

Diana Ray is reporting her luggage loss to an airline employee at the airport in Lima. First, try learning these key phrases: **Estoy seguro/a de que aparecerá** *I'm sure it will appear*, **Espero que la encuentren** *I hope you find it*, **cuando aparezca** *when it appears*, **Es muy posible que llegue ...** *It's very likely that it may arrive ...*

Diana	Buenos días.
Empleada	Buenos días. ¿Qué desea?
Diana	Acabo de llegar en el vuelo 435 de Aerolatina que venía de Londres, pero mi maleta no ha llegado.
Empleada	Perdone, ¿en qué vuelo dice que venía?
Diana	En el vuelo 435 de Aerolatina.
Empleada	Y usted tomó el avión en Londres, ¿verdad?
Diana	Sí, en Londres.
Empleada	¿Cuál es su nombre?
Diana	Diana Ray, r-a-y, Ray.
Empleada	¿Tiene usted el ticket de su equipaje?
Diana	Sí, aquí está.
Empleada	Este vuelo hizo escala en París, y posiblemente, por error, su maleta fue enviada a París. No se preocupe usted. Estoy segura de que aparecerá.
Diana	Espero que la encuentren. Tengo toda mi ropa en la maleta. Es una maleta grande, de color verde oscuro. Tiene una etiqueta con mi nombre.
Empleada	Deme la dirección y el teléfono del hotel donde se quedará para llamarla cuando aparezca. Mañana hay otro vuelo de Aerolatina que viene de París. Es muy posible que llegue en ese vuelo. Yo misma me encargaré de buscarla.
Diana	Muchas gracias.

acabo de llegar	*I have just arrived*
fue enviado/a	*it was sent*
aparecer	*to appear*
esperar	*to hope*
encontrar	*to find*

verde oscuro/a	*dark green*
la etiqueta	*label*
encargarse	*to see to, to take care of*
buscar	*to look for*

Say it in Spanish

Can you find the Spanish for the following expressions in the dialogue?

a It stopped over in Paris.
b by mistake
c I'll take care of (looking for) it myself.

▶2 Una habitación ruidosa
A noisy room

Diana's room at the hotel is rather noisy, so she complained to the hotel receptionist about it. First, try learning these key sentences: **No pude dormir** *I could not sleep,* **debido a la bulla del tráfico** *due to the traffic noise,* **La habitación es demasiado ruidosa** *The room is too noisy.*

Diana	Buenos días.
Recepcionista	Buenos días. ¿En qué puedo servirle?
Diana	Yo estoy en la habitación número 315 y anoche no pude dormir debido a la bulla del tráfico. La habitación es demasiado ruidosa. ¿No tendría una más tranquila?
Recepcionista	Un momentito, por favor. Veré qué habitación puedo darle.
	(*The receptionist comes back to the desk.*)
	Sí, puedo darle una habitación interior si no le importa. Es un poco oscura, pero muy tranquila.
Diana	No me importa. Prefiero cambiarme ahora mismo.
Recepcionista	Muy bien, señora. La habitación 420, en el cuarto piso, estará lista dentro de un momento. Acaba de irse la persona que estaba allí.
Diana	Muchas gracias.

anoche	*last night*
dormir	*to sleep*
interior	*at the back*
oscuro/a	*dark*
no me importa (importar)	*I don't mind (to mind, to matter)*
dentro de un momento	*in a moment*

Say it in Spanish

What expressions are used in the dialogue to say the following?

a Can I help you?
b Wouldn't you have a quieter room?
c If you don't mind.
d Right now.
e The person who was there has just left.

▶ 3 Doble a la izquierda *Turn left*

Diana's suitcase has appeared, so she is now ready to tour the city. She asks the hotel receptionist how to get to the museum. Note how she asks whether this is very far: **¿Podría decirme si está muy lejos ...?** As you read or listen to the dialogue, make a note of the directions given by the receptionist. Try guessing their meaning before you look at the vocabulary.

Diana Perdone, ¿podría decirme si está muy lejos el Museo Nacional de Arte?

Recepcionista No, no está lejos. Está a unas siete u ocho cuadras de aquí, en el Paseo Colón. Al salir del hotel doble a la izquierda y siga derecho por la avenida Garcilaso de la Vega hasta el Paseo Colón. Allí tuerza a la izquierda otra vez y continúe por esa calle. El museo está en la segunda cuadra, a la derecha.

Diana Muchas gracias.

Recepcionista De nada.

u	*or (before a word beginning with o or ho)*
al salir	*as you leave*
siga derecho	*go straight on*
hasta	*as far as*

tuerza (torcer)	*turn (to turn)*
otra vez	*again*
continúe (continuar)	*go on, continue (to go on, to continue)*

What do these directions mean?

It is your first day in a Latin American town and you are trying to find your way around. Can you give the English for these directions?

a Está a unas tres o cuatro cuadras de la catedral, a la izquierda.
b Siga derecho hasta el parque, y después doble a la derecha.
c En la esquina, tuerza a la izquierda, y continúe por esa calle hasta el final.
d Al llegar a la plaza verá un edificio grande de color amarillo. Ése es el museo.

▶4 Un dolor de estómago
A stomach ache

Diana is at the chemist's buying something for a stomach ache. First, try learning these key sentences: **Me cayó mal** *It didn't agree with me*, **¿Tiene fiebre?** *Have you got a fever?*, **Me duele el estómago** *I have a stomach ache*, **Tengo náuseas** *I feel sick*.

Empleada	Buenas tardes. ¿Qué desea?
Diana	Quisiera algo para el dolor de estómago. Anoche comí algo que me cayó mal. No dormí en toda la noche.
Empleada	¿Tiene fiebre?
Diana	No, fiebre no tengo, pero no me siento bien. Todavía me duele un poco el estómago y tengo náuseas.
Empleada	No creo que sea nada serio. Posiblemente se trata de una infección muy leve. Le daré estas pastillas que son muy buenas. Tome una cada cuatro horas con un poco de agua hasta que se sienta mejor. Y trate de comer sólo comidas livianas. Nada de frituras.
Diana	Muchas gracias. ¿Cuánto es?
Empleada	Son cuatro soles.

sentirse (e > ie)	*to feel*
doler (o > ue)	*to ache*
no creo que sea ...	*I don't think it is ...*
se trata de (tratarse de)	*it is (to be, to have to do with)*
leve	*slight*
la pastilla	*tablet, pill*
cada	*every, each*
trate de (tratar de)	*try to (to try to)*
la comida liviana	*light meal*
la fritura	*fried food*

How is the following expressed in the dialogue?

a Anoche no pude dormir.
b No tengo fiebre.
c Me siento mal.
d Creo que no es nada serio.

Key phrases

Expressing hope

Espero que la encuentren / aparezca.	*I hope you find it / it appears.*
Espero que sí / no.	*I hope so / not.*

Expressing certainty, uncertainty and possibility

Estoy seguro/a de que aparecerá / la encontraremos.	*I'm sure it will appear / we'll find it.*
Es muy posible que llegue / la encontremos.	*It's very likely that it will arrive / we'll find it.*
No creo que sea nada serio.	*I don't think it's anything serious.*
Posiblemente se trata de una infección.	*It's probably an infection.*

Asking for and giving directions

¿Podría decirme si está muy lejos / dónde está?	*Could you tell me if it's very far / where it is?*
Siga derecho.	*Go straight on.*
Doble / tuerza a la derecha / / izquierda.	*Turn right / left.*
Continúe/siga por esa calle.	*Go on along that street.*

Describing minor ailments

No me siento/encuentro bien.	*I don't feel well.*
Me duele el estómago / la cabeza.	*I have a stomach / head ache.*
Tengo dolor de estómago / cabeza	
Tengo fiebre/gripe/náuseas.	*I have a fever / cold / feel sick.*
La comida me cayó mal.	*The food didn't agree with me.*

Grammar

1 The subjunctive

Alongside *indicative* tenses, all the ones you have learned in this book, with the exception of the *imperative*, a form of the verb used for giving commands, Spanish uses a small range of other tenses, corresponding to what is known as the *subjunctive*.

The indicative is used for statements of fact.

Viven en Costa Rica (*present indicative*)	*They live in Costa Rica.*
Trabajaba conmigo (*imperfect indicative*)	*He / she used to work with me.*

The subjunctive is used in sentences expressing unreality, uncertainty, possibility and probability, and some kind of emotion, such as hope.

Espero que **sea** cierto.	*I hope it's true.*
Es posible que **vuelvan**.	*They may come back.*
Es probable que **llueva**.	*It may rain.*
No creo que **estén** en casa.	*I don't think they are at home.*

Note that positive sentences with **creer** require an indicative verb.

Creo que **están** en casa.	*I think they are at home.*

The subjunctive is little used in English nowadays, except in sentences such as *If I were you...*, *I wish you were here!* In Spanish, however, the subjunctive is quite common, in the spoken language as well as in writing. Read the notes below to find out how to use this so called *mood* of the verb.

Using the subjunctive

a Look at this sentence: *I hope (that) she arrives soon.*

It has two clauses: a main clause, *I hope*, and a subordinate clause, *(that) she arrives soon*. The verb in the main clause and the one in the subordinate clause are both in the same tense: the present tense. In Spanish, however, certain verbs, such as those expressing hope (e.g. esperar *to hope*), some kind of wish (e.g. querer *to want*), doubt or possibility (e.g. dudar *to doubt*), require the use of the subjunctive in the subordinate clause.

Espero que ella **llegue** pronto.	*I hope (that) she arrives soon.*
Queremos que nos **acompañes.**	*We want you to accompany us.*
Dudo que me **llamen.**	*I doubt (that) they will call me.*
Es muy posible que **llegue** en ese vuelo.	*It's very likely (that) it will come on that flight.*
No creo que **tenga** suficiente dinero.	*I don't think he / she has enough money.*

In these sentences, the verbs which follow the clause introduced by **que** are all in the subjunctive, in this case the *present subjunctive*. The word *that* is optional in these English sentences, whereas **que** cannot be omitted. Note also that in all the examples above the subject of the main verb is different from that of the verb in the subordinate clause. If this is not the case, use the infinitive and not the subjunctive.

Espero **llegar** pronto.	*I hope to arrive soon.*
Queremos **acompañarte.**	*We want to accompany you.*

b The subjunctive is also used after certain conjunctions, such as those indicating purpose (e.g. **para que** *in order that*) and time (e.g. **cuando** *when,* **hasta que** *until*), but only when these refer to the future.

Lo traeré **para que lo veas.**	*I'll bring it so that you can see it.*
La llamaré **cuando aparezca.**	*I'll call you when it appears.*
Trabajaré **hasta que termine.**	*I'll work until I finish.*

The verbs following these conjunctions are in the present subjunctive. This is the most frequently used subjunctive tense, and it is the only one covered in this book. If you wish to study the remaining subjunctive tenses, the *imperfect,* the *perfect* or the *pluperfect,* refer to one of the reference grammar books in the **Taking it further** section on page 275.

2 The present subjunctive

The *present subjunctive* normally occurs in sentences with the verb in the main clause in the present indicative, the future, the perfect or the imperative.

No **creo** que **esté** en casa.   *I don't think he / she is at home.*
Le **diré** que **venga**.   *I'll tell him / her to come.*
Me **han pedido** que vaya.   *They have asked me to go.*
Dile que me **llame**.   *Tell him / her to call me.*

Formation of the present subjunctive

Like the imperative, which you learned in Unit 12, the present subjunctive is formed from the first person singular of the present tense, e.g. **viajo** *I travel*, **como** *I eat*, **subo** *I go up*. Drop the **-o** and add the appropriate ending: there is one set of endings for **-ar** verbs and another for **-er** and **-ir** verbs. The first and third person singular of the present subjunctive have the same form as the polite imperative that you learned in Unit 12. Here are three examples:

viajar (*to travel*)	viaje, viajes, viaje, viajemos, viajen
comer (*to eat*)	coma, comas, coma, comamos, coman
subir (*to go up*)	suba, subas, suba, subamos, suban

Here are some further examples demonstrating the use of the present subjunctive:

Es probable que ellos **escriban**.   *They may write.* (possibility)

Espero que él **viaje** a Venezuela.   *I hope he travels to Venezuela.* (hope)

No creo que él **llame**.   *I don't think he will call.* (doubt)

Irregular forms of the present subjunctive

As with imperatives, verbs which are irregular or stem-changing in the first person of the present tense, e.g. **tener** *to have*, and **encontrar** *to find*, are also irregular or stem-changing in the present subjunctive. Here is an example:

Present tense: **tengo** (*I have*)
Present subjunctive: tenga, tengas, tenga, tengamos, tengan

No creo que él **tenga** dinero.   *I don't think he has money.*
Espero que **tengamos** tiempo.   *I hope we have time.*

For other examples of irregular forms look at irregular imperatives in Unit 12.

Some verbs are irregular in a different way:

dar	to give	dé, des, dé, demos, den
estar	to be	esté, estés, esté, estemos, estén
haber	to have	haya, hayas, haya, hayamos, hayan
ir	to go	vaya, vayas, vaya, vayamos, vayan
ser	to be	sea, seas, sea, seamos, sean

Espero que esta habitación
sea mejor.

I hope this room is better.

No creo que él esté allí.

I don't think he is there.

Cuando **vayas** a Lima llámalo.

When you go to Lima, call him.

For other irregular present subjunctive forms, see the table of irregular verbs starting on page 215.

3 Giving directions: present tense or imperative

Directions are normally given using the present tense (see Unit 3) or the imperative form (see Unit 12). Both forms are equally frequent in this context, and it may be easier for you to use the present tense, but you will need to understand the imperative form when native speakers use it.

Present tense	Imperative
(Usted) **dobla** a la derecha.	**Doble** a la derecha. *Turn right.*
(Usted) **tuerce** a la izquierda.	**Tuerza** a la izquierda. *Turn left.*
(Usted) **sigue** por esa calle.	**Siga** por esa calle. *Go on along that street.*

Note that the polite imperative has the same form as the first and third person singular of the present subjunctive.

4 *Al* + infinitive

This construction with **al** followed by the infinitive is fairly frequent in Spanish and translates into English in more than one way.

Al salir del hotel...

When you leave / On leaving the hotel ...

Al llegar al parque tuerza
a la izquierda.

When you reach the park turn left.

| Al **volver** entramos en un café. | *When we were coming back / On our way back we went into a café.* |

5 *Acabar de* + infinitive *to have just...*

To talk about actions or events which have just taken place, as in *I have just arrived*, use the present tense of **acabar** (lit. *to finish*) followed by the preposition **de** and the infinitive.

Acabo de llegar.	*I have just arrived.*
Acaba de irse.	*He / she has just left.*
Acabamos de almorzar.	*We have just had lunch.*

An alternative to this is the construction with **recién** followed by a verb in the preterite tense (see Unit 10).

| **Recién llamó.** | *He / she has just called.* |
| **Recién lo vimos.** | *We have just seen him.* |

6 *¿Le / te importa?* *Do you mind?*

To ask people whether they mind something, use the following construction with **importar** *to mind*, in a construction similar to that with **gustar** *to like* (see Unit 6), with the verb in the third person singular.

| **¿Le / te importa?** | *Do you mind?* (formal/informal) |
| **Si no le/te importa.** | *If you don't mind* (formal/informal) |

To say whether you don't mind something or doing something, use sentences like the following:

| **No me importa.** | *I don't mind.* |
| **No me importa hacerlo.** | *I don't mind doing it.* |

Practice

1 You have just arrived in a Latin American country. Unfortunately, your luggage is missing, so you decide to go to the airline desk to complain.

| **Empleada** | ¿Qué desea? |
| **Ud.** | *Say you have just arrived on flight 310 of Hispanair which was coming from ..., but unfortunately your luggage has not arrived.* |

Empleada	¿Qué equipaje traía usted?
Ud.	*You had two suitcases, one large one and one small one. Say you have the luggage receipts. Both suitcases have labels with your name (say your name).*
Empleada	Lo siento mucho. Estas situaciones ocurren a veces, pero normalmente el equipaje aparece uno o dos días después. Seguramente no lo enviaron, o lo enviaron a otra ciudad. El vuelo hizo escala en Amsterdam y Madrid.
Ud.	*Say you hope they find them. You have all your clothes in them and also some presents you brought for friends.*
Empleada	No se preocupe usted. Seguramente aparecerán. Yo misma me encargaré de buscarlas y lo / la llamaré por teléfono cuando aparezcan. Por favor, deme su nombre completo, su teléfono y su dirección.

una maleta grande y una pequeña

lo siento mucho	*I am very sorry*
ocurrir	*to happen*
traer	*to bring*
el nombre completo	*full name*

2 Put the infinitives in brackets in the appropriate form of the present subjunctive.

a Cuando (nosotros, ir) a Perú, visitaremos Machu Picchu.
b Posiblemente (ellos, pasar) sus vacaciones en Chile.
c Llamaré a la recepción para que (ellos, enviar) el desayuno.
d Esperaremos aquí hasta que el avión (llegar).
e Espero que mañana no (hacer) mucho calor. Quiero salir de compras.
f No creo que Carmen (venir) hoy. Está muy ocupada.
g Te traje un regalo. Espero que te (gustar).
h Está muy nublado. Es posible que (llover).

3 Your first night at a hotel was a nightmare (**una pesadilla**). Several things went wrong, so you want to complain to the hotel management. Here is what you want to say. How would you express it in Spanish?

a The air conditioning didn't work.
b There was no hot water.
c The washbasin was blocked.
d There were no towels in the bathroom.
e The room is too noisy. You couldn't sleep last night.
f You want to move into a quieter room.

el baño	bathroom
no había ...	there was no ...
el aire acondicionado	air conditioning
el lavabo / lavatorio / lavamanos	washbasin

▶ 4 Some people are never happy! Listen to these complaints, then say in English what each person is complaining about. The first complaint takes place in an airplane and both speakers are Chilean. The second and third take place in a restaurant and the people complaining are first a Venezuelan and then a Chilean. First, look at these new words:

el asiento	seat
¡lo siento tanto!	I am so sorry!
No es culpa nuestra.	It is not our fault.
cambiar	to change
¡epa muchacho!	Lit. come on boy! (Venezuela, very informal)
¿vale?	OK? (very frequent in Venezuela)
pedí	I ordered
la sopa de mariscos	seafood soup
pasar	to happen
tan ocupados	so busy
hoy día	today
tantos clientes	so many customers

5 Your hotel is at the corner of **avenida Abancay** and **calle Miró Quesada**, number 2 on the map opposite. Today you want to visit the Cathedral, number 1 on the map. How would you get there from your hotel? Choose the correct directions, **a**, **b** or **c**.

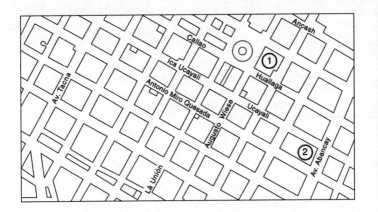

a   Siga derecho por Miró Quesada hasta la calle Augusto
    Wiese. Allí doble a la izquierda y camine tres cuadras
    hasta llegar a la Catedral.

b   Al salir del hotel, doble a la derecha y camine tres
    cuadras hasta la calle Augusto Wiese. En Augusto
    Wiese doble a la derecha. La Catedral está a dos
    cuadras de allí, a la derecha, en la esquina de la calle
    Huallaga.

c   Cuando salga del hotel, siga por la calle Miró Quesada
    y continúe hasta la calle La Unión que está pasado
    Augusto Wiese. Doble a la derecha y siga por esa calle
    hasta que encuentre la Catedral, que está en la esquina
    de las calles Callao y La Unión.

▶ 6   While you are waiting to ask for information in the
tourist office in Lima, you hear another tourist asking for
directions. Listen to the conversation and complete the
transcript below with the missing words. If you do not have the
recording, try guessing what those words are.

Turista	Buenas tardes. Para _____ al Teatro Segura, por favor.
Recepcionista	Sí, cómo no. Al _____ de aquí, _____ por la calle Ucayali, camine de frente hacia Abancay. Ahí _____ a la _____ izquierda, camine dos _____ y media, y ahí está el Teatro Segura.
Turista	Gracias.
Recepcionista	_____.

camine de frente	walk straight on
hacia	towards
ahí	there

7   You are not feeling very well and decide to see a doctor. It probably has something to do with some food you had last night. Use the guidelines to complete this conversation with the doctor.

Doctor   ¿Qué le pasa?
Ud.   *Say you are feeling unwell. You have a stomach ache and diarrhoea.*
Doctor   ¿Desde cuándo se siente así?
Ud.   *It started last night. You went out for a meal with some friends and you had fish and fried potatoes. Surely that was it. Later when you got back to your hotel you started to feel unwell.*
Doctor   ¿Ha tenido vómitos?
Ud.   *Yes, you have vomited and you seem to have a fever too.*
(The doctor examines you and gives you a prescription, una receta.)
Doctor   No creo que sea nada grave. Se trata simplemente de una infección estomacal. Con esta receta vaya a la farmacia y compre estas pastillas que son muy buenas. Tome dos cada seis horas. Estoy seguro de que se sentirá mejor.
Ud.   *Say you hope so.*

¿qué le pasa?	what's wrong with you?
empezar	to start
grave	serious
la diarrea	diarrhoea
la infección estomacal	stomach infection

▶ 8   You might not like the idea of visiting a doctor who needs to advertise on the radio to get patients, but if you had to, here is one from Veracruz, in Mexico! Listen to the advertisement, then answer the questions that follow. First, look at these key words:

la fractura	fracture
la luxación	dislocation
la cirugía	surgery
la traumatología	orthopaedic surgery
la ortopedia	orthopaedics
las consultas	surgery hours

Complete these sentences:

a   Las horas de consulta del doctor Manuel Loyo de Valdés son de _____ a _____ y de _____ a _____ .

b   El doctor atiende en González Pajés número _____ .

c   El número de teléfono del doctor es el _____ .

▶ 9   A patient arrives at a doctor's surgery in Peru. Listen to his conversation with the receptionist and note down the days and times when the surgery is open. First look at these key words:

| pedir hora | to ask for an appointment (with doctor or dentist) |
| atender | to be available |

Congratulations on completing *Teach Yourself Latin American Spanish*!

We hope you have enjoyed working your way through the course. We are always keen to receive feedback from people who have used our courses, so why not contact us and let us know your reactions? We'll be particularly pleased to receive your praise, but we should also like to know if things could be improved. We always welcome comments and suggestions, and we do our best to incorporate constructive suggestions into later editions. You can contact us at: Teach Yourself Books, Hodder Headline Ltd, 338 Euston Road, London NW1 3BH, UK

We hope you will want to build on your knowledge of Spanish and have made a few suggestions to help you do this in the section entitled **Taking it further**, on page 275.

¡Buena suerte!

Juan Kattán-Ibarra

testing yourself

1 How would you express the following in Spanish?
a What's your name? (formal)
b Pleased to meet you (give two alternatives)
c Sit down, please (formal, sing).
d What part of Mexico are you from? (familiar, sing)
e I'm very glad to see you (familiar, sing)
f You are Colombian, aren't you? (familiar, sing)
g Excuse me, are you señor García?
h What is señora Roble's room number, please?
i It's on the third floor, on the right.
j They are at the end of the corridor, on the left.

(Units 1, 2)

2 Complete the following sentences with the appropriate present tense form of the verbs in brackets.

a '¿Dónde (*vivir*, tú)?' '(*Vivir*, yo) en la avenida de Las Américas.'
b No (*tener*, nosotros) mucho tiempo. La película (*empezar*) a las seis.
c '¿Qué (*pensar*, ustedes) hacer este verano?' (*Pensar*, nosotros) ir a México.'
d Carmen (*entender*) bastante el inglés, pero no lo (*hablar*) muy bien.
e '¿(*Saber*, tú) dónde (*estar*) las llaves?' 'No lo (*saber*, yo). Yo no las (*tener*).'
f (*Ir*, yo) al supermercado. Si Luis (*llamar*) por teléfono, ¿le (*decir*, tú) que (*volver*, yo) pronto?
g '¿A qué hora (*salir*, tú) para el trabajo?' 'Normalmente (*salir*, yo) a las 9.00.'
h ¿(*Poder*, usted) abrir la puerta un momento, por favor? (*Hacer*) mucho calor.

i '¿Cómo (*venir*, tú) a la universidad?' 'Normalmente (*venir*, yo) en autobús.'

j Cuando (*llegar*, yo) a casa (*oír*, yo) la radio o (*ver*, yo) la televisión.

(Units 3, 4)

3 What questions would you ask for each of the following replies? Use the familiar form.

a Estoy bien, gracias.
b Soy de Chile.
c Vivo en Santiago.
d Tengo treinta y cinco años.
e ¿Mi horario de trabajo? Bueno, empiezo a las nueve y termino a las seis.
f Me levanto a las siete.
g Me acuesto a las once.
h Los fines de semana salgo fuera de la ciudad.
i No, no conozco Nueva York.
j Son las cuatro y media.

(Units 3, 4)

4 Fill in the blanks with the appropriate verb: **hay** or the present tense form of **ser** or **estar**.

a Carlos _____ arquitecto. Su oficina _____ en el centro de la ciudad.
b '¿ _____ algún banco por aquí?' 'Sí, _____ dos, uno en la plaza y otro frente a la estación, pero _____ un poco lejos de aquí.'
c '¿Cuándo _____ la fiesta de María?' '_____ el sábado.'
  '¿Y dónde _____ ?' '_____ en su casa, pero no sé dónde _____ .'
d '¿A cuánto _____ el cambio del dólar?' 'No lo sé, pero allá _____ una casa de cambio. Vamos a ver.'
e '¿Qué hora _____ ?' '_____ las dos y cuarto.'
f '¿Qué (tú) _____ haciendo?' '_____ escribiendo una carta.'
g La ciudad _____ muy interesante. En ella _____ una gran cantidad de museos. Y _____ bastante cerca de aquí.
h '¿Cuáles _____ sus maletas?' 'Ésas, las que _____ allí.'
i Luisa _____ muy elegante hoy. ¿Adónde va?

j Antonio _____ una persona muy activa, pero hoy _____ un poco cansado.

(Units 1–3, 6, 10)

5 Match each question or request on the left with an appropriate answer on the right.

a ¿Qué va a tomar?
b El pollo, ¿cómo lo quiere?
c ¿Qué va a comer de postre?
d ¿Me trae la cuenta, por favor?
e ¿Cuánto vale esa camisa?
f ¿En qué color la prefiere?
g ¿Le gusta ésta?
h ¿Puedo pagar con tarjeta de crédito?
i ¿Va a pagar en efectivo?
j ¿Algo más?

1 Seis mil pesos.
2 Quiero un helado.
3 Por supuesto.
4 Me encanta.
5 Un agua mineral.
6 No, con cheque.
7 Asado.
8 Nada más.
9 Enseguida se la traigo.
10 En amarillo.

(Units 5, 6)

6 Fill in the blanks with an appropriate verb from the box, without repeating any. Use the future tense.

quedarse	volver	presentar	ir	hacer	salir	poder
	estar	gustar	venir	enviar		

Querida Amelia:

En tu última carta me preguntas qué (1) _____ (yo) en mis vacaciones. Bueno, este año José y yo (2) _____ a Cuba y (3) _____ (nosotros) allí dos semanas. (4) _____ (nosotros) de aquí el día 20 de julio y (5) _____ (nosotros) a casa el 5 de agosto.

En La Habana (6) _____ (nosotros) en casa de unos amigos cubanos, y en Varadero en un hotel. Te (7) _____ (yo) una postal.

Y tú, ¿cuándo (8) _____ a vernos? Tenemos una nueva casa, muy bonita. Estoy segura de que te (9) _____. Está

muy cerca de la playa y (10) _____ (tú) tomar el sol y nadar todos los días. Te (11) _____ a mis nuevos amigos _____.

(Unit 7)

7 While on holiday in a Spanish-speaking country you visit a friend. Follow the guidelines to complete your part of the conversation.

Tu amigo	¿Cuánto tiempo hace que estás aquí?
Tú	*Say you've been here for two days only. You arrived on Saturday,*
Tu amigo	¿Y qué tal el viaje?
Tú	*Say it was very pleasant, but it was a bit long.*
Tu amigo	¿Cuánto tiempo vas a estar aquí?
Tú	*Say you are going to stay two weeks.*
Tu amigo	¡Qué bien! Tendremos bastante tiempo para salir juntos. ¿Has visto ya algo de la ciudad?
Tú	*Yes, on Sunday you visited the museum and the cathedral. You liked the cathedral very much. And in the evening you went to the theatre (**el teatro**). On Monday you had lunch with a friend and then you bought some presents for your family.*
Tu amigo	¿Tienes algo que hacer esta noche?
Tú	*No, nothing, you are free.*
Tu amigo	¿Qué te parece si cenamos juntos? Conozco un restaurante muy bueno, y estoy seguro de que te va a gustar.

(Units 8, 9)

8 Fill in the blanks with the appropriate form of the preterite tense.

a '¿Has estado alguna vez en Argentina?' 'Sí, (*estar*) allá el año pasado.

b '¿Qué (*hacer*, tú) ayer?' '(*Ir*, yo) al cine con Gabriel. (*Ver*, nosotros) una película muy buena.'

c Estoy muy cansada. Anoche no (*poder*, yo) dormir.

d ¿Dónde (*poner*, tú) las llaves? No las puedo encontrar.

e Le (*decir*, yo) a Juan sobre la fiesta, pero me (*decir*, él) que no podrá venir.

f '¿Cuándo (*llegar*, usted)?' '(*llegar*, yo) la semana pasada.'

g Pablo (*levantarse*) muy tarde y no (*ir*) a clase.

h '¿Por qué no (*venir*, usted) ayer?' '(*tener*, yo) que trabajar en casa.'

i Su madre (*morir*) hace muchos años.

j Ayer (*llover*) toda la tarde. (*quedarse*, nosotros) en casa.

(Unit 9)

9 Choose the correct tense, the preterite or the imperfect.

a En aquel tiempo yo (viví / vivía) en los Estados Unidos. (Estuve / estaba) allí varios años.

b Ana (fue / era) una persona muy especial. A mí me (gustó / gustaba) mucho.

c Ricardo y yo nos (conocimos / conocíamos) hace más de tres años.

d Yo (estuve / estaba) en casa cuando él (llegó / llegaba).

e (Trabajaron / Trabajaban) aquí durante cuatro años.

f El año pasado (pasamos / pasábamos) nuestras vacaciones en Costa Rica.

g No (fui / iba) a la fiesta de Raquel porque me (dolió / dolía) el estómago.

h No lo compré porque (fue / era) demasiado caro.

i Su casa (fue / era) muy bonita y (estuvo / estaba) frente al mar.

j '¿Cómo se (llamó / llamaba) tu profesor de español?' 'Su nombre (fue / era) Manuel.'

(Units 9, 10)

10 How would you express the following in Spanish?

a What would you like to do? (formal, sing)

b I would like to hire a car. What car do you recommend? (formal)

c Could you tell me how much it costs?

d 'Is this the first time you come to Ecuador?' 'No, I have been here several times.'

e We have booked a room at the hotel San Martín.

f Will you wake us at seven o'clock tomorrow? We have to leave the hotel at 9.00.

g I hope you come back here soon.

h 'Could you tell me where the museum is?' 'Go straight on as far as avenida Bolívar, and then turn right. The museum is on the left.'

i I'd like something for a stomach ache.

j I'm not feeling well and I have a fever.

(Units 11–13)

adjectives Adjectives are words which provide more information about nouns: *His / her house is very nice.* **Su casa es muy bonita.**

adverbs Adverbs are used to provide more information about verbs, adjectives or other adverbs: *He / she spoke clearly.* **Habló** *claramente. It was incredibly easy.* **Fue** *increíblemente* fácil. *She sang extremely well.* **Cantó** *extremadamente* bien.

articles There are two types of articles, *definite* and *indefinite*. Definite articles in Spanish are **el, la, los, las,** *the* in English. Indefinite articles are **un, una,** *a, an,* and **unos, unas,** *some* in English: *the book* **el libro,** *the books* **los libros,** *a chair* **una silla,** *some chairs,* **unas sillas.**

clause A clause is a group of words within a sentence which has its own verb. A *main clause* functions on its own; a *subordinate clause* is dependent on another clause. In *I'll buy it when I have money* **Lo compraré cuando tenga dinero,** *I'll buy it,* the main clause, can function on its own; *when I have money,* the subordinate clause, is dependent on the main clause.

comparative and superlative When we make comparisons we need the comparative form of the adjective. In English this usually means adding *–er* to the adjective or putting *more* in front of it. The Spanish equivalent is **más:** *She is taller than her sister.* **Es** *más alta* **que su hermana.** *This chair is more comfortable.* **Esta silla es** *más cómoda.* The most extreme version of a comparison is known as *superlative,* **el/la más** in Spanish: e.g. *this hotel is the cheapest.* **Este hotel es** *el más barato.*

definite article See **articles**.

demonstratives Words like este, esta *this*, esos, esas *those*, are called demonstrative adjectives when they go before a noun: *this* boy, *este chico*, *those keys, esas* llaves. If these demonstratives are used instead of a noun, they are called demonstrative pronouns, and have a written accent: *these* are nice, son **éstas** están lindas, deme *ése/ésa give me that*.

direct object See **object**.

finite verb A verb form such as the one in *they work hard* is said to be *finite* because it indicates *tense, person* and *number*. Gerunds, infinitives and past participles are non-finite verb forms.

gender In Spanish, all nouns are either masculine or feminine. For example, *el* avión, *the aeroplane,* is masculine, while *la* bicicleta, *the bicycle,* is feminine. Nouns referring to male people are masculine and those referring to female persons are feminine.

gerund In Spanish, the word gerund refers to the forms of the verb ending in -**ando** and -**iendo**, e.g. habl**ando**, com**iendo**, viv**iendo**. Some of its uses correspond to those of the verb form ending in -*ing* in English, e.g. She *is eating* Está *comiendo*.

imperative See **mood**.

indefinite article See **articles**.

indicative mood See **mood**.

indirect object See **object**.

infinitive The basic form of the verb, as found in the dictionary, is known as infinitive. In Spanish, infinitives end in –**ar**, -**er**, and -**ir**, for example habl**ar** *to speak*, com**er** *to eat*, viv**ir** *to live*.

irregular verbs Verbs which do not behave according to a set pattern are known as irregular verbs.

mood Mood refers to the forms verbs can take depending on how these are used. There are three moods of the verb: *indicative mood*, normally associated with statements of fact, e.g. He *works* here *Trabaja* aquí, *imperative mood*, used for commands, directions and instructions, e.g. *Come* back tomorrow *Vuelva* mañana, *and subjunctive mood*, normally associated with doubt, possibility, wishes, etc., e.g. I don't think she *knows* No creo que *sepa*. See also **subjunctive**.

nouns Nouns are words like *magazine* revista, *dog* perro, *beauty* belleza.

number The word number is used to indicate whether something is *singular* or *plural*, for example *the train* **el tren** is singular, *the trains* **los trenes** is plural.

object In a sentence such as I gave *him the keys* **Le di *las llaves***, the phrase *the keys*, which undergoes the action of the verb in a direct way, is said to be the direct object, while *him*, the recipient of the giving, is the indirect object. An object can be a noun or noun phrase, e.g. *the keys,* or a pronoun, e.g. *him.*

personal pronouns As their name suggests, personal pronouns refer to persons, for example *I* **yo,** *he* **él,** *she* **ella,** *we* **nosotros,** *him* **lo, le,** *us* **nos.** See also **pronouns**.

plural see **number**.

possessives Words like *my* **my,** *mine* **mío,** *her* **su,** *hers* **suyo** are called possessives.

prepositions Prepositions are words such as *to* **a,** *in* **en,** *between* **entre,** which provide information such as direction, location, time.

pronouns Pronouns are words which stand in place of nouns or noun phrases which have already been mentioned, for example My sister went to Cuba. *She* went to Cuba. **Mi hermana fue a Cuba. *Ella* fue a Cuba.** This restaurant is cheaper. *This* is cheaper. **Este restaurante es caro. *Éste* es caro.** My house is small. *Hers* is big. **Mi casa es pequeña. La *suya* es grande.**

reflexive pronouns Words such as *myself* **me,** *yourself* **te, se,** *ourselves* **nos** are known as reflexive pronouns.

reflexive verbs When the subject and the object of a verb are one and the same, the verb is said to be reflexive, for example *I enjoyed myself* very much. **Me *divertí* mucho.** *He washed himself.* **Se lavó.**

singular see **number**.

subject In a sentence such as, *My son finished his studies* **Mi hijo terminó sus estudios,** *my son,* the person performing the action denoted by the verb, is the subject of the sentence. A subject can be a single word or a group of words.

subjunctive mood The so-called subjunctive mood is used very rarely in modern English, but there are remnants of it in sentences such as the following: I insist that you *do* it. **Insisto en que lo *hagas*.** I wish he *were here.* **Ojalá *estuviera* aquí.** Spanish uses the subjunctive much more frequently than English.

subordinate clause See **clause**.

superlative comparative and **superlative**.

tense Changes in the verb which indicate aspects of time are referred to as tenses, for example present tense, future tense, preterite tense. In She *lives* in Mexico now. **Ahora *vive* en México,** the verb is in the present tense. In She *lived* here for many years *Vivió* **aquí durante muchos años,** the verb is in the preterite tense.

verbs Verbs are words such as *to speak* **hablar,** *to exist* **existir,** *to feel* **sentir,** which can denote actions, states, sensations.

1 Definite and indefinite articles (the, a / an) (Units 1, 2)

a The word for *the* for singular nouns is **el** for masculine and **la** for feminine, e.g. **el hotel, la habitación**. The plural forms are **los, las**, e.g. **los hoteles, las habitaciones**.

b The word for *a / an* is **un** for masculine and **una** for feminine, e.g. **un señor, una señora**.

c A + el becomes **al**, e.g. **Voy al cine**, *I'm going to the cinema.*

d De + el becomes **del**, e.g. **Vengo del supermercado**, *I'm coming from the supermarket.*

2 Nouns

Masculine and feminine (Unit 1)

a In Spanish, all nouns are either masculine or feminine. Nouns ending in **-o** are usually masculine while those ending in **-a** are usually feminine, e.g. **el desayuno, la cena**.

b Words referring to males and females, such as occupations, must change. To form the feminine, change **-o** to **-a** or add **-a** to the consonant, e.g. **el doctor, la doctora**.

c Nouns ending in **-ista** and many of those ending in **-nte** are invariable, e.g. **el / la artista, el / la estudiante**.

d Some nouns have different forms for male and female, e.g. **el padre, la madre**.

Singular and plural (Unit 2)

e Nouns ending in a vowel form the plural by adding **-s**, e.g. **el libro, los libros**.

f Nouns ending in a consonant add -es, e.g. **la ciudad, las ciudades.**

g The masculine plural of some nouns may be used to refer to members of both sexes, e.g. **el padre, la madre, los padres.**

3 Adjectives (Units 1 and 5)

Number and gender agreement

Adjectives must agree in gender and number with the noun they describe.

a Adjectives ending in -o change -o to -a with feminine nouns, e.g. **un hotel pequeño, una habitación pequeña.**

b As a general rule, adjectives ending in a letter other than -o or -a do not change for masculine and feminine, e.g. **el vestido azul, la camisa azul.**

c Adjectives indicating nationality form the feminine by changing -o into -a or by adding -a to the consonant, e.g. **un amigo mexicano, una amiga mexicana.**

d To form the plural of adjectives follow the same rules as for nouns, e.g. **los carros antiguos.**

Position of adjectives

a The great majority of adjectives come after the noun, e.g. **una persona inteligente.**

b Adjectives are sometimes used before nouns for emphasis or to convey some kind of emotion, e.g. **un excelente hotel.**

c Certain adjectives, among them **grande** *big, large,* **pequeño** *small,* **bueno** *good,* **malo** *bad,* usually precede the adjective, e.g. **un pequeño problema.**

d **Grande** normally follows the noun when its meaning is *big* or *large,* but it goes before it when it means *great.* Before the noun, **grande** becomes **gran,** e.g. **una persona grande, una gran persona.**

e **Bueno** and **malo** become **buen** and **mal** before masculine singular nouns, e.g. **un buen / mal momento.**

4 Adverbs (Unit 4)

a To form an adverb from an adjective, add -**mente** to the singular form of the adjective, e.g. **posible, posiblemente.**

b If the adjective ends in **-o**, change the **-o** to **-a** and then add -mente, e.g. **rápido, rápidamente.**

b Many adverbs are not derived from adjectives, e.g. **ahora, mañana, aquí, bien.**

5 Pronouns

Subject pronouns (Unit 1)

singular	
yo	*I*
tú	*you* (familiar)
usted	*you* (formal)
él, ella	*he, she*
plural	
nosotros / as	*we* (m / f)
ustedes	*you* (formal / informal)
ellos / as	*they* (m / f)

Subject pronouns are usually omitted in Spanish, unless you want to show emphasis or to avoid ambiguity.

Direct and indirect object pronouns (Unit 5)

a Object pronouns can be direct, e.g. <u>La</u> invité *I invited her*, or indirect, as in <u>Le</u> dije *I said to her / him / you* (formal).

b In the first and second person singular and plural there is no distinction between direct and indirect object pronouns, e.g. <u>Me</u> invitó *He / She invited me*, <u>Me</u> dijo *He / She said to me*.

singular		plural	
me	*me, to me*	nos	*us, to us*
te	*you, to you* (informal)		

c In the third person, direct and indirect object pronouns differ, e.g. **Lo / la invité** *I invited him / her*, **Le dije** *I said to him / her*.

Direct object pronouns: third person

Singular		Plural	
Masc. lo	*you* (formal) / *him / it*	los	*you* (formal / informal) / *them*
Fem. la	*you* (formal) / *her / it*	las	*you* (formal / informal) / *them*

Indirect object pronouns: third person

Singular	Plural
Le (to) you (formal) /	les (to) you (formal / informal) /
him / her / it	them

Le and les become se before lo, la, los, las, Se lo daré *I'll give it to you / him / her / it / them.*

Position of object pronouns (Unit 5)

a Object pronouns normally precede the verb, e.g.¿Me trae un café? *Will you bring me a coffee?*
b In sentences with two object pronouns, the indirect one comes first,e.g. Te las daré, *I'll give them to you.*
c With imperatives, they follow positive forms but come before negative ones, e.g. Dígale *Tell him / her,* No le diga *Don't tell him / her.*
d In constructions with a finite verb followed by an infinitive (e.g. llevar) or a gerund (e.g. haciendo), the object pronoun can either precede the finite verb or be attached to the infinitive or gerund, e.g. Voy a llevarlo or Lo voy a llevar, *I'm going to take it,* Estoy escribiéndola or La estoy escribiendo, *I'm writing it.*

Pronouns with prepositions (Unit 11)

a With prepositions, use mí, ti, for the first and second person singular, and subject pronouns, él, ella, etc., for the remaining persons, e.g. Un café para mí / él, *Coffee for me / him.*
b Note the use of this construction in A mí me gusta *I like it.*
c Note the special use of con in conmigo, *with me,* contigo, *with you* (informal). But con él / ella / usted, etc.

Reflexive pronouns (Unit 4)

These are me, te, se, nos, se, and they accompany reflexive verbs such as levantarse, e.g. me levanto *I get up.*

6 Possessives (Unit 4)

To say *my, your, his, her,* etc. use the following set of words, which agree in number (singular and plural) with the thing possessed, not with the possessor. The first person plural, nuestro *our,* also agrees in gender (masculine and feminine).

mi(s)	*my*
tu(s)	*your* (informal)
su(s)	*your* (formal), *his, her, its*
nuestro / a(s)	*our*
su(s)	*your* (formal / informal), *their*

To say *mine, yours, his, hers*, etc. use the following set of words, which agree in number and gender with the thing possessed.

mío / a(s)	*mine*
tuyo / a(s)	*yours* (informal)
suyo / a(s)	*yours* (formal), *his, hers, its*
nuestro / a(s)	*ours*
suyo / a(s)	*yours* (formal / informal), *theirs*

7 Prepositions (Units 4, 5, 11)

Only the most common single word prepositions and meanings are given here.

a

at: a las cuatro
on: a la derecha / izquierda
per: una vez a la semana
personal a: used before the direct object when this is a person, e.g. Invité a Manuel

con

with: café con leche

de

from: Julio es de Granada.
made of: es de cristal.
in: la ciudad más grande de Venezuela

desde

from: desde las 2.00 de la tarde
for: desde hace cinco años

en

in: viven en Buenos Aires
on: las llaves están en la cama
at: trabaja en la Universidad de México

hasta

until: hasta las 5.00
as far as: hasta el semáforo

para

for (direction): el tren para Lima
for (with pronouns): para mí, un café
for / by: (with time phrases) para el lunes
in order to: iré a Bogotá para ver a María

por

by: por avión, por correo electrónico
during: por dos días
via: viajaron a Chile por Buenos Aires
through: pasaron por Guatemala
along: por esa calle
around: por aquí
per: por ciento
because of: lo hago por ti
by: este libro fue escrito por García Márquez

8 Types of verbs

a According to the ending of the infinitive, Spanish verbs may be grouped into three main categories: -**ar**, e.g. **hablar** *to speak*, -**er**, e.g. **comer** *to eat*, and -**ir**, e.g. **vivir** *to live*. (Unit 3)
b Most Spanish verbs are regular, that is, they follow a fixed pattern in their conjugation, but some very common verbs are irregular. A list of these will be found on pages 215–218.
c Stem-changing verbs (see opposite)
d Reflexive verbs (Unit 4)

9 Present tense (Units 1, 2, 3, 4)

Here are the present tense forms of three regular verbs, **hablar** *to speak*, **comer** *to eat*, **vivir** *to live*.

yo	habl<u>o</u>	com<u>o</u>	viv<u>o</u>
tú	habl<u>as</u>	com<u>es</u>	viv<u>es</u>
usted / él / ella	habl<u>a</u>	com<u>e</u>	viv<u>e</u>
nosotros / as	habl<u>amos</u>	com<u>emos</u>	viv<u>imos</u>
ustedes / ellos / ellas	habl<u>an</u>	com<u>en</u>	viv<u>en</u>

Ella **habla** muy bien español. *She speaks Spanish very well.*
¿Dónde **vives**? *Where do you live?*

Stem-changing verbs (Unit 3)

Some verbs undergo a vowel change in the stem in all persons but **nosotros/as**. Their endings remain the same as for regular verbs. The main types of changes are:

a From **e** to **ie**, e.g. **empezar** *to begin, start,* **entender** *to understand,* **pensar** *to think,* **preferir** *to prefer,* e.g. **Yo empiezo,** *I start.*
b From **o** to **ue**, e.g. **acostarse** *to go to bed,* **poder** *to be able to, can,* **volver** *to come back,* e.g. ¿**Puedes** hacerlo? *Can you do it?*
c From **e** to **i**, e.g. **pedir** *to ask for,* **seguir** *to follow,* **servir** *to serve,* e.g. ¿Le **sirvo** un poco más? *Shall I give (serve) you some more?*

10 Preterite tense (Unit 9)

To say what you did at some point in the past and to talk about events which lasted over a definite period and ended in the past, you use the preterite tense. There are two sets of endings for this tense, one for -**ar** verbs and another one for verbs in -**er** and -**ir**.

hablar	**comer**	**vivir**
habl**é**	com**í**	viv**í**
habl**aste**	com**iste**	viv**iste**
habl**ó**	com**ió**	viv**ió**
habl**amos**	com**imos**	viv**imos**
habl**aron**	com**ieron**	viv**ieron**

Ayer **hablé** con él. *I spoke to him yesterday*
Viví dos años allí. *I lived there for two years.*

11 Imperfect tense (Unit 10)

The imperfect tense is used to talk about what you were doing, what you used to do, and to say what people, places and things were like. Unlike the preterite, the imperfect cannot be used to indicate a definite and completed action in the past. Note that verbs in –**er** and –**ir** share the same endings.

hablar	comer	vivir
hablaba	comía	vivía
hablabas	comías	vivías
hablaba	comía	vivía
hablábamos	comíamos	vivíamos
hablaban	comían	vivían

¿Con quién **hablabas**? *Who were you speaking to?*
Comíamos siempre en casa. *We always used to eat at home.*

12 Perfect tense (Unit 12)

The perfect tense is used for talking about recent events as well as actions which have taken place over a period of time which has not yet ended. Usage of this tense varies among Latin Americans who, by and large, tend to use the preterite tense when talking about past events, even recent ones.

The perfect tense is formed with the present tense of **haber** followed by the past participle. This ends in **-ado** for -**ar** verbs and **-ido** for -**er** and -**ir** verbs.

	hablar	comer	vivir
he	hablado	comido	vivido
has	hablado	comido	vivido
ha	hablado	comido	vivido
hemos	hablado	comido	vivido
han	hablado	comido	vivido

Todavía no **he hablado** *I still have not spoken*
  con Juan.   *to Juan.*
¿Has comido ya? *Have you eaten already?*

The pluperfect tense is used to say what one had done:

Gloria **había estado** *Gloria had been here before.*
  aquí antes.

13 Future tense (Unit 7)

The future tense is more common in the written language. In the spoken language it is normally used to make predictions, promises, and to express probability. In the spoken language, future actions and events are normally expressed with the construction **ir a** followed by the infinitive (see Unit 5).

The future tense is formed with the whole infinitive, to which the endings are added, the same set of endings for **-ar**, **-er** and **-ir** verbs.

hablar	comer	vivir
hablar**é**	com**eré**	viv**iré**
hablar**ás**	com**erás**	viv**irás**
hablar**á**	com**erá**	viv**irá**
hablar**emos**	com**eremos**	viv**iremos**
hablar**án**	com**erán**	viv**irán**

Te prometo que **hablaré** con él.
¿Dónde **vivirá**?

I promise you I'll speak to him.
I wonder where he / she lives.

14 Conditional tense (Unit 11)

The conditional is used to say what you *would* do, as in *I would go if I could*. Like the future tense, the conditional is formed with the whole infinitive, to which the endings are added, the same for **-ar**, **-er** and **-ir** verbs.

hablar	comer	vivir
hablar**ía**	comer**ía**	vivir**ía**
hablar**ías**	comer**ías**	vivir**ías**
hablar**ía**	comer**ía**	vivir**ía**
hablar**íamos**	comer**íamos**	vivir**íamos**
hablar**ían**	comer**ían**	vivir**ían**

Yo **hablaría** con ella, pero no tengo su número de teléfono.

Con todo ese dinero **viviríamos** muy bien.

I would speak to her, but I haven't got her telephone number.
With all that money we would live very well.

15 Present subjunctive (Unit 13)

The subjunctive is little used in English nowadays, except in sentences such as *If I were you, I wish he were more careful.* The subjunctive is not a tense, but a different *mood* of the verb, just as the indicative (all the tenses above) and the imperative (see 16 below) are also moods of the verb (see **Glossary of grammatical terms**).

The subjunctive usually occurs in *subordinate* clauses, in sentences expressing unreality, uncertainty, or some kind of emotion, for example joy, fear, regret, hope, anger, sadness, etc. It also occurs on its own, in independent clauses.

The subjunctive has several tenses, but only the present subjunctive, the most common of all, has been covered in this book.

To form the present subjunctive, remove the **-o** of the first person of the present indicative tense and add the endings, one set for **-ar** verbs, another for verbs in **-er** and **-ir**.

present indicative (1st person)	present subjunctive
hablo	hable, hables, hable, hablemos, hablen
como	coma, comas, coma, comamos, coman
vivo	viva, vivas, viva, vivamos, vivan

Necesitamos una persona que **hable** español.	*We need a person who speaks Spanish.*
Espero que **viva** muchos años.	*I hope he / she lives for many years.*
No creo que **coman** esto.	*I don't think they'll eat this.*

16 Imperative (Units 12 and 13)

The imperative or command form of the verb is used for giving directions, instructions and commands. Spanish uses different imperative forms depending on who you are talking to – formal or familiar – and whether you are speaking to one or more than one person, singular or plural. The familiar imperative has different positive and negative forms.

With the exception of the positive form for **tú**, imperative forms are the same as the corresponding person of the present subjunctive.

Imperative forms for *usted* and *ustedes*
   hable (Ud.) hablen (Uds.)
   coma (Ud.) coman (Uds.)
   viva (Ud.) vivan (Uds.)

Imperative forms for *tú*

Positive	*Negative*
habla (tú)	no hables (tú)
come (tú)	no comas (tú)
vive (tú)	no vivas (tú)

For irregular imperative forms see **Irregular verbs** on pages 215–18.

17 The gerund (Unit 10)

Gerunds are forms like **trabajando** *working*, **comiendo** *eating*, which are used with **estar** to refer to actions in progress at the moment of speaking, e.g. **Estoy trabajando** *I'm working*.

18 Ser and estar *to be* (Units 1, 2, 3, 6, 7, 10)

Ser is used

a   To give personal information such as who you are, nationality, where you are from, occupation, marital status (see also **estar**), e.g. **Ana es mexicana** *Ana is Mexican*.

b   To describe people, places and things, e.g. **Cuzco es una ciudad muy interesante** *Cuzco is a very interesting city*.

c   With the time and certain time phrases, e.g. **Mañana es domingo** *Tomorrow is Sunday*.

d   To refer to the material something is made of, e.g. **Esta camisa es de algodón** *This shirt is made of cotton*.

e   To denote possession, e.g. **Éste es mi libro**, *This is my book*.

f   To ask and say how much something is, e.g. **¿Cuánto es?** *How much is it?*

g   To indicate where an event will take place, e.g. **La fiesta es aquí** *The party is here*.

Estar is used

a   To ask and say where something is, e.g. **La catedral está en la plaza** *The cathedral is in the square*.

b   To express marital status, e.g. **Pancho está soltero** *Pancho is single.*

c   To ask people how they are and respond, e.g. **¿Cómo estás? Estoy bien** *How are you? - I'm fine.*

d   To denote a temporary state or condition, e.g. **Gloria está muy guapa hoy** *Gloria looks very pretty today.*

e   To refer to cost when prices fluctuate, e.g. **¿A cuánto está el cambio?** *What is the rate of exchange?*

f   With past participles, to denote a condition resulting from an action, e.g. **El restaurante está abierto** *The restaurant is open.*

g   With gerunds, to talk about actions in progress, e.g. **Está hablando con Carmen** *He / she is speaking with Carmen.*

19 Using *se* (Units 4, 5, 8)

Se is used with the third person of the verb

a   To form impersonal sentences, e.g. **¿Cómo se va al aeropuerto desde aquí?** *How does one go to the airport from here?*

b   To convey the idea that something *'is done'*, e.g. **Aquí se habla español** *Spanish is spoken here.*

c   With reflexive verbs (e.g. **levantarse** *to get up*), e.g. **Se levantaron a las seis** *They got up at six.*

d   As an indirect object pronoun in place of **le**, before **lo(s)**, **la(s)**, e.g. **Se lo dije** *I told him / her.*

The following list includes only the most common irregular verbs. Only irregular forms are given (verbs marked with an asterisk are also stem-changing). The **vosotros** form, used in Spain, is included here.

abrir *to open*
past participle: abierto

andar *to walk*
preterite: anduve, anduviste, anduvo, anduvimos, anduvisteis, anduvieron

caer *to fall*
present indicative: (yo) caigo
present subjunctive: caiga, caigas, caiga, caigamos, caigáis, caigan
gerund: cayendo
preterite: (él, ella, Ud.) cayó, (ellos, ellas, Uds.) cayeron

conducir *to drive*
present indicative: (yo) conduzco
present subjunctive: conduzca, conduzcas, conduzca, conduzcamos, conduzcáis, conduzcan
preterite: conduje, condujiste, condujo, condujimos, condujisteis, condujeron

cubrir *to cover*
past participle: cubierto

dar *to give*
present indicative: (yo) doy
preterite: di, diste, dio, dimos, disteis, dieron
present subjunctive: dé, des, dé, demos, deis, den

decir* to say
present indicative: (yo) digo
present subjunctive: diga, digas, diga, digamos, digáis, digan
preterite: dije, dijiste, dijo, dijimos, dijisteis, dijeron
future: diré, dirás, dirá, diremos, diréis, dirán
conditional: diría, dirías, diría, diríamos, diríais, dirían
imperative (familiar, singular): di
gerund: diciendo
past participle: dicho

escribir *to write*
past participle: escrito

estar *to be*
present indicative: estoy, estás, está, estamos, estáis, están
present subjunctive: esté, estés, esté, estemos, estéis, estén
preterite: estuve, estuviste, estuvo, estuvimos, estuvisteis, estuvieron
imperative (familiar, singular): está

hacer *to do, make*
present indicative: (yo) hago
present subjunctive: haga, hagas, haga, hagamos, hagáis, hagan
preterite: hice, hiciste, hizo, hicimos, hicisteis, hicieron
future: haré, harás, hará, haremos, haréis, harán
conditional: haría, harías, haría, haríamos, haríais, harían
imperative: (Ud.) haga, (tú) haz
past participle: hecho

ir *to go*
present indicative: voy, vas, va, vamos, vais, van
present subjunctive: vaya, vayas, vaya, vayamos, vayáis, vayan
imperfect: iba, ibas, iba, íbamos, ibais, iban
preterite: fui, fuiste, fue, fuimos, fuisteis, fueron
imperative: (Ud.) vaya, (tú) ve
gerund: yendo

leer *to read*
preterite: (él, ella, Ud.) leyó, (ellos, ellas, Uds.) leyeron
gerund: leyendo

morir* *to die*
past participle: muerto

oír *to hear*
present indicative: oigo, oyes, oye, oímos, oís, oyen
present subjunctive: oiga, oigas, oiga, oigamos, oigáis, oigan

preterite: (él, ella, Ud.) oyó, (ellos, ellas, Uds.) oyeron
imperative: (Ud.) oiga, (tú) oye
gerund: oyendo

poder* *to be able to, can*
preterite: pude, pudiste, pudo, pudimos, pudisteis, pudieron
future: podré, podrás, podrá, podremos, podréis, podrán
conditional: podría, podrías, podría, podríamos, podríais,
  podrían
gerund: pudiendo

poner *to put*
present indicative: (yo) pongo
present subjunctive: ponga, pongas, ponga, pongamos,
  pongáis, pongan
preterite: puse, pusiste, puso, pusimos, pusisteis, pusieron
future: pondré, pondrás, pondrá, pondremos, pondréis,
  pondrán
conditional: pondría, pondrías, pondría, pondríamos,
  pondríais, pondrían
imperative: (Ud.) ponga, (tú) pon
past participle: puesto

querer* *to want*
preterite: quise, quisiste, quiso, quisimos, quisisteis, quisieron
future: querré, querrás, querrá, querremos, querréis, querrán
conditional: querría, querrías, querría, querríamos, querríais,
  querrían

romper *to break*
past participle: roto

saber *to know*
present indicative: (yo) sé
present subjunctive: sepa, sepas, sepa, sepamos, sepáis, sepan
preterite: supe, supiste, supo, supimos, supisteis, supieron
future: sabré, sabrás, sabrá, sabremos, sabréis, sabrán
conditional: sabría, sabrías, sabría, sabríamos, sabríais, sabrían
imperative: (Ud.) sepa

salir *to go out*
present indicative: (yo) salgo
present subjunctive: salga, salgas, salga, salgamos, salgáis, salgan
future: saldré, saldrás, saldrá, saldremos, saldréis, saldrán
conditional: saldría, saldrías, saldría, saldríamos, saldríais,
  saldrían
imperative: (Ud.) salga, (tú) sal

ser *to be*
present indicative: soy, eres, es, somos, sois, son
present subjunctive: sea, seas, sea, seamos, seáis, sean
preterite: fui, fuiste, fue, fuimos, fuisteis, fueron
imperfect indicative: era, eras, era, éramos, erais, eran
imperative: (Ud.) sea, (tú) sé

soltar *to loosen*
past participle: suelto

tener* *to have*
present indicative: (yo) tengo
present subjunctive: tenga, tengas, tenga, tengamos, tengáis, tengan
preterite: tuve, tuviste, tuvo, tuvimos, tuvisteis, tuvieron
future: tendré, tendrás, tendrá, tendremos, tendréis, tendrán
conditional: tendría, tendrías, tendría, tendríamos, tendríais, tendrían
imperative: (Ud.) tenga, (tú) ten

traer *to bring*
present indicative: (yo) traigo
present subjunctive: traiga, traigas, traiga, traigamos, traigáis, traigan
preterite: traje, trajiste, trajo, trajimos, trajisteis, trajeron
imperative: (Ud.) traiga
gerund: trayendo

venir* *to come*
present indicative: (yo) vengo
present subjunctive: venga, vengas, venga, vengamos, vengáis, vengan
preterite: vine, viniste, vino, vinimos, vinisteis, vinieron
future: vendré, vendrás, vendrá, vendremos, vendréis, vendrán
conditional: vendría, vendrías, vendría, vendríamos, vendríais, vendrían
imperative: (Ud.) venga, (tú) ven
gerund: viniendo

ver *to see*
present indicative: (yo) veo
present subjunctive: vea, veas, vea, veamos, veáis, vean
imperfect indicative: veía, veías, veía, veíamos, veíais, veían
imperative: (Ud.) vea
past participle: visto

volver* *to go back, return*
past participle: vuelto

This glossary is intended as a reference section and includes essential words which vary within major Latin American countries or in relation to Spain. Words which are the same in all countries have not been included.

The words in bold in each group, after their English equivalent, are those normally used in Spain. Most of these words are not exclusive to Spain, as they are also used, unless specified, in some Latin American countries. And even in places where they are not normally used they will be understood. Thus, the word **el autobús** (*bus*), which many countries do not use, will probably be understood everywhere. Therefore, with a few exceptions, you will be able to get along with the words used in Spain, but you will need to understand what different native speakers mean when they use other terms. Words which do not indicate a specific country in brackets are used in several places. Other, more restricted terms show the country where they are used. For a general list of word groups in Spanish, consult a phrase book.

Transport and travel

bus
el autobús
el bus
el camión (Mex, Central Am)
el pesero o el colectivo (Mex, minibus in which fare depends on distance you travel)
el colectivo (in Chile a shared taxi with a fixed route; in Argentina and Venezuela, the word refers to a city bus)

la guagua (Caribbean) (in Chile, Peru and Bolivia, **la guagua** is
  a baby)
el ómnibus
el / la micro (from **el microbús**), Argentina; la micro (Chile)

to take (a bus, train, etc.)
coger (a taboo word in some Latin American countries)
tomar

underground, subway
el metro
el subte (Arg)

car
el coche
el carro
el auto (esp. Southern Cone; i.e. Argentina, Chile and Uruguay)

car park
el aparcamiento
el estacionamiento

to park
aparcar
estacionar

ticket (bus, train, etc.)
el billete
el boleto
el pasaje

to hire, rent
alquilar (un coche, etc.)
rentar
arrendar

ticket office
la taquilla
la boletería

petrol
la gasolina
la bencina (Chile)
la nafta (Arg)

service station
la estación de servicio
la bomba
el grifo (Perú)
la gasolinera o gasolinería (Mex)

tyre
el neumático
la llanta (in Spain and some other countries, **la llanta** is the
metal rim of a car wheel)
la goma (Arg)

to drive
conducir
manejar

driving licence
el carnet (or **carné**) / **el permiso de conducir**
la licencia de conducir / manejar
el pase (Col)
el registro (de conductor) (Arg)
el brevete (Perú)

House and hotel

reservation
la reserva
la reservación

room
la habitación
el cuarto
la pieza

single room
una habitación individual
una habitación sencilla
una habitación simple
una single
un cuarto sencillo (Mex)

bedroom
el dormitorio
el cuarto
la recámara (Mex)
la alcoba

blanket
la manta
la cobija
el cobertor
la frazada

washbasin
el lavabo
el lavatorio
el lavamanos
la pileta (Arg)

water tap
el grifo
la llave (del agua)
la canilla (Arg)
la pluma (Col)
el caño (Peru)

shower
la ducha
la regadera (Mex)

bath tub
la bañera
la tina
la bañadera (Arg)

light bulb
la bombilla
el bombillo (Col, Ven)
la ampolleta (Chile)
el foco (Mex)
la bombita (River Plate, i.e. Argentina and Uruguay)
la bujía (Central Am)

swimming pool
la piscina
la alberca (Mex)
la pileta (River Plate)

flat, apartment
el apartamento (also **el piso**)
el departamento

lift
el ascensor
el elevador

Restaurants and food

Words for different dishes are not given, as in this area there are many more variations within Latin America and between Latin America and Spain. With a few exceptions, most basic food and farm produce carry the same names everywhere. However, as you travel in Latin America, you will encounter many names for products which are typical of certain countries or regions, and which you may not hear anywhere else.

waiter, waitress
el camarero, la camarera
el mesero, la mesera
el mozo, la señorita (Arg, Chile, Peru)
el mesonero, la mesonera (Ven)

to have breakfast
desayunar
tomar (el) desayuno

dinner
la cena
la comida

set-price meal
el menú (del día)
el plato del día
la comida corrida (Mex)

potatoes
las patatas
las papas

beans
las judías / alubias
los frijoles / frejoles
los porotos
las caraotas (Ven)

peas
los guisantes
los chícharos (Mex, Central Am)
las arvejas

chilli
el chile
el ají (Arg, Chile, Peru)

avocado
el aguacate
la palta (Southern Cone)

peach
el melocotón
el durazno

apricot
el albaricoque
el damasco
el melocotón (Col)
el chabacano (Mex)

strawberry
la fresa
la frutilla (Southern Cone)

black coffee
un café solo
un café
un tinto (Col)

to drink
beber
tomar

toilets
el lavabo
el servicio / los servicios
el baño / los baños
el sanitario (Col, Ven, Mex)

Telephone and postal services

Hello?
¿Díga(me)?
¿Sí?
¿Aló?
¿Bueno? (Mex)
¿Holá? (River Plate)

extension
la extensión
el anexo (Chile, Peru)
el interno (Arg)

call
una llamada
un llamado

a reverse-charge call
un(a) llamado/a a / con cobro revertido
un(a) llamado/a a / por cobrar/pagar (allá)

it is engaged
está comunicando
está ocupado

stamp
el sello
la estampilla
el timbre (Mex)

post office
correos
el correo
la oficina de correos

post box
el apartado (de correos)
el apartado (postal)
la casilla (de correos) (Southern Cone)
el buzón

pronunciation

The aim of this brief pronunciation guide is to offer hints which will enable you to produce sounds recognizable to a speaker from any part of the Spanish-speaking world. It cannot by itself teach you to pronounce Spanish accurately. The best way to acquire a reasonably good accent is to listen to and try to imitate native speakers.

This guide gives hints on individual sounds and it also provides an overview of main pronunciation features within certain regions of Latin America.

Vowels

Spanish vowels are generally shorter, clearer and more precise than English vowels. Unstressed vowels are not weakened as in English but are given much the same value in pronunciation as those which are stressed. For example, in the English word *comfortable*, the vowels which follow the syllable *com* are weak, while in Spanish every vowel in the word **confortable** has the same quality.

There are only five vowel sounds in Spanish:

a	like the **u** in *butter*, as in standard south of England pronunciation	gracias
e	like the **e** in *end*	él
i	like the **i** in *marine*	inglés
o	like the **o** in *God*	sol
u	like the **oo** in *moon*	uno

Note:
When **i** occurs before another vowel, it is
pronounced like the **y** in *yes*.
When **u** occurs before another vowel, it is
pronounced like the **w** in *wind*.
After **q**, **u** is not pronounced at all.
u is also silent in **gui** and **gue**.
u is pronounced in **güi** and **güe**,
a very infrequent sound combination
in Spanish.

tiene

bueno

que
guía, guerra
lingüística
vergüenza

Consonants

The pronunciation of Spanish consonants is generally similar to
that of English consonants. But note the following features:

b and v	in initial position and after **n**, like the **b** in *bar*.	bien, invierno
	in other positions, more like the **v** in *very*.	Caribe, El Salvador
c	before **a**, **o**, **u**, like the **c** in *coast*.	castellano
	before **e**, **i**, like the **s** in *sea*.	hacer, gracias
ch	like the **ch** in *chair*.	Chile
d	like the **d** in *day*.	día
	between vowels and after **r**, more like the **th** in *those*.	nada, tarde
g	before **a**, **o**, **u**, like the **g** in *government*.	hago, Guatemala
	before **e**, **i**, like the **h** in *hand* in Central America and the Caribbean, but more like the Scottish **ch** in *loch* in other countries.	Argentina, Sergio
j	like the **h** in *hand* in Central America and the Caribbean, but more like the Scottish **ch** in *loch* in other countries.	Juan
h	is silent.	ahora
ll	like the **y** of *yawn*.	llamar
ñ	like the **ni** in *onion*.	mañana
q(u)	like the **c** in *cake*.	que
r	in initial position is strongly rolled.	río
rr	strongly rolled.	carro
y	like the **y** in *yes*.	mayo
z	like the **s** in *sale*.	Venezuela

Note: In Mexico, there are many words derived from indigenous languages which carry an **x**. The pronunciation of **x** varies, as can be seen from these examples:

Ixtapa	pronounced as **ks**
Xochimilco	pronounced as **s**
Oaxaca	pronounced as **h**
mexica	pronounced as **sh**

Latin American pronunciation

As it occurs in the English-speaking world, most of the countries in Latin America can be said to have their own pronunciation and intonation features. As a non-native speaker, you may not notice these differences at first, but increased familiarity with the spoken language will gradually allow you to distinguish them, perhaps not in terms of specific countries but in terms of larger areas or regions.

Among general characteristics of Latin American Spanish, we find the *seseo*, that is, the pronunciation of *z* (e.g. *González*) and *c* before *e* and *i* (e.g. *cien, quince*) as *s* and not like the *th* in *think*, which is what you will hear in most parts of Spain. Also, the distinction made in some parts of Spain between *y* and *ll* (e.g. *yo, llamo*) where *y* is pronounced like the *y* in *yes*, and *ll* more like the *lli* in *million*, is not made in Latin America. A single sound, not unlike the *y* in *yes*, is used in both instances in most regions.

In terms of specific areas or countries, Mexican accent and pronunciation is one of the most distinctive in Latin America. In general, there is a weakening of vowel sounds, for example in *buen(a)s noch(e)s*, unlike what happens in many other Latin American countries, where it is consonant sounds which are reduced or even omitted altogether in certain positions. The pronunciation of final *s* and *s* before a consonant, as in *buenas noches*, for example, is fully pronounced in Mexico, unlike what happens in places like the Caribbean or Venezuela, where it tends to be substituted by an aspirated *h*, rendering a pronunciation more like *buena(h) noche(h)*. The latter is also characteristic of southern Spain.

Colombians claim they speak the best Spanish in Latin America. Even if you are reluctant to accept adjectives such as *good* or *bad* regarding a particular language or dialect, one must admit that the Spanish spoken in some areas of Colombia may seem, to foreign ears at least, clearer and easier to follow than that of some other countries or areas. However, within Colombia there are wide differences between the Spanish spoken in places like Bogotá or Cali, for example, usually associated with 'good, clear Spanish', and that spoken around the Caribbean. This bears some of the characteristics of Caribbean Spanish in general, that is, weakening or even disappearance of consonant sounds in certain positions, e.g. *do(h), tre(h)*, instead of *dos, tres*, or *pe(h)cao* instead of *pescado*.

This weakening or disappearance of certain consonant sounds is also a feature of Chilean pronunciation and to a large extent also of Argentinian accent, except in deliberate and more careful speech. Further features of Chilean accent are the pronunciation of the combination *tr*, which is pronounced by most people like the *tr* in *country*, and the rendering of *ch* (e.g. *Chile*), not unlike the *sh* in *ship*. The latter is particularly common among less educated speakers.

The Argentinian accent is a very distinctive one, particularly as regards the pronunciation of *y* (e.g. *yo*) and *ll* (e.g. *allá*), which are pronounced much like the *j* in *John* or the *s* in *pleasure*. In parts of Argentina, especially in the west and north, the *r* is not rolled in words such as *río* and *perro*. What you hear instead sounds more like *rj, rjío, perjo*.

Stress and accentuation

Words which end in a vowel, **n** or **s** stress the last syllable but one.	**bueno, amigos**
Words which end in a consonant other than **n** or **s** stress the last syllable.	**hotel, señor**
Words which do not follow the above rules carry a written accent over the stressed syllable.	**América, autobús**
Differences in meaning between certain similar words are shown through the use of an accent.	**sí** *yes* **si** *if* **él** *he* **el** *the*, m **sé** *I know* **se** *pronoun* **dé** *give* **de** *of, from* **mí** *me* **mi** *my* **sólo** *only* **solo** *alone*
Question words carry an accent, and are preceded by an inverted question mark.	**¿dónde?** *where?* **¿cuándo?** *when?* **¿qué?** *what?*

¿cuál? *which?*
¿cómo? *how?*

In exclamations, **que** carries
an accent. Notice also the inverted
exclamation mark at the beginning.

¡Qué lindo! *How beautiful!*
¡Qué difícil! *How difficult!*

Spelling

Note the following changes in spelling.

Verbs may change their spelling in certain forms in order to keep
the sound of the infinitive. For example:

lle**gar** *to arrive*   but lle**gué** *I arrived*
pa**gar** *to pay*   but pa**gué** *I paid*
bus**car** *to look for*   but bus**qué** *I looked for*

Liaison

If a word ends in a vowel and is followed by a word beginning
with a vowel, the two vowels are normally pronounced as
though both were part of the same word. When the two vowels
are the same, these are usually pronounced as one, for example:

¿Cómo‿está‿usted?   No‿está‿aquí.   ¿Habla‿español?

Pronouncing the alphabet

a	**a**	j	**jota**	r	**ere**
b	**be**	k	**ka**	s	**ese**
c	**c**	l	**ele**	t	**te**
d	**de**	m	**eme**	u	**u**
e	**e**	n	**ene**	v	**uve***
f	**efe**	ñ	**eñe**	w	**doble u***
g	**ge**	o	**o**	x	**equis**
h	**ache**	p	**pe**	y	**i griega**
i	**i**	q	**cu**	z	**zeta**

* As Spanish does not make a distinction in pronunciation
between **b** and **v**, when spelling a word **v** is normally qualified
as **ve pequeña**, **ve chica** or **ve corta**, depending on the country,
or else, examples are given: **be de bonito**, or **de burro**, **ve de
Venezuela** or **de vaca**.

* **w** is called **doble uve** in some countries and **doble ve** in others.

Unit 1

Practice 8

a

Entrevistador	Buenas tardes. ¿Cómo se llama usted?
Initia	Buenas tardes. Mi nombre es Initia Muñoz García.
Entrevistador	Initia, ¿de qué país es usted?
Initia	Soy de aquí de México. Soy mexicana.
Entrevistador	¿De qué parte de México?
Initia	De la ciudad de Córdoba. Veracruz.

b

Entrevistador	Buenas tardes.
Clotilde	Buenas tardes.
Entrevistador	¿Cómo se llama usted?
Clotilde	Me llamo Clotilde Montalvo Rodríguez, para servirle.
Entrevistador	Clotilde, ¿de dónde es usted?
Clotilde	Soy de aquí de Veracruz.
Entrevistador	Veracruz. ¿Es usted mexicana?
Clotilde	Sí, soy mexicana.

c

Elizabeth	Me llamo Elizabeth. Soy de Panamá, de la Ciudad de Panamá.

Unit 2

Practice 5

a

Señor	Disculpe, señorita.
Señorita	A sus órdenes.
Señor	¿Hay una casa de cambio por aquí?
Señorita	Sí, hay una en la calle Amazonas.
Señor	¿Dónde está la calle Amazonas?
Señorita	Está a cinco cuadras de aquí, a la izquierda.
Señor	Muchas gracias. Muy amable.
Señorita	Para servirle.

b

Sr. Ramos	Buenos días.
Recepcionista	Buenos días. ¿Qué desea?
Sr. Ramos	¿Está el señor Silva?
Recepcionista	Sí, sí está. Está en su oficina.
Sr. Ramos	¿Cuál es el número de la oficina?
Recepcionista	La oficina del señor Silva es la doscientos cuarenta. Está en el segundo piso, al final del pasillo, a la derecha.
Sr. Ramos	¿Dónde está el elevador?
Recepcionista	Está allá.

Practice 7

Turista	Por favor, ¿dónde está la estación?
Colombiana	Está en la carrera diecisiete, al final de la calle dieciséis.
Turista	¿Está lejos de aquí?
Colombiana	¿A pie?
Turista	Sí, a pie.
Colombiana	Está a quince minutos más o menos.
Turista	Muchas gracias.
Colombiana	De nada.

Practice 8

Jorge	Soy director de un centro de lenguas modernas.
Entrevistador	¿Dónde … dónde está el centro?
Jorge	El Centro de Lenguas Modernas está localizado en la ciudad de Veracruz, a media cuadra de la

calle principal, es decir, a una y media cuadra
del parque principal de la ciudad.

Unit 3

Practice 5

En la mañana abren a las nueve de la mañana y, entonces,
trabajan de nueve a una, nueve de la mañana a una de la tarde,
cierran de una a cuatro, abren a las cuatro, para trabajar hasta
las ocho de la noche.

Practice 8

a

Entrevistador	Dime, ¿cuáles son las comidas principales en México, y cuál es el horario de cada comida?
Jorge	O.K. Las comidas principales en México son el desayuno entre las ocho y las nueve; el almuerzo entre la una y media y las tres y media; la cena, entre ocho y media y nueve; y, opcionalmente, hay una ... podríamos llamarle poscena, que puede ser a las once y media de la noche, si nos acostamos tarde.

a

Entrevistador	Coty, buenas tardes. Coty, ¿cuáles son las comidas principales en México y cuáles son los horarios de las comidas?
Coty	Las comidas ... la comida principal es la de mediodía, que varía entre una y dos de la tarde, en que se toma. El desayuno ..., pues, bueno, tenemos tres en el día: desayuno, almuerzo y cena. El desayuno es temprano, a las ocho de la mañana, almuerzo entre una y dos, y cena, pues, de las siete en adelante.

Unit 4

Practice 4

Entrevistador	Coty, ¿en qué trabaja usted?
Coty	Yo soy secretaria, eh … mi horario de trabajo es …, por la mañana entro a las diez de la mañana, salgo a almorzar a la una de la tarde, regreso a las cuatro de la tarde a seguir laborando y salgo a las nueve de la noche.

Practice 6

En las vacaciones normalmente aprovecho para visitar a mis sobrinos. Tengo tres sobrinos que viven en Tijuana, Baja California. En la frontera con Estados Unidos. Es un viaje largo, porque de Veracruz hasta allá son varios días, pero lo disfruto, porque veo a la familia muy de vez en cuando.

Practice 8

Entrevistador	¿Cómo se llama usted?
Clotilde	Mi nombre es Clotilde Montalvo Rodríguez.
Entrevistador	Clotilde, ¿cuántos años tiene usted?
Clotilde	Tengo cuarenta y cuatro años.
Entrevistador	¿Está casada o soltera?
Clotilde	Estoy casada.
Entrevistador	¿Cuántos hijos tiene?
Clotilde	Tengo dos hijas, una de veintitrés años y una pequeña de seis años y medio.
Entrevistador	¿En qué trabaja usted?
Clotilde	Soy secretaria y trabajo en el Centro Cultural de Lenguas Modernas.
Entrevistador	Y su esposo, ¿qué hace?
Clotilde	Mi esposo, pues … maneja, es chofer de carretera.

Unit 5

Practice 4

Mesero	¿Qué le traigo, señorita?
Señorita	¿Qué tiene de almuerzo?

Mesero	Tenemos sopa de pollo, sopa de verduras, crema de espárragos, de champiñones ...
Señorita	Tráigame una crema de espárragos. No, no, no, mire, prefiero tomar una sopa de pollo.
Mesero	¿Y qué otra cosa? Tenemos arroz con pollo, pollo en salsa de mostaza, soufflé de calabaza, carne guisada ...
Señorita	¿Pescado no tiene?
Mesero	No, no queda. Le recomiendo el soufflé de calabaza. Está muy bueno.
Señorita	Sí, tráigame eso.
Mesero	¿Y para tomar? ¿Una cerveza, vino, un jugo ...?
Señorita	Una cerveza.
Mesero	Muy bien, señorita.

Unit 6

Practice 3

Clienta	Buenos días.
Vendedor	Buenos días. ¿A la orden?
Clienta	¿Podría decirme cuánto valen esos zapatos?
Vendedor	¿Cuáles?
Clienta	Ésos, los negros.
Vendedor	Ésos valen treinta y dos mil pesos, pero hay un descuento del diez por ciento. Con descuento son veintiocho mil ochocientos pesos.
Clienta	Sí, está bien. Quisiera probármelos.
Vendedor	¿Qué número?
Clienta	Cuarenta y dos.
Vendedor	Sí, un momento, por favor.

Practice 4

Almacenes García, calidad y economía. García. Por fin de temporada todas las camisas sport manga larga y manga corta para caballeros, cuarenta por ciento de descuento. Todos los pantalones para caballero, treinta, cuarenta y cincuenta por ciento de descuento. No incluye promociones. García.

Practice 7

Cliente	¿Cuánto es todo?
Vendedora	Bueno, tenemos ciento cuarenta y siete mil … ochenta y ocho mil …ciento sesenta y cinco mil … doscientos ochenta y seis mil … quince mil … ciento noventa y ocho mil … ciento cincuenta y un mil. El total es … un millón cincuenta mil pesos.

Unit 7

Practice 5

Entre la gloria y el paraíso está Motel Miraflores, con todos los servicios para que usted disfrute cómodamente de su estancia. Habitaciones con aire acondicionado, cama de agua, jacuzzi, suites con alberca, antena parabólica y música ambiental. Motel Miraflores, el lugar al que siempre deseará volver. Carretera Boticaria-Mocambo s/n (sin número), Veracruz.

Practice 6

El hotel tiene doscientas dieciséis habitaciones, una piscina en la parte trasera con un gran espacio verde, patios bien grandes, dos restaurantes, uno de primera categoría, que es el Techo del Mundo, la otra la cafetería y muchos … y varios salones donde se hacen muchas convenciones. Es de cinco estrellas. Aparte, tiene casino y la discoteca.

Practice 8

a

Entrevistador	¿Cómo es el clima en Panamá?
Elizabeth	Hace calor. Es de una temperatura promedio de veintiocho grados centígrados todo …, durante todo el año. Es un país netamente tropical; tiene dos estaciones, la de invierno, que es lluviosa, y la de verano, que es seca.

b

Lima, la capital del Perú, es una ciudad bonita, grande, moderna, y donde en algunos lugares se conservan las características de la época colonial. También tiene bonitas playas, museos, zoológicos y, en cuanto al clima, es cálido y casi no existen las lluvias.

Unit 8

Practice 6

Guillermo	Me gustaría ir a Mendoza. No sé en qué ir, si en bus o en avión. ¿Qué me recomiendas?
Carlos	Bueno, mira, yo te recomiendo el bus, porque el viaje es mucho más interesante. El bus demora aproximadamente cinco o seis horas. El avión demora treinta minutos, pero en bus vas a ver muchísimo más. Hay buses dos o tres veces por día y el pasaje no te va a costar mucho. Ahora, si tú quieres que te recomiende algún hotel en Mendoza, te puedo recomendar un hotel bastante bueno y económico, el hotel Plaza que está a dos cuadras de la calle principal de Mendoza. Tengo la dirección y el teléfono y te los puedo dar.

Unit 9

Practice 3

a

Sra. Puig	Buenas tardes ¿Está el señor Solís, por favor?
Recepcionista	El señor Solís está ocupado. Está en una reunión. ¿Quiere dejarle algún mensaje?
Sra. Puig	Dígale, por favor, que vino Carmen Puig, de Caracas, que yo necesito hablar urgentemente con él. Dígale que me llame al hotel, al hotel Sheraton. Yo estoy en la habitación 500. Pero tiene que ser ahora, porque yo me voy a Caracas mañana.
Recepcionista	Muy bien, señora.

b

Srta. Pérez	Buenas tardes. ¿Está el señor Solís?
Recepcionista	No, el señor Solís no está. Está en una reunión en este momento.

Srta. Pérez	¿A qué hora llega?
Recepcionista	Va a llegar a las 2.00.
Srta. Pérez	Por favor, dígale que vino Marilú Pérez. Estoy en el hotel Gala, en la habitación 324. Aquí tengo el teléfono. Es el 687951.
Recepcionista	Muy bien, señorita. Yo le daré su recado.
Srta. Pérez	Gracias.
Recepcionista	De nada.

Practice 6

| Marilú | En las vacaciones fui con mi familia a la costa y estuvimos dos semanas en un hotel frente a la playa. Disfrutamos mucho, ya que el lugar donde fuimos es agradable, tranquilo y tiene unas playas maravillosas, y el aire es tan puro. Salimos mucho, harto, tomamos el sol, nadamos, hicimos deportes. Y volvimos pero llenos de energía a la ciudad. |

Note that **pero** (*but*) in the last sentence is emphatic.

Unit 10

Practice 4

Entrevistador	Carlos, ¿siempre has vivido en Buenos Aires?
Carlos	No, no siempre, también viví en San Pablo, Brasil.
Entrevistador	¿Y qué hacías en San Pablo?
Carlos	En San Pablo daba clases de pintura.
Entrevistador	¿Y en qué parte de San Pablo vivías?
Carlos	Vivía en el barrio de Vila Mariana.
Entrevistador	¿Y qué tal era el barrio?
Carlos	Era excelente. Uno de los más arborizados y con más vegetación de San Pablo.
Entrevistador	¿Vivías en una casa o un departamento?
Carlos	Vivía en un departamento.
Entrevistador	¿Un buen departamento tenías allí?
Carlos	Sí, pequeño, pero agradable.
Entrevistador	Y tus vecinos, ¿qué tal eran?
Carlos	Muy buenos vecinos, como todos los brasileros.
Entrevistador	¿Tenías muchos amigos en San Pablo?

Carlos	Muchos, muchos que todavía tengo.
Entrevistador	¿Y por qué volviste a Buenos Aires?
Carlos	Bueno, porque extrañaba mucho la ciudad.

Practice 7

Entrevistador	Carlos, ¿cómo describirías Buenos Aires?
Carlos	Buenos Aires es una ciudad muy grande, con muchos rincones diferentes, pero con una unidad común. Es una ciudad con mucho movimiento cultural y la expresión que más … este … la representa, para mí, es que es una ciudad que tiene alma.
Entrevistador	¿Y qué es lo que más te gusta de Buenos Aires?
Carlos	Me gusta su vida nocturna, me gusta la posibilidad de expresarse que le da a la gente que vive en ella. Me gusta su movimiento cultural.
Entrevistador	¿Hay algo que no te guste de Buenos Aires?
Carlos	Sí, hay algo que no me gusta, que es la tendencia que tenemos los porteños a entristecer y a la melancolía extrema.

Unit 11

Practice 5

Entrevistador	Carlos. ¿dónde te gustaría pasar tus próximas vacaciones?
Carlos	Me gustaría pasarlas en Bariloche.
Entrevistador	¿Y por qué en Bariloche?
Carlos	Porque fui hace muchos años y su imagen quedó profundamente grabada en mí.
Entrevistador	¿Irías solo o acompañado?
Carlos	No, iría con mi familia o con amigos.
Entrevistador	¿Y por cuánto tiempo irías?
Carlos	Bueno, iría por quince días o veinte.
Entrevistador	¿Y qué harías allí?
Carlos	Recorrería todo lo que de naturaleza se pueda visitar. No me gusta demasiado la vida … frívola del lugar.

Practice 6

Entrevistador	¿Tienes coche?
Carlos	No tengo.
Entrevistador	¿Te gustaría tener uno?
Carlos	Sí, me gustaría mucho.
Entrevistador	¿Y qué marca de coche preferirías?
Carlos	Preferiría un Ford.
Entrevistador	Un Ford ... ¿Y comprarías uno grande o uno chico?
Carlos	Me gustan más los autos grandes.
Entrevistador	¿Preferirías un coche deportivo o tradicional?
Carlos	Preferiría un coche tradicional.
Entrevistador	¿Y qué color comprarías?
Carlos	Un color gris o azul.
Entrevistador	¿Lo usarías para ir al trabajo o para salir a pasear?
Carlos	Por supuesto, para las dos cosas.
Entrevistador	¿Y adónde irías, por ejemplo, a pasear el fin de semana o en las vacaciones?
Carlos	Iría a lugares cercanos, pero donde abunde la naturaleza.

Unit 12

Practice 3

Entrevistador	Karina, ¿has estado en el Cuzco alguna vez?
Karina	Sí, estuve cuando yo tenía once años de edad.
Entrevistador	¿Y qué tal es la ciudad?
Karina	Es muy bonita. Es muy tradicional, pues (que) conserva las características de la cultura incaica.
Entrevistador	¿Y está ...? ¿Cómo se puede ir desde Lima al Cuzco?
Karina	Bueno, se puede viajar mediante bus, avión o tren.
Entrevistador	¿Y el avión cuánto demora?
Karina	Aproximadamente dos horas.
Entrevistador	Dos horas. Y para ir a Machu Picchu desde el Cuzco, ¿está muy lejos?
Karina	Exactamente, no sé a cuánto tiempo está. Está lejos de Machu Picchu y la única forma de llegar es mediante el tren.

Unit 13

Practice 4

a

Señor	Señorita, mire, yo pedí un asiento en la sección de *no* fumadores.
Azafata	Lo siento, tanto, señor, pero no es culpa nuestra. Inmediatamente voy a ver qué puedo hacer para cambiarlo.
Señor	Gracias.

b

Señora	¡Epa, muchacho!
Mesero	Sí, señora.
Señora	Mire, yo le pedí pescado con puré y usted ... usted me trajo pescado con papas fritas, ¿vale?
Mesero	Disculpe, se lo cambio ahorita.

c

Señorita	¡Mozo!
Mozo	Señorita, ¿sí?
Señorita	Mire por favor, hace quince minutos que pedí una sopa de mariscos y todavía no me la traen. ¿Qué pasa?
Mozo	Perdone, señorita, pero estamos tan ocupados hoy día. Hay tantos clientes. Mire, voy a ver lo que pasó. Se la traigo enseguida.

Practice 6

Turista	Buenas tardes. Para ir al Teatro Segura, por favor.
Recepcionista	Sí, cómo no. Al salir de aquí, doble por la calle Ucayali, camine de frente hacia Abancay. Ahí doble a la mano izquierda, camine dos cuadras y media, y ahí está el Teatro Segura.
Turista	Gracias.
Recepcionista	De nada.

Practice 8

Doctor Manuel Loyo de Valdés, fracturas, luxaciones, cirugía, traumatología y ortopedia. Doctor Manuel Loyo de Valdés.

Consultas, de 11.00 a 13.00 horas y de 18.00 a 21.00 horas, en González Pajés 1016, entre Iturbide y Mina. Teléfono 325228, en Veracruz.

Practice 9

Paciente	Quisiera pedir hora con el doctor Martínez, por favor. ¿Qué días atiende?
Recepcionista	Atiende los lunes, miércoles y viernes. Los lunes atiende de cuatro a seis y los miércoles y viernes de once de la mañana a una de la tarde.

Unit 1

Dialogues

4 a Me llamo (*your name*). **b** Soy de (*country or city*). **5 a** ¿Cómo te llamas? **b** ¿De dónde eres?

Practice

1 Buenos días. / Tengo una reservación. / Mi nombre es . . . *or* Me llamo . . . (*name*). / Gracias. **2** Buenas tardes. / No, no soy Emilio/a Zapata. Soy . . . (*your name*). / No se preocupe. **3** Mi nombre es . . . *or* Me llamo . . . (*name*), soy de . . . (*place where you come from*). / Mucho gusto *or* Encantado/a. / Siéntese, por favor. **4** No, no soy americano/a. Soy inglés / inglesa (*or* Sí, soy americano/a). / Soy de (*city*). / Me llamo . . . (*name*). ¿Y tú? / Mucho gusto *or* Encantado/a. **5 a** Buenas tardes. **b** ¿Cuál es su nombre? *or* ¿Cómo se llama Ud.? **c** ¿De dónde es (usted)? **d** ¿Es usted mexicano/a? **e** ¿De qué parte de México es? **7** Pablo Miranda Frías es venezolano. Pablo es de Caracas. **8 a** Initia is from Córdoba in Veracruz. **b** ¿De qué país es Ud.? **c** Clotilde is from Veracruz. **d** ¿De dónde es Ud.? **e** Elizabeth is from Panama City. **f** Hola, me llamo Elizabeth.

Unit 2

Dialogues

3 La oficina del señor Martínez. **4** ¿Cómo le va? **5 a** ¿Hay una casa de cambio por aquí? **b** ¿Hay un banco por aquí? **c** Está a tres cuadras de aquí, a la izquierda. **d** Está a cuatro cuadras de aquí, a la derecha.

Practice

1 habitación doscientos veinte, en el segundo piso; habitación cuatrocientos treinta, en el cuarto piso; habitación quinientos cincuenta, en el quinto piso (*follow the model to complete the dialogues*). **2** Hola, ¿cómo estás? *or*

¿cómo te va? / Estoy muy bien. Siéntate. Me alegro mucho de verte. / ¿Cómo están tus papás? **3** Buenos días, ¿cómo está usted? *or* ¿Cómo le va? / Bien, gracias. Siéntese, por favor. Me alegro mucho de verla. **5 a** He is looking for a bureau de change. **b** There is one in the calle Amazonas. **c** Five blocks away. **d** He is in his office. **e** 240 **f** On the second floor. **g** At the end of the corridor, on the right. **6 a** ¿Hay una (*or* alguna) estación (de metro) por aquí? **b** ¿Dónde está? *or* ¿Está lejos? **c** ¿Hay un (*or* algún) hotel por aquí? **d** ¿Está lejos? **e** ¿Dónde está el Banco Nacional, por favor? **f** ¿Dónde está la calle Pánuco? *or* ¿Está cerca / lejos la calle Pánuco? **7 a** F. **b** F. **c** V. **8 a** It is half a block from the main street. **b** It is one and a half blocks from the main park. **9 a** It is in a valley, at an altitude of 2,240 m. **b** It has a rich cultural and artistic life, and is the intellectual centre of Latin America. **c** It is a mixture of old and new. It is a modern city, with wide avenues and lively squares, elegant districts, popular markets, futuristic buildings, colonial buildings and barroque churches.

Unit 3

Dialogues

1 a ¿Qué hora es? Son las dos y media. **b** Son las seis y media. **c** Son las diez y media. **3 a** ¿A qué hora abren el banco? Abren a las nueve. **b** ¿A qué hora abren el museo? Abren a las nueve y media. **c** ¿A qué hora abren la oficina de turismo/ Abren a las diez. **4 a** ¿A qué hora cierran las tiendas? **b** ¿A qué hora cierran los museos? **c** ¿A qué hora cierran las casas de cambio? **5 a** ¿A qué hora es el desayuno? Es a las siete y media. **b** ¿A qué hora es el almuerzo? Es a la una. **c** ¿A qué hora es la salida? Es a las ocho. **6 a** Rosa has breakfast at 8.30 a.m. **b** Raúl has breakfast at 7.00 a.m. **c** Raúl has lunch between 12.30 and 1.00 p.m. **d** Rosa has lunch at 2.00 p.m.

Practice

1 a Es la una y media. **b** Son las seis veinticinco. **c** Son las siete y cuarto. **d** Son veinte para las nueve. *or* Son las nueve menos veinte. **e** Es un cuarto para las diez. *or* Son las diez menos cuarto. **f** Son las once. **2 a** Son las diez. **b** Son las cinco. **c** Es la una. **d** Son las seis. **3 a** Está detrás del Auditorio Nacional. **b** El viernes quince hay una función. **c** Es a las ocho de la noche. **d** Es a las doce. **4 a** ¿A qué hora abren las tiendas? **b** ¿A qué hora abre(n) el supermercado? **c** ¿A qué hora cierra(n) el correo? **d** ¿A qué hora cierran los museos? **5 a** F. **b** V. **c** F. **6** Disculpe, ¿qué hora tiene? / Son las dos y media. / ¿A qué hora abren las casas de cambio? / Abren a las cuatro. / ¿Hay una casa de cambio por aquí? / Sí, La Internacional está a dos cuadras de aquí . . . **7 a** Tomo el desayuno (*or* Desayuno) a las . . . (*time*). **b** Almuerzo a las . . . (*time*). **c** Almuerzo en (casa / la oficina / una cafetería / un restaurante / un bar). **d** No, no muy tarde. *or* Sí, bastante / muy tarde. Ceno a las . . . (*time*). **8 a** Breakfast between 8.00 and 9.00 a.m., lunch between 1.30 and 3.30 p.m. and dinner between 8.30 and 9.00 p.m. **b** It is at 11.30 p.m. **c** mediodía. **d** 1.00 y 2.00. **e** de las 7.00 en adelante.

Unit 4

Dialogues

1 **a** ¿Cómo estás? Pues, un poco cansado. **b** Tengo mucho trabajo. **c** Está aquí de vacaciones. **d** Éste es Juan. **e** Trabajo en una agencia de viajes. 2 **a** Because it is a beautiful place and it has a good climate. **b** She starts at nine in the morning and finishes at seven. 3 **a** Sometimes he goes out of Santiago, to the beach or the countryside. When he stays in Santiago he goes to the cinema or out with friends. **b** She normally watches television, reads or listens to music. 4 **a** She has two children. **b** They are aged twelve and ten.

Practice

1 Hola, Raúl. Te presento a mi mamá. Éste es Raúl. / Encantada. 2 *Ud.*: Buenas tardes, señor Molina. ¿Cómo está Ud.? *Sr. Molina*: Muy bien, gracias. ¿Y Ud.? *Ud.*: Bien, gracias. Le presento a mi colega John Evans. Éste es el señor Molina. *Sr. Molina*: Encantado. *J. Evans*: Mucho gusto. *Sr. Molina*: Siéntense, por favor. 3 **a** ¿Dónde vives? / Vivo en . . . (*place*). ¿En qué trabajas? / Soy . . . (*occupation or profession*) or Trabajo en . . . (*place of work*). **b** ¿De dónde son ustedes? / Soy de . . . (*country*). ¿Dónde viven (ustedes)? / ¿Y en qué trabajan? / Yo soy . . . (*occupation or profession*) or Trabajo en . . . (*place of work*). 4 **a** F. **b** V. **c** F. 5 Soy . . . (*occupation*) or Trabajo en . . . (*place of work*) or Estudio en . . . (*place where you are studying*). Trabajo de lunes a viernes or Voy a la universidad / al colegio de lunes a viernes. Empiezo a las . . . (*time*) y termino a las . . . (*time*). Generalmente almuerzo en . . . (*place*). Cuando salgo del trabajo / de la universidad / del colegio, generalmente (veo la televisión / leo el periódico / escucho música / estudio / visito a mis amigos/as / riego el jardín / cocino, etc.). Los fines de semana (me levanto tarde / trabajo en casa / salgo de compras / juego al tenis / voy al cine / salgo a caminar / salgo a correr, etc.). 6 **a** She visits her nephews in Tijuana. **b** Because she very rarely sees her family. 8 *Name*: Clotilde Montalvo Rodríguez. *Age*: 44 *Marital status*: Married. *Profession*: Secretary. *Husband's profession*: Coach or lorry driver. *No of children*: 2. *Ages*: 23, 6½. 9 **a** Soy casado/a or Soy soltero/a. **b** Tengo (dos) hijos. / No tengo hijos. **c** Tengo (tres) hermanos. / No tengo hermanos. **d** John tiene (doce) años, Anne tiene (siete). **e** Vivo en . . . (*city or town*).

Unit 5

Dialogues

1 Prefiero filetes de pescado / Quiero . . . / Quiero (café / té). 2 **a** ¿Tiene una mesa para tres? **b** Quiero un aperitivo. **c** ¿Nos trae una botella de vino tinto, por favor? 3 **a** ¿Me trae una sopa de verduras? **b** Quiero pollo asado con puré. **c** ¿Nos trae una ensalada mixta? **d** Para mí, café, por favor. 4 ¿Tiene helados? / Prefiero de . . . y quisiera / quiero un café también.

Practice

1 Buenos días, quisiera reservar una mesa para dos (personas). / Sí, para hoy. / Para la una y media. / A nombre de … (*your name*). **2** Buenas tardes, tengo (*or* tenemos) una reservación para la una y media. / Mi nombre es … *or* Me llamo … (*your name*). **3** Mesero: ¿Qué van a comer? Para empezar tenemos… También tenemos sopas y cremas / Ud. Para empezar yo quiero … / **Colega** Y para mi… / M ¿Y qué más? / **Ud.** Yo quisiera… M ¿Con qué lo / la quiere? Ud. Lo / la quiero con … M ¿Y usted señor/a? C Yo quiero / prefiero … con … M ¿Qué van a tomar? Ud. Traíganos … M ¿Qué desean de postre? Ud. Tráigame… C Para mí … M ¿Van a tomoar café? Ud. Yo sí / no, gracias. C Yo… **4 a** Sopa de pollo. **b** Soufflé de calabaza. **c** Una cerveza. **5 a** Because the food tastes good, the service is good, the prices are low and it's a nice place. **b** They serve fish, seafood and meat. **6 a** Potatoes and tomatoes **b** It is difficult to imagine European cuisine without these products. **7 a** Tortillas, like maize bread. Another basic ingredient in Mexican food is chilli. **b** The staple food in Central America is maize. **c** A typical dish in many South American countries is chicken and rice. **d** Argentinians and Uruguayans prefer to eat beef.

Unit 6

Dialogues

1 a Quisiera ver esa maleta. **b** Es un poco cara. ¿Tiene una / otra más barata? **c** Esa no me gusta mucho. **d** Voy a llevar la negra. **e** ¿Puedo pagar con cheques de viaje? **2** Quisiera ver los / esos pantalones que están en la vitrina / el escaparate / Sí, ésos / Talla (size) / Los quiero en (*colour*) / ¿Me los puedo probar? **3 a** ¿Cuánto valen / cuestan los tomates? / ¿Qué precio tienen …? **b** ¿Qué precio tienen los mangos? **c** Deme dos libras / kilos. **d** Quiero un kilo y medio. **4 a** ¿Dónde está la oficina de correos? **b** ¿Cuánto vale / cuesta enviar una carta a (*destination*)? **c** Quisiera tres estampillas / sellos de ochocientos pesos.

Practice

1 Quisiera ver ese bolso que está en la vitrina. / Ése, el café (*or* marrón). / Es muy bonito. ¿Es de cuero? / ¿Cuánto cuesta? / ¿(No) tiene otro más barato? / Me gusta mucho. / Lo voy a llevar. ¿Puedo pagar con tarjeta de crédito? / Sí, es para regalo. **2** Quisiera ver (una chaqueta), por favor. / Talla . . . (*your size*). / ¿Qué colores tiene? / La prefiero en blanco. / No me gusta mucho el modelo. ¿Tiene otras? / Sí, ésas me gustan más. / ¿Me la puedo probar? / Me queda muy bien. ¿Cuánto cuesta (*or* vale)? / Sí, la voy a llevar. / Voy a pagar en efectivo. **3** *Precio sin descuento*: 32,000 pesos. *Precio con descuento*: 28,800 pesos. *Color*: negro. *Número*: 42. **4 a** Long and short sleeved sport shirts are on offer. **b** Men's trousers have a 30, 40 and 50% discount. **c** Todos los pantalones para caballeros. No incluye promociones. **5 a** ¿Cuánto valen (*or* cuestan) los aguacates? **b** ¿Tiene mangos? **c** ¿Qué precio tienen los duraznos? **d** Quiero un kilo de zanahorias. **e** Deme una lechuga. **f** Quiero dos repollos. **g** Eso es todo. **h** ¿Cuánto es? **6** mandar *or* enviar; a; pesos; estampilla; de; Eso; es; tres mil cuatrocientos; buzón; a. **7** A bedroom suite, a double sofabed, a 10-foot refrigerator, a washing machine, a TV table, a stereo system, a 14" TV. The total is 1,050,000 pesos.

Unit 7

Dialogues

1 Iré a Cuba con un amigo / Vamos a estar cuatro días en La Habana y tres días en Santiago de Cuba. Y tú, ¿qué piensas hacer? / Es un país muy lindo. Espero que lo pases muy bien. 2 a No, not at this time of the year. b She proposes to take something for the rain.

Practice

1 Pienso ir a México y Quito. / No, voy a estar allí doce días en total. / Sí, es un tour y no es muy caro. Cuesta novecientos cuarenta y nueve dólares. / Sí, incluye el pasaje aéreo (or el vuelo), hoteles de cuatro estrellas, excursiones y traslados. / No, voy a viajar con un colega (or amigo/a). Y tú ¿qué vas a hacer este verano? 2 a Coyoacán is a typical district, with good restaurants and some important monuments. b You will be able to visit the Frida Khalo Museum. c Cuernavaca and Taxco. d No. 3 a It is quite pleasant. b It is a little cold. c It does not rain much. d A sweater for the mornings and evenings. 4 está; tiene; hay; tiene. 5 Facilities include air conditioning in the rooms, water bed, jacuzzi, suites with a pool, satellite TV and piped music. 6 a It has 216 rooms. b It has two restaurants. c It has a swimming pool, conference rooms, a casino and a disco. 7 a Voy a ir (or Iré) al banco a comprar cheques de viaje. b Voy a tener (or Tendré or Tengo) una reunión con el director de producción. c Voy a almorzar con el gerente. d Voy a estar (or Estaré or Estoy) libre entre las dos y media y las tres. 8 a F. b V. c V. d She says Lima is a nice, big and modern city, which retains some of the characteristics of colonial culture. e Lima has nice beaches, museums and zoos. f The weather is warm and there is almost no rain. 9 a Es una ciudad grande / mediana / pequeña / moderna / antigua / industrial / agrícola. b Tiene . . . habitantes. c (No) hace mucho frío. or (No) llueve mucho. or En verano (generalmente) hace calor (or sol). 10 a No, en México está nublado. b En Londres está despejado. c No, en París está despejado. d En Madrid está lloviendo (or lluvioso).

Unit 8

Dialogues

1 a ¿A qué hora sale el tren? b ¿A qué hora llega? c ¿Cuánto cuesta un boleto de ida y vuelta? d ¿Tiene boletos para el viernes 12? Quiero dos. 2 a El desayuno es aparte. b ¿Cuántos días van a quedarse? c Dos días solamente. d Nos vamos el martes. 3 a ¿Tiene una habitación individual / sencilla? b ¿Tiene baño la habitación? / ¿La habitación tiene baño? c Tiene agua caliente? d ¿Sirven desayuno? 4 a ¿Qué haces aquí? b Estoy aquí de vacaciones. c Nos vamos pasado mañana. d Llevamos dos días (aquí) solamente.

Practice

1 Ud: ¿A qué hora hay tren a Concepción? *Empleado/a*: Hay uno a las veintidós treinta (10.30 p.m.). Ud: ¿A qué hora llega a Concepción? *E*: Llega a

las siete y media de la mañana. *Ud*: ¿Tiene (*or* Lleva) coche dormitorio? *E*: Sí, sí tiene (*or* lleva). *Ud*: ¿Cuánto cuesta la cama? *E*: La cama baja vale veintitrés mil quinientos pesos y la alta diecinueve mil novecientos. *Ud*: ¿De ida o de ida y vuelta? *E*: De ida y vuelta. *Ud*: Muy bien. Deme un boleto de ida y vuelta para el lunes veinte de julio. Prefiero una cama baja. **2** Voy a viajar a Concepción. / Me voy el veinte de julio. / No, voy a viajar en tren. / Demora nueve horas. / No, para en San Rosendo. **3** *Ud*: Buenos días. ¿Tiene una habitación? *Recepcionista*: Sí, sí tenemos. ¿Quiere una habitación doble o sencilla? *Ud*: Sencilla. ¿Cuánto vale? *R*: Veinticinco mil pesos. *Ud*: ¿Está incluido el desayuno? *R*: No, el desayuno es aparte. ¿Cuánto tiempo va a quedarse? *Ud*: Cinco días solamente. *R*: Bien, me da su nombre, por favor. *Ud*: (*Say your name.*) *R*: ¿Cómo se escribe? *Ud*: (*Spell your name.*) *R*: ¿Y la dirección? *Ud*: (*Give your address.*) *R*: Gracias. Su habitación es la 320, en el tercer piso. Aquí tiene la llave. El ascensor está al fondo. **4 a** It lasts three days. **b** It leaves early on Friday morning. **c** It returns on Sunday night. **d** It includes return air ticket from Santiago, land transport, food, accommodation in tents, equipment and professional guides. **e** There are discounts for groups of over eight people. **5 a** Llega en el vuelo 173. **b** Viaja en LAN Chile. **c** Llega a las veintiuna cincuenta y cinco (9.55 p.m.). **6 a** F. **b** F. **c** V. **d** F. **7 a** Most people in Latin America travel by bus. **b** In Mexico, there is a first-class bus service with air conditioning and toilet. Seats can be booked in advance, and the service is much more comfortable than the second-class service. **c** During holiday time you have to book in advance because many people travel by bus.

Unit 9

Dialogues

1 a ¿Puede repetir su nombre? **b** ¿Cuándo hizo la reserva? **c** No la hice yo. **2 a** ¿Aló? **b** She went out to have lunch with a client. **c** He says he arrived in Santiago yesterday and that he is at the hotel Santiago Park Plaza. **3** Buenas tardes / noches. ¿Podría decirme si volvió Alfonso? / De parte de (your name) **4** Estuve en Santiago hace dos años. Me gustó mucho. / Llegué el sábado en la mañana. / Fue un poco largo.

Practice

1 *Ud*: Buenas tardes. Mi nombre es . . . (*name*). Tengo una habitación reservada. *Recepcionista*: Perdone, ¿puede repetir su nombre, por favor? *Ud*: (*Say your name again and spell it.*) *R*: ¿Cuándo hizo la reserva (*or* reservación*)? *Ud*: No la hice yo, mi secretaria reservó la habitación por teléfono desde (*town*) hace cinco días más o menos. *R*: Ah sí, aquí está. Es la habitación número cincuenta en el quinto piso. ¿Podría llenar esta ficha, si es tan amable? **2 a** ¿Aló? **b** Quiero el anexo dos, cinco, cinco, dos (*or* veinticinco cincuenta y dos), por favor. **c** Quisiera hablar con el señor Juan Miguel García, por favor. *or* ¿Está el señor . . .? **d** ¿De parte de quién? – De parte de (*your name*). **e** Encantado de conocerlo, señor García. **f** Por favor, dígale que llamó ... (*your name*). Llegué a Santiago hace dos días y estoy en el hotel Plaza, en la habitación número cincuenta. **3 a** Carmen Puig, from Caracas, needs to speak to señor Solís urgently. She wants him to phone her at the Sheraton Hotel, room 500, where she is staying. But it has to be now, as she is leaving for

Caracas tomorrow. **b** Marilú Pérez came to see señor Solís. She is staying at the Gala Hotel, in room 324. The telephone number is 687951. **4** fue, fui, estuvimos, entramos, gustó, levanté, tomé. **5** a ¿Cuándo llegó (usted)? **b** ¿Qué tal el viaje? **c** ¿Volvió (ya) la señorita Alonso? **d** ¿Es la primera vez que viene (usted) a Santiago? **e** ¿Le gustó Chile? **f** ¿Cenó (usted) ya? **6** a She went to the coast with her family. **b** They stayed in a hotel opposite the beach. **c** She says the place is pleasant, quiet, has wonderful beaches and that the air is very clean. **d** Salimos mucho, tomamos el sol, nadamos, hicimos deportes. **7** a Fui a . . . (*place*). **b** Fui solo/a / acompañado/a. **c** Me quedé en . . . (*place*). **d** Estuve . . . (*length of time*) allí. **e** *Possible replies*: nadé, tomé el sol, salí a pasear, fui a bailar, comí mucho, bebí mucho, etc.

Unit 10

Dialogues

1 a-3, b-1, c-4, d-2. **2** era, estaba, era, era, tenía, compartía, estudiaba, era, trabajaba, era.

Practice

1 vivía; trabajaba; viajaba; pasaba; compartía; se llamaba; vivían; era; tenía; estaba… gustaba; había. **2** a Ella vivía en Bariloche. **b** Trabajaba como guía en una agencia de viajes. **c** Era muy agradable. **d** Estaba frente al lago. **e** La vida era muy tranquila y a veces un poco monótona. **f** Porque ella extrañaba a su familia. **3** a Tenía dos dormitorios. **b** Tenía dos baños. **c** La cocina estaba entre el dormitorio dos y el estar-comedor. **d** Había una cama. **4** a V. **b** F. **c** F. **d** V. **e** F. **5** a Hace cinco/diez años yo vivía en . . . (*town or old address*). **b** Estaba soltero/a / casado/a. **c** Vivía con . . . (mis padres / mi novio/a / mi marido / mujer / mis hijos, etc.). **d** Estudiaba / Trabajaba. **e** Estudiaba / Trabajaba en . . . (*place*). *or* Trabajaba en una empresa / compañía / con un colegio que se llamaba . . . (*name*). **f** (No) me gustaba (mucho). **g** Mi casa / departamento / apartamento era grande / chico / agradable / cómodo, etc. **6** a ¿Dónde vivías antes? **b** ¿En qué parte de Ecuador vivías? **c** ¿Qué hacías allá? **d** ¿Y qué estás haciendo acá? **7** a He describes Buenos Aires as a very large city, with many different corners, but with a unity. A city with a cultural life, a city which has 'a soul'. **b** He likes its nightlife, and the possibility it gives its people for expressing themselves. He likes its cultural life. **c** He does not like the tendency the 'porteños' have towards sadness and melancholy. **8** Él era guapo. / Ella era bonita / linda. Era trigueño/a (moreno/a *in certain countries*), alto/a y delgado/a. Tenía pelo negro y ojos verdes. Tenía unos … años y era muy simpático/a.

Unit 11

Dialogues

1 a Nos gustaría / Quisiéramos alquilar / arrendar un coche / auto / carro. **b** ¿Podría recomendarnos una agencia? **c** Está a media cuadra de aquí. **d** Está cuatro cuadras más abajo, a la izquierda. **2 a** A car with room for four people, comfortable and economical. **b** 90 dollars per day. **c** It includes tax and insurance. **c** He wants it for two days. **3 a** He asks the attendant to fill the petrol tank and to check the tyre pressure. **b** ¿Me podría decir ...? **4 a** ¿Podrían repararme ...? **b** ¿Para cuándo la quiere? **c** Se la puedo tener lista. **5 a** Llamo desde la habitación veinticinco. **b** ¿Sería posible hacer una llamada a (*place*) desde mi habitación? **c** Es una llamada de persona a persona, al número (*number*). El nombre de la persona es (*name*) *or* La persona se llama (*name*).

Practice

1 *Ud*: Buenos días. Quisiera alquilar un coche. ¿Me podría recomendar una agencia? *Recepcionista*: Sí, en la calle Agustinas, frente al cerro Santa Lucía, hay una agencia. *Ud*: ¿Frente al cerro Santa Lucía me dijo? *R*: Sí, dos cuadras más abajo por calle Moneda, después a la izquierda en Santa Lucía y a la izquierda otra vez en calle Agustinas. *Ud*: Gracias. **2** Quisiera alquilar un coche. ¿Qué me recomienda? / Quiero un coche chico, no demasiado caro. / ¿Cuánto cuesta el alquiler por día? / ¿Y por semana? / ¿Es con kilometraje ilimitado? / ¿El IVA y el seguro están incluidos? / Está bien. Lo llevaré (*or* Me lo llevo) / Sí, aquí está. / ¿Sería posible dejar el coche en otra ciudad? Me gustaría viajar al sur y dejar el coche allí. Quiero volver en tren. **3 a** ¿Hay una estación de servicio por aquí? **b** Me lo llena, por favor. *or* ¿Podría llenármelo? **c** ¿Podría revisar el aceite y la presión de las ruedas, por favor? *or* Me revisa .. . **d** ¿Podría limpiar el parabrisas, por favor? *or* Me limpia . . . **e** ¿Me podría reparar esta llanta (*or* este neumático), por favor? *or* Me repara . . . **f** ¿Falta mucho para llegar a Santa Isabel? **4** *Telefonista*: ¿Dígame? *or* ¿Aló? *or* ¿Hola? *or* ¿Bueno? *Ud*: ¿Sería posible hacer una llamada internacional con cobro revertido desde mi habitación? *T*: Sí, cómo no. ¿Adónde quiere llamar? *Ud*: A . . . (*place*). *T*: ¿Y a qué número? *Ud*: (*telephone number*). *T*: ¿Y con quién desea hablar? *Ud*: Con . . . (*name*). *T*: ¿Su nombre, por favor? *Ud*: Me llamo *or* Mi nombre es . . . (*name*). *Y*: Un momento, por favor. Cuelgue y yo lo vuelvo a llamar. **5 a** Because he went there many years ago and its image is deeply engraved in him. **b** He would go with his family or friends, for fifteen or twenty days. **6 a** grande **b** tradicional **c** gris o azul **d** ir al trabajo y salir a pasear.

Unit 12

Dialogues

1 a F **b** F **c** V **2 a** Lléveme al aeropuerto, por favor. **b** Llévenos a la calle San Martín, por favor. **3 a** ¿Me da la cuenta de la habitación ciento cincuenta? Me voy mañana en / por la mañana. **b** ¿Me despierta a las siete y media? Tengo que estar en el aeropuerto a las nueve. **4** Tenemos dos maletas / Tenemos dos mochilas pequeñas / No fumador, y prefiero un asiento junto a la ventanilla.

Practice

1 Sí, es la primera vez. Me gusta mucho. Es un país bonito, aunque todavía no he visto mucho. / No, todavía no he ido al Cuzco (or Todavía no he estado en ...), pero espero ir la próxima semana. Voy a visitar Machu Picchu también. Me han dicho que es muy interesante. ¿Usted ha estado en Europa alguna vez? / Sí, he estado allí varias veces. Me gusta mucho España, especialmente el sur. / Gracias. Estudié español en el colegio. ¿Usted habla inglés? / Está bien. / No, gracias. Ya he tomado dos. Es suficiente. Y, además, mañana tengo que levantarme temprano, así que debo volver pronto al hotel. 2 a Sí, ya estuve allí. b No, todavía no lo he visitado. c Sí, ya lo vi. d No, todavía no lo he conocido. 3 a She was there when she was 11 years old. b She says the city is very beautiful. It is a traditional city, as it still retains the characteristics of Inca culture. c From Lima, you can travel to Cuzco by bus, train or plane. d The only way of getting to Machu Picchu is by train. 4 a Deme (or Me da) la cuenta, por favor. b Por favor, me despierta (or Despiérteme) a las seis y media. c ¿Me podría enviar (or ¿Podría enviarme) el desayuno a la habitación, por favor? d Lléveme (or Me lleva) al aeropuerto, por favor. 5 a 6 b 3 c 1 d 5 e 2 f 4. 6 Recommendations for tourists. For your own security, the National Tourist Service in our country makes the following suggestions: Change your money and travellers cheques only in banks or at authorised bureaux de change. Do not change money in the street. Leave your valuables in the safe deposit box at your hotel. Do not go out carrying large sums of money. When you take a taxi, see what the meter shows, as that is the amount that you will have to pay. In our country, there are no additional surcharges. If possible, use the taxi services of your own hotel.

Unit 13

Dialogues

1 a Hizo escala en París. b por error. c Yo misma me encargaré de buscarla. 2 a ¿En qué puedo servirle? b ¿No tendría una (habitación) más tranquila? c Si no le importa. d Ahora mismo. e Acaba de irse la persona que estaba allí. 3 a It's three or four blocks from the cathedral, on the left. b Go straight on as far as the park, and then turn right. c Turn left at the corner and continue as far as the end of that street. d When you reach the square you will see a large yellow building. That is the museum. 4 a No dormí en toda la noche. b Fiebre no tengo. c No me siento bien. d No creo que sea nada serio.

Practice

1 Recién llegué (or Acabé de llegar) en el vuelo trescientos diez de Hispanair que venía de . . . (city or country), pero desgraciadamente mi equipaje no ha llegado (or no llegó). / Traía dos maletas, una grande y una chica. Aquí tengo los tickets (or talones) del equipaje. Las dos maletas tenían etiquetas con mi nombre (say your name). / Espero que las encuentren. Tengo toda mi ropa en ellas y también unos regalos que traía para unos amigos. 2 a vayamos,

b pasen, **c** envíen, **d** llegue, **e** haga, **f** venga, **g** guste, **h** llueva. **3 a** El aire acondicionado no funcionó. **b** No había agua caliente. **c** El lavatorio estaba tapado. **d** En el baño no había toallas. **e** La habitación es muy ruidosa. No pude dormir anoche. **f** Quiero cambiarme a una habitación más tranquila.
4 a The man had asked for a seat in the non-smoking section of the plane.
b The Venezuelan lady in the restaurant had ordered fish with mashed potatoes and the waiter brought her fish with fried potatoes instead. **c** The young Chilean lady ordered a seafood soup 15 minutes ago and it still hasn't arrived. **5 b 6** ir; salir; doble; doble; mano; cuadras; de nada. **7** No me siento bien. Tengo dolor de estómago (*or* Me duele el estómago) y tengo diarrea. / Empezó anoche. Salí a comer (*or* cenar) con unos amigos y comí pescado y papas fritas. Seguramente fue eso. Más tarde, cuando volví al hotel empecé a sentirme mal. / Sí, he vomitado y parece que tengo fiebre también. / Espero que sí. **8 a** 11.00 a 13.00; 18.00 a 21.00. **b** 1016 **c** 325228 **9** Surgery days and hours are Mondays from 4.00 to 6.00 p.m. and Wednesdays and Fridays from 11.00 a.m. to 1.00 p.m.

1   a ¿Cómo se llama (usted)? b Mucho gusto, Encantado/a de conocerlo/a. c Siéntese, por favor. d ¿De qué parte de México eres? e Me alegro mucho de verte. f Eres colombiano/a, ¿verdad? / ¿no? g Disculpe / Perdone, ¿es usted el señor García? h ¿Cuál es el número de habitación de la señora Roble, por favor? i Está en el tercer piso, a la derecha. j Están al final del pasillo, a la izquierda.

2   a vives, Vivo b tenemos, empieza c piensan, pensamos d entiende, habla e Sabes, están, sé, tengo f Voy, llama, dices, vuelvo g sales, salgo, h Puede, Hace i vienes, vengo j llego, oigo, veo.

3   a ¿Cómo estás? b ¿De dónde eres? c ¿Dónde vives? d ¿Cuántos años tienes? e ¿Cuál es tu horario de trabajo? f ¿A qué hora te levantas? g ¿A qué hora te acuestas? h ¿Qué haces los fines de semana? / ¿Dónde sales los fines de semana? i ¿Conoces Nueva York? j ¿Qué hora es?/¿Tienes hora?

4   a es, está b Hay, hay, están c es, Es, es, es, Está d está, hay e es, Son f estás, Estoy g es, hay, está h son, están i está j es, está

5   a 5, b 7, c 2, d 9, e 1, f 10, g 4, h 3, i 6, j 8

6   (1) haré (2) iremos (3) estaremos (4) Saldremos (5) volveremos (6) nos quedaremos (7) enviaré (8) vendrás (9) gustará (10) podrás (11) presentaré.

7   Hace sólo (or solamente) dos días que estoy aquí. Llegué el sábado. / Fue muy agradable, pero fue un poco largo. / Me voy a quedar (or Voy a quedarme) dos semanas. / Sí, el domingo visité el museo y la catedral. Me gustó mucho la catedral. Y en / por la noche fui al teatro. El lunes

almorcé con un amigo y después compré unos (*or* algunos) regalos para mi familia. / No, nada. Estoy libre.

8   a estuve b hiciste, Fui, Vimos c pude d pusiste e dije, dijo f llegó, Llegué g se levantó, fue h vino, Tuve i murió j llovió, Nos quedamos.

9   a vivía, estuve b era, gustaba c conocimos d estaba, llegó e trabajaron f pasamos g fui, dolía h era i era, estaba j llamaba, era.

10 a ¿Qué le gustaría hacer? b Me gustaría / Quisiera alquilar un carro (auto / coche). ¿Qué carro (auto / coche) me recomienda? c ¿Podría decirme cuánto cuesta? d '¿Es (ésta) la primera vez que viene a Ecuador?' – 'No, he estado aquí varias veces' e Hemos reservado una habitación en el hotel San Martín f ¿Nos despierta / Podría despertarnos a las siete mañana? Tenemos que salir del hotel a las nueve g Espero que vuelva (*or* vuelvan) pronto aquí h '¿Podría decirme dónde está el museo?' 'Siga derecho / todo recto hasta la avenida Bolívar, y después doble / tuerza a la derecha. El museo está en la izquierda' j Quisiera algo para el dolor de estómago j No me siento bien y tengo fiebre.

a   *to, at, on*
abajo: más –   *further down*
abrazar   *to embrace, hug*
abrir   *to open*
abuelos (m, pl)   *grandparents*
acabar de   *to have just*
aceite (m)   *oil*
acerca de   *about*
acompañado/a   *accompanied*
acostarse   *to go to bed*
acuerdo: de –   *fine, OK, agreed*
activar   *to activate*
adelante   *see:* en adelante
además   *besides*
adentro   *inside*
adicional   *additional*
adiós   *goodbye*
aeropuerto (m)   *airport*
afuera   *outside*
agencia (f)   *agency*
agencia de viajes (f)   *travel agency*
agradable   *pleasant*
agua (f)   *water*
ahora   *now*
ahora mismo   *right now*
ahorita   *right now* (diminutive)
aire (m)   *air*
aire acondicionado (m)   *air
   conditioning*
a la derecha   *on the right*
a la izquierda   *on the left*
al (a + el)   *to the, on the, at the*
al final de   *at the end of*
al fondo de   *at the end of*

al lado de   *next to*
alberca (f)   *swimming pool* (Mex)
alegrarse   *to be glad*
algo   *something*
algún (m)   *some, any*
alguna (f)   *some, any*
alguna vez   *ever*
alimento (m)   *food*
allá   *there*
allí   *there*
alma (f)   *soul*
almacenes (m pl)   *department store*
almorzar   *to have lunch*
almuerzo (m)   *lunch*
aló   *hello* (on the phone)
alojamiento (m)   *accommodation*
alquilar   *to rent*
alquiler (m)   *rent*
alto/a   *tall; top; upper*
amable   *kind*
amarillo/a   *yellow*
ambos/as   *both*
americano/a   *American*
amigo/a (m/f)   *friend*
amplio/a   *wide*
andén (m)   *platform*
anexo (m)   *extension* (Chile)
animado/a   *animated*
anoche   *last night*
antena (f)   *aerial, antenna*
antes   *before*
antiquísimo/a   *very ancient*
anunciar   *to announce*
año (m)   *year*

año pasado (m)   *last year*
a partir de   *starting in / on*
a pesar de   *although, despite,
  in spite of*
aparecer   *to appear*
aparte   *separate*
apellido (m)   *surname*
aprender   *to learn*
aprovechar   *to take the opportunity*
aproximadamente   *approximately*
aquí   *here*
arquitecto (m)   *architect*
arquitectónica   *architectural*
arquitectura (f)   *architecture*
arroz (m)   *rice*
artículo (m)   *article*
arvejas (f pl)   *peas*
a sus órdenes   *at your service*
asado/a   *roast*
así   *thus*
asiento (m)   *seat*
asistir   *to attend*
aunque   *although, even though*
auto (m)   *car*
autorización (f)   *permission*
a veces   *sometimes*
avenida (f)   *avenue*
aventura (f)   *adventure*
avión (m)   *plane*
ayer   *yesterday*
azafata (f)   *stewardess*
azteca (m / f)   *Aztec*
azul   *blue*

bajar   *to go down*
bajo/a   *low, lower*
balsa (f)   *raft*
bañarse   *to take a bath*
banco (m)   *bank*
baño (m)   *toilet, bathroom*
bar (m)   *bar*
barato/a   *cheap*
barrio (m)   *district, area*
barroco/a   *barroque*
bastante   *quite*
beber   *to drink*
bebida gaseosa (f)   *fizzy drink*
bien   *well*
bienvenido/a   *welcome*

blanco/a   *white*
blusa (f)   *blouse*
boleto (m)   *ticket*
bonito/a   *pretty*
botella (f)   *bottle*
brasileño/a   *Brazilian*
brasilero/a   *Brazilian*
brevedad: a la –   *as soon as possible*
bueno/a   *good*
bueno   *well*
bulla (f)   *noise*
bus (m)   *bus*
buscar   *to look for*
buzón (m)   *post box*

caballero (m)   *gentleman*
cada   *each, every*
caer mal   *to be ill* (from food)
café (m)   *coffee, café*
calabaza (f)   *pumpkin*
calidad (f)   *quality*
cálido/a   *warm*
caliente   *hot*
calle (f)   *street*
calor (m)   *heat;* (adj) *warm, hot*
cama de agua (f)   *water bed*
cambiar   *to change*
cambiarse   *to move*
caminar   *to walk*
camino (m)   *road*
camión (m)   *bus* (Mex)
camioneta (f)   *van*
camisa (f)   *shirt*
campo (m)   *countryside*
cansado/a   *tired*
capacidad (f)   *room*
carne (f)   *meat*
carne asada   *roast / grilled meat*
carnet de conducir (m)   *driving
  licence*
caro/a   *expensive*
carrera (f)   *street* (Colombia)
carretera (f)   *highway*
carro (m)   *car*
carta (f)   *menu, letter*
casa (f)   *house, home*
casa de cambio (f)   *bureau de change*
casado/a   *married*
caso (m)   *case*

castellano (m)   *Castilian*
catedral (f)   *cathedral*
categoría (f)   *category*
cena (f)   *dinner*
cenar   *to have dinner*
centro (m)   *centre*
Centroamérica   *Central America*
cerca   *near*
cerdo (m)   *pig, pork*
cerrado/a   *closed*
cerrar   *to close*
cerveza (f)   *beer*
chamarra (f)   *jacket* (Mex)
chao   *goodbye*
chaqueta (f)   *jacket*
chico/a   *boy, girl*
chileno/a   *Chilean*
chofer (m)   *driver*
cine (m)   *cinema*
ciudad (f)   *city*
cliente (m / f)   *client*
clima (m)   *climate*
coche (m)   *car*
coche dormitorio (m)   *sleeping car*
colega (m / f)   *colleague*
colgar   *to hang up*
colombiano/a   *Colombian*
color (m)   *colour*
comedor (m)   *dining room*
comer   *to eat*
comida (f)   *meal, food, dinner*
cómo   *how?, what?*
como   *such as, like, as*
como también   *as well as*
cómodo/a   *comfortable*
compañía (f)   *company*
comparación (f)   *comparison*
compartir   *to share*
completo/a   *complete, full*
comprar   *to buy*
computadora (f)   *computer*
computarizado/a   *computerized*
con   *with*
concluyendo   *finishing*
conectar   *to connect*
conmigo   *with me*
conocer   *to know*
conseguir   *to get*
contar   *to tell*

contar con   *to have, depend on*
contento/a   *happy*
contigo   *with you* (fam sing)
continuar   *to continue*
copa (f)   *glass*
correo (m)   *post office*
correr   *to run*
corto/a   *short*
costa (f)   *coast*
costar   *to cost*
costoso/a   *expensive*
creer   *to believe, think*
crema (f)   *soup; cream*
crema de espárragos (f)   *asparagus soup*
crema del día (f)   *soup of the day*
creo que sí   *I think so*
cuadra (f)   *block*
cuál   *what?, which?*
cuándo   *when?*
cuando   *when*
cuanto: en – a   *as regards*
cuánto   *how much?*
cuántos   *how many?*
cuarto (m)   *quarter, room*
cuarto/a   *fourth*
cuenta (f)   *bill*
cuero (m)   *leather*
culpa (f)   *fault*
cultura (f)   *culture*
curso (m)   *course*
cuyo/a   *whose*

dar   *to give*
dar paseos   *to walk*
de   *of, from, on*
debido a   *due to*
decidir   *to decide*
decir   *to say*
dejar   *to leave*
del (de + el)   *of the*
demasiado/a   *too, too much*
deme   *give me*
demora (f)   *delay*
demorar   *to take* (time)
de nada   *don't mention it, not at all*
dentro de   *within*
departamento (m)   *flat, apartment*
dependiente/a   *shop assistant*

derecha (f)   *right*
desayunar   *to have breakfast*
desayuno (m)   *breakfast*
descansar   *to rest*
describir   *to describe*
descuento (m)   *discount*
desde   *from*
desear   *to wish, to want*
despejado/a   *clear*
despertar   *to wake up*
después   *after, afterwards*
destino (m)   *destination*
detenerse   *to stop*
detrás   *behind*
devolver   *to return* (something)
día (m)   *day*
día: al –   *valid*
día siguiente (m)   *following day*
diario   *per day*
diarrea (f)   *diarrhoea*
diciembre   *December*
diferente   *different*
difícil   *difficult*
dígale   *tell him/her*
dígame   *Hello* (on the phone), *Can I help you?*
digamos   *let's say*
dinero (m)   *money*
dirección (f)   *address*
discoteca (f)   *disco*
disculpe/a   *I am sorry, excuse me*
disfrutar   *to enjoy*
Distrito Federal (m)   *Federal District* (Mexico City)
doblar   *to turn*
dolor (m)   *pain*
dolor de estómago (m)   *stomach ache*
domingo (m)   *Sunday*
dónde   *where?*
donde   *where*
dormir   *to sleep*
dormitorio (m)   *bedroom*
durante   *during*
durazno (m)   *peach*

e   *and (*before i*)*
edificio (m)   *building*
efectivo   *see: en efectivo*
ejecutivo/a   *executive*

el (m)   *the*
elevador (m)   *lift*
ello   *this, that*
embarcar   *to board*
empezar   *to begin*
empleado/a   *employee, clerk*
empresa (f)   *company*
en   *in, on, at*
en adelante   *onwards*
en efectivo   *in cash*
en todo caso   *in any case*
encantado/a   *pleased to meet you*
encantar   *to love, like*
encargarse   *to be responsible*
encontrar   *to find*
energía (f)   *energy*
enero   *January*
enfrente   *in front*
enorme   *huge*
ensalada (f)   *salad*
ensalada de fruta (f)   *fruit salad*
ensalada mixta (f)   *mixed salad*
enseguida   *right away*
enseñar   *to show, teach*
entonces   *then*
entrar   *to begin, start*
entre   *between, among*
entrevista (f)   *interview*
enviar   *to send*
época (f)   *time*
equipaje (m)   *luggage*
equipaje de mano (m)   *hand luggage*
equipo (m)   *equipment*
es decir   *that is to say*
escalera (f)   *stairs*
escribir   *to write, spell*
escritorio (m)   *desk*
escuchar   *to listen*
ese/a   *that*
esos/as (pl)   *those*
espárragos (f pl)   *asparagus*
esperar   *to hope, wait, expect*
esposo/a   *husband, wife*
esquina (f)   *corner*
establecimiento (m)   *establishment*
estación (f)   *station, season*
estación de metro (f)   *underground station*
estación de servicio (f)   *petrol station*

estadía (f)   *stay*
Estados Unidos (m pl)   *United States*
estampilla (f)   *stamp*
estancia (f)   *stay*
estar   *to be*
estar seguro/a   *to be sure*
este/a   *this*
estomacal   *stomach* (adj)
estómago (m)   *stomach*
estos/as (pl)   *these*
estrella (f)   *star*
estudiante (m / f)   *student*
estudiar   *to study*
estudios (m pl)   *studies*
estupendo/a   *very good, fantastic*
etiqueta (f)   *label*
excitante   *exciting*
experimentado/a   *experienced*
explicadas   *explained*
extrañar   *to miss*

falda (f)   *skirt*
faltar   *to be lacking*
familia (f)   *family*
famoso/a   *famous*
febrero   *February*
felicitar   *to congratulate*
ficha (f)   *registration form*
fiebre (f)   *fever*
filete de pescado (m)   *fillet of fish*
fin (m)   *end*
fin de semana (m)   *weekend*
final (m)   *end*
finalmente   *finally*
fino/a   *good, of good quality*
firma (f)   *signature*
flan (m)   *creme caramel*
fondo   *see: al fondo de*
frente a   *opposite*
fresa (f)   *strawberry*
frío (m)   *cold*
frito/a   *fried*
fritura (f)   *fried dish*
frontera (f)   *border*
fruta (f)   *fruit*
fuera   *outside*
fumador   *smoker*
fumar   *to smoke*

galleta (f)   *biscuit*
ganar   *to earn, win*
general: por lo –   *usually*
generalmente   *generally, usually*
gente (f)   *people*
gerente (m / f)   *manager*
gesticular   *to gesticulate*
gloria (f)   *glory*
goma pinchada (f)   *flat tyre*
gracias   *thank you*
grado (m)   *degree*
gran   *big*
grande   *big, great*
gris   *grey*
guía (m / f)   *guide* (person)
guisado/a   *stewed*
gustar   *to like*
gusto: mucho –   *pleased to meet you*

había   *there was / were*
habitación (f)   *room*
habitante (m)   *inhabitant*
hablar   *to speak*
hace   *for, ago*
hace sol   *it is sunny*
hacer   *to do, make*
hacer deportes   *to practise sports*
hacer escala   *to stop over*
hacer frío / calor   *to be cold / warm*
harto   *a lot*
hasta   *until, as far as*
hay   *there is, there are*
helado (m)   *ice-cream*
hermano/a   *brother / sister*
hermanos (m pl)   *brothers and sisters*
hijo/a   *son, daughter*
hijos (m pl)   *children*
Hispanoamérica   *Spanish-speaking
countries in the Americas*
hispanoamericano/a   *Spanish American*
historia (f)   *history*
hola   *hello*
hora (f)   *time, hour*
hora: a la –   *on time*
horario (m)   *times, timetable*
horario de trabajo (m)   *working
hours*
hoy   *today*
huésped (m / f)   *guest*

ida (f) *single* (ticket)
ida y vuelta (f) *return* (ticket)
idioma (m) *language*
iglesia (f) *church*
ilimitado/a *unlimited*
importar: si no le importa *if you don't mind*
no me importa *I don't mind*
impuesto (m) *tax*
incluido/a *included*
incluir *to include*
independiente *independent*
individual (adj) *single*
infección (f) *infection*
informe (m) *report*
ingeniería (f) *engineering*
ingeniero/a *engineer*
Inglaterra *England*
inglés (m) *English*
inglesa (f) *English*
inmediatamente *immediately*
inmediato: de – *immediately*
instituto de idiomas (m) *school of languages*
interesante *interesting*
interesar *to be interested*
interior *at the back*
interrupción (f) *interruption*
invierno (m) *winter*
ir *to go*
ir de compras *to go shopping*
irse *to leave*
izquierda (f) *left*

jefe (m) *boss, manager*
jugo (m) *juice*
junto a *next to*
juntos *together*

kilometraje (m) *mileage*
kilometraje ilimitado (m) *unlimited mileage*

la (f) *the, it, her*
laborar *to work*
lado *see: al lado de*
lago (m) *lake*
largo/a *long*
las (f pl) *the, them*

lástima (f) *pity, shame*
le *to him, to her, to you* (pol)
lechuga (f) *lettuce*
leer *to read*
legumbre (f) *vegetable, pulse*
lejos *far*
lengua (f) *language, tongue*
levantarse *to get up*
leve *slight*
libra (f) *pound*
libre *free*
licencia de conducir (m) *driving licence*
limpiar *to clean*
lindo/a *pretty, beautiful*
listo/a *ready*
liviano/a *light*
llamada (f) *telephone call*
llamar *to call*
llamarse *to be called*
llave (f) *key; water tap*
llegada (f) *arrival*
llegar *to arrive, get to*
llenar *to fill in*
llevar *to take*
llevarse bien *to get on well*
llover *to rain*
lluvia (f) *rain*
lluvioso/a *rainy*
lo *you* (pol)*, him, it*
lo siento *I am sorry*
localizar *to trace, look for*
los (m, pl) *the*
lugar (m) *place*
luna (f) *moon*
lunes (m) *Monday*

madre (f) *mother*
maestro/a *teacher*
mal *bad*
maleta (f) *suitcase*
maletín (m) *briefcase*
mamá (f) *mother*
mandar *to send*
manejar *to drive*
manga (f) *sleeve*
mantequilla (f) *butter*
manzana (f) *apple*
mañana (f) *morning*

mañana   *tomorrow*
maravilla (f)   *marvel*
maravilloso/a   *marvellous*
marido (m)   *husband*
mariscos (m pl)   *seafood*
marrón   *brown*
más   *more, else*
más o menos   *more or less*
materno/a   *maternal*
mayor   *elder, eldest, bigger*
mayoría (f)   *majority*
me   *me, to me, myself*
mediano/a   *medium sized*
médico/a   *doctor*
medio/a   *half*
mediodía (m)   *midday*
mejor   *better*
menor   *younger, youngest*
mensaje (m)   *message*
mercado (m)   *market*
mes (m)   *month*
mesa (f)   *table*
mesero/a   *waiter / waitress*
mexicano/a   *Mexican*
mí   *me*
mi   *my*
millón (m)   *million*
minuto (m)   *minute*
mira   *look* (fam)
mire   *look* (pol)
mismo/a   *same, itself*
mitad (f)   *half*
mixto/a   *mixed*
mochila (f)   *rucksack*
modelo (m)   *model*
momentito (m)   *moment* (diminutive)
moneda (f)   *coin*
monedero (m)   *purse*
monótono/a   *monotonous*
monumento (m)   *monument*
mostaza (f)   *mustard*
mostrador (m)   *desk*
mostrar   *to show*
mozo (m)   *waiter*
muchas gracias   *thank you very much*
mucho/a   *much, a lot*
mucho gusto   *pleased to meet you*
muchos/as   *many*
mundo (m)   *world*

museo (m)   *museum*
música ambiental (f)   *piped music*
muy   *very*
muy bien   *very well*

nacionalidad (f)   *nationality*
nada   *nothing*
nadar   *to swim*
naranja   *orange* (colour)
negocio (m)   *business*
negro/a   *black*
neumático (m)   *tyre*
nevar   *to snow*
ni   *nor*
niño/a   *boy/girl, child*
niños (m, pl)   *children*
no dejar de   *not to fail to*
no me digas   *you don't say*
noche (f)   *night*
nocturno/a   *night* (adj)
nombre (m)   *name*
normalmente   *normally*
norte (m)   *north*
Norteamérica   *North America*
nos   *us, to us*
nublado/a   *cloudy*
nuestro/a   *our*
número (m)   *number*
número de teléfono (m)   *telephone number*
nunca   *never*

o   *or*
ocupado/a   *occupied, engaged*
ocurrir   *to happen, occur*
oficial   *official*
oficina (f)   *office*
ofrecer   *to offer*
ómnibus (m)   *bus*
opcionalmente   *optionally*
oportunidad (f)   *opportunity, chance*
orden: a la – / a sus órdenes   *can I help you?*
otoño (m)   *autumn*
oscuro/a   *dark*
otra vez   *again*
otro/a   *other, another*
otros/as   *others*

padre (m)   *father*
padres (m pl)   *parents*
pagar   *to pay*
país (m)   *country*
paisaje (m)   *landscape*
palacio (m)   *palace*
pantalones (m pl)   *trousers*
papa (f)   *potato*
papas doradas / fritas (f pl)   *golden potatoes / chips*
papá (m)   *father*
papás (m pl)   *parents*
par (m)   *pair*
para   *for, to, in order to*
para que   *so that*
para servirle   *at your service*
paralela   *parallel*
parecer   *to seem*
pariente (m / f)   *relative*
parque (m)   *park*
parte (f): ¿de – de quién?   *who is speaking?*
   ¿de qué –?   *what part of?*
pasado   *past*
pasado mañana   *the day after tomorrow*
pasaje (m)   *ticket*
pasaje aéreo (m)   *air fare*
pasaporte (m)   *passport*
pasar   *to come in, spend* (time)
pasar: ¿qué le pasa?   *what's the matter with you?*
pasarlo bien   *to have a good time*
pasear   *to go for a walk*
pasillo (m)   *corridor*
paso (m)   *step*
pastel (m)   *pie, cake*
pastilla (f)   *tablet, pill*
pedir   *to ask for*
película (f)   *film*
pensar   *to think*
pensión (f)   *boarding house*
pequeño/a   *small*
perdón   *excuse me, sorry*
periódico (m)   *newspaper*
periodista (m / f)   *journalist*
pero   *but*
persona (f)   *person*
persona a persona   *personal*

(telephone call)
pescado (m)   *fish*
pescado frito (m)   *fried fish*
peso (m)   *Latin American currency*
pinchazo (m)   *puncture*
pintura (f)   *painting*
pirámide (f)   *pyramid*
piscina (f)   *swimming pool*
piso (m)   *floor*
planta alta (f)   *upper floor*
planta baja (f)   *ground floor*
plata (f)   *money, silver*
playa (f)   *beach*
plaza (f)   *square*
plazoleta (f)   *small square*
poco   *a little*
pocos/as   *few*
poder   *to be able, can*
podríamos   *we could*
policía (f)   *police*
pollo (m)   *chicken*
pollo asado / rostizado   *roast chicken*
por   *for, by, along, per*
por aquí   *near here, nearby*
por ciento   *per cent*
por ejemplo   *for example*
por error   *by mistake*
por favor   *please*
por la noche   *in the evening, at night*
por lo general   *usually, generally*
por qué   *why?*
por semana   *per week*
por si acaso   *just in case*
por supuesto   *of course, certainly*
porque   *because*
porteño/a (m/f)   *inhabitant of Buenos Aires*
posgrado   *postgraduate*
posible   *possible*
posiblemente   *possibly*
postal: tarjeta – (f)   *postcard*
postre (m)   *dessert*
precio (m)   *price*
precioso/a   *very beautiful*
preferir   *to prefer*
preocuparse   *to worry*
presentar   *to introduce*
presente (m)   *present*
presión (f)   *pressure*

primavera (f)   *spring*
primero/a   *first*
privado/a   *private*
probador (m)   *fitting room*
probar   *to try on*
procedencia (f)   *place of origin*
programa (m)   *programme*
promedio (m)   *average*
prometer   *to promise*
pronto   *soon*
propio   *itself*
proporcionar   *to provide*
próximo/a   *next*
psicólogo/a   *psychologist*
puerta (f)   *gate, door*
pues   *well*
puré de papa (m)   *mashed potatoes*
puro/a   *pure*

que   *than, that*
qué   *what?, which?, who?, how?*
quedar bien   *to fit well*
quedarse   *to stay*
querer   *to want*
querido/a   *dear*
queso (m)   *cheese*
quién   *who?*
quien   *who*
quinto/a   *fifth*
quisiera   *I would like*
quizá(s)   *perhaps*

rápidos (m pl)   *rapids*
realizar   *to carry out*
recado (m)   *message*
recargo (m)   *surcharge*
recepción (f)   *reception*
recepcionista (m/f)   *receptionist*
receta (f)   *prescription*
recién   *just (now)*
recomendar   *to recommend*
reconfirmar   *to reconfirm*
recorrido (m)   *tour*
recuerdos (m pl)   *memories*
regalo (m)   *gift, present*
regresar   *to come back*
reparar   *to repair*
repetir   *to repeat*
repollo (m)   *cabbage*

reservación (f)   *reservation, booking*
reservado/a   *booked, reserved*
reservar   *to book, reserve*
residencia (f)   *house, residence*
retrasado/a   *delayed*
retraso (m)   *delay*
reunión (f)   *meeting*
revisar   *to check*
rincón (m)   *corner*
rojo/a   *red*
ropa (f)   *clothing*
rueda (f)   *wheel*
ruido (m)   *noise*
ruidoso/a   *noisy*

sábado (m)   *Saturday*
sala de conferencia (f)   *conference room*
salir   *to go out*
salir a   *to go to*
salón (m)   *railway carriage with wider and more comfortable seats (Chile)*
salsa (f)   *sauce*
se   *to you*
se   *yourself* (pol), *himself, herself, one*
sección (f)   *area, section*
secretario/a   *secretary*
seguir   *to continue, follow, go on*
seguir derecho   *to go straight on*
segundo/a   *second*
seguramente   *surely*
seguridad (f)   *security*
seguro (m)   *insurance*
seguro: estar –   *to be sure*
seleccionado/a   *chosen, of your choice*
semana (f)   *week*
sencillo/a: habitación –   *single room*
sentarse   *to sit*
sentirse   *to feel*
señor   *Mr, sir*
señora (f)   *lady, Mrs, wife*
señorita (f)   *young lady, Miss*
ser   *to be*
serio/a   *serious*
servicio (m)   *service*
servir   *to serve*
servirse   *to help oneself*
si   *if, whether*

sí   *yes*
siempre   *always*
siéntate   *sit down (*fam)
siéntense   *sit down* (pl)
siguiente   *following*
simpático/a   *nice*
sin   *without*
situado/a   *situated*
sobrino/a   *nephew, niece*
sol (m)   *sun; Peruvian currency*
solamente   *only*
solo/a   *alone*
sólo   *only*
soltero/a   *single*
sopa (f)   *soup*
sopa de pollo (f)   *chicken soup*
sopa de verduras (f)   *vegetable soup*
sorpresa (f)   *surprise*
sos   *you are* (fam, Arg)
su   *your* (pol), *his her*
suave   *mild*
sueldo (m)   *salary*
suerte (f)   *luck*
suéter (m)   *sweater*
suficiente   *enough, suficient*
sugerencia (f)   *suggestion*
sugerir   *to suggest*
suma (f)   *amount, sum*
sur (m)   *south*

tableta (f)   *tablet*
tal: ¿qué –?   *how are you?* (fam), *how
  about it?*
talla (f)   *size* (clothes)
talón (m)   *receipt*
tamaño (m)   *size*
también   *also*
tampoco   *neither*
tan   *so*
tan amable   *so kind*
tantos/as   *so many*
tarde   *late*
tarde (f)   *afternoon, early evening*
tarjeta (f)   *card*
tarjeta de crédito (f)   *credit card*
tarjeta de embarque (f)   *boarding
  card*
te   *you, to you, yourself* (fam)
té (m)   *tea*

teléfono (m)   *telephone*
teléfono celular (m)   *cell / mobile
  phone*
templo (m)   *temple*
temporada (f)   *season*
temprano   *early*
tendencia (f)   *tendency*
tener   *to have*
tercero/a   *third*
terminar   *to finish*
terrestre   *land* (adj)
ti   *you* (fam)
tiempo (m)   *weather; time*
tiempo libre (m)   *spare time*
tienda (f)   *shop*
tienda de regalos (f)   *gift shop*
tinto   *red* (wine), *coffee* (Colombia)
típico/a   *typical*
todavía   *still, yet*
todo/a   *all, every*
tomar   *to drink, to have; to take, to
  catch* (bus, train, etc.)
tomar el desayuno   *to have breakfast*
tomar (el) sol   *to sunbathe*
tomate (m)   *tomato*
torcer   *to turn*
trabajar   *to work*
trabajo (m)   *work*
traer   *to bring*
tráfico (m)   *traffic*
tranquilo/a   *quiet*
traslado (m)   *transfer*
tratar de   *to try to*
tratarse de   *to have to do with, to be
  a question of*
tren (m)   *train*
tú   *you* (fam)
tu   *your* (fam)

último/a   *last*
universidad (f)   *university*
uno/a   *a, one*
urgentemente   *urgently*
usar   *to use*
usted   *you* (pol)
ustedes   *you* (pl)
utilizar   *to use*

vacaciones (f pl)   *holidays*

valer   *to cost*
valija (f)   *suitcase* (Arg)
variar   *to vary*
veces (f pl)   *times*
vecino/a   *neighbour*
vender   *to sell*
venir   *to come*
ventana (f)   *window*
ver   *to see*
verano (m)   *summer*
verdad   *true*
verdadero/a   *true, real*
verde   *green*
verdura (f)   *vegetable*
vez (f)   *time*
   de vez en cuando   *from time to time*
viajar   *to travel*
viaje (m)   *journey, trip*
viaje: cheque de – (m)   *traveller's cheque*
vida (f)   *life*

viento (m)   *wind*
viernes (m)   *Friday*
vino (m)   *wine*
visitar   *to visit*
vitrina (f)   *shop window*
vivienda (f)   *housing, house*
vivir   *to live*
volver   *to come back*
vos   *you* (fam, Argentina)
vuelo (m)   *flight*

y   *and*
ya   *already, soon*
ya que   *since, as, for*
yo   *I*
yo mismo/a   *I myself*

zanahoria (f)   *carrot*
zapato (m)   *shoe*
zócalo (m)   *plaza* (Mexico)
zona (f)   *district, zone*

English–Spanish vocabulary

a *un/a; uno*
able: to be – *poder*
about *acerca de*
accommodation *alojamiento* (m)
accompanied *acompañado/a*
activate: to – *activar*
additional *adicional*
address *dirección* (f)
adventure *aventura* (f)
aerial *antena* (f)
after *después*
afternoon *tarde* (f)
afternoon: good – *buenas tardes*
afterwards *después*
again *otra vez, de nuevo,*
  nuevamente
agency *agencia* (f)
ago *hace*
air *aire* (m)
air conditioning *aire acondicionado*
  (m)
airport *aeropuerto* (m)
all *todo/a*
alone *solo/a*
along *por*
already *ya*
also *también*
although *aunque, a pesar de*
always *siempre*
American *americano/a,*
  norteamericano/a
among *entre*
ancient *antiguo*
ancient: very – *antiquísimo/a*
and *y, e* (before i, hi)
animated *animado/a*
announce: to – *anunciar*
another *otro/a*

apartment *departamento* (m),
  apartamento (m)
appear: to – *aparecer*
April *abril*
architect *arquitecto/a*
area *barrio* (m), *sección* (f)
arrival *llegada* (f)
arrive: to – *llegar*
article *artículo* (m)
as *ya que, como*
as far as *hasta*
as regards *en cuanto a*
as soon as possible *a la brevedad, lo*
  más pronto posible, lo antes posible
as well as *como también*
ask: to – for *pedir*
asparagus *espárragos* (m pl)
asparagus soup *crema de espárragos*
  (f)
at *en*
attend: to – *asistir*
August *agosto*
avenue *avenida* (f)
average *promedio* (m)
Aztec *azteca* (m / f)

bad *mal, malo/a*
bank *banco* (m)
bar *bar* (m)
bath: to take a – *bañarse*
bathroom *baño* (m)
be: to – *ser, estar*
beach *playa* (f)
beautiful *lindo/a, bonito/a*
beautiful: very – *precioso/a*
because *porque*
bed *cama*
bed: to go to – *acostarse*

bedroom *dormitorio* (m)
beer *cerveza* (f)
before *antes*
begin : to – *empezar; entrar* a (to begin work)
believe: to – *creer*
besides *además*
better *mejor*
between *entre*
big *gran, grande*
bigger *más grande, mayor*
bill *cuenta* (f)
black *negro/a*
block *cuadra* (f)
blue *azul*
board: to – *embarcar*
boarding card *tarjeta de embarque* (f), *pase de abordar* (m)
boarding house *pensión* (f)
book: to – *reservar*
booked *reservado/a*
booking *reservación* (f), *reserva* (f)
border *frontera* (f)
boss *jefe/a* (m / f)
bottle *botella* (f)
boy *niño, chico, muchacho*
Brazilian *brasileño/a, brasilero/a*
breakfast *desayuno* (m)
breakfast: to have – *tomar (el) desayuno, desayunar*
briefcase *maletín* (m), *portafolio* (m)
bring: to – *traer*
brother *hermano*
brothers and sisters *hermanos* (m,pl)
brown *marrón, café*
building *edificio* (m)
bureau de change *casa / oficina de cambio* (f)
bus *autobús* (m), *ómnibus* (m), *camión* (m Mex), *colectivo* (m Arg)
business *negocio* (m), *empresa* (f)
but *pero*
butter *mantequilla* (f), *manteca* (f) (Arg)
buy: to – *comprar*
by *por*

cafe *café* (m)
call: telephone – *llamada* (f), *llamado* (m)
called: to be – *llamarse*
can *poder*
car *carro* (m), *auto* (m), *coche* (m)
card *tarjeta* (f)

carry: to – out *realizar*
case *caso* (m)
case: just in – *por si acaso*
cash *efectivo*
cash: in – *en efectivo*
Castilian *castellano* (m)
catch: to – *tomar, coger* (bus, train, etc.)
category *categoría* (f)
cathedral *catedral* (f)
cell phone *teléfono celular* (m)
Central America *Centroamérica*
centre *centro* (m)
certainly *por supuesto*
chance *oportunidad* (f)
change: to – *cambiar*
cheap *barato/a*
check: to – *revisar*
chicken *pollo* (m)
chicken soup *sopa de pollo* (f)
child *niño/a, chico/a, hijo/a*
children *niños/as, chicos/as, hijos/as*
Chilean *chileno/a*
chosen *seleccionado/a, escogido/a*
church *iglesia* (f)
cinema *cine* (m)
city *ciudad* (f)
clear *despejado/a*
clerk *empleado/a*
client *cliente/a*
climate *clima* (m)
close: to – *cerrar*
clothing *ropa* (f)
cloudy *nublado/a*
coast *costa* (f)
coffee *café* (m), *tinto* (m Colombia)
cold *frío* (m)
cold: to be – *hacer / sentir / frío*
colleague *colega* (m / f), *compañero/a de trabajo*
Colombian *colombiano/a*
colour *color* (m)
come: to – *venir*
come: to – back *volver, regresar*
come: to – in *pasar, entrar*
comfortable *cómodo/a*
company *empresa* (f), *compañía* (f)
comparison *comparación* (f)
complete *completo/a*
computerized *computarizado/a*
conference room *sala de conferencia* (f)
congratulate: to – *felicitar*
connect: to – *conectar*

continue: to – *continuar, seguir*
corner *esquina* (f), *rincón* (m)
corridor *pasillo* (m)
cost: to – *costar, valer*
country *país* (m)
countryside *campo* (m)
course *curso* (m)
course: of – *por supuesto*
credit card *tarjeta de crédito* (f)
culture *cultura* (f)

dark *oscuro/a*
daughter *hija* (f)
day *día* (m)
day: following – *día siguiente* (m)
dear *querido/a, estimado/a*
December *diciembre* (m)
decide: to – *decidir*
degree *grado* (m)
delay *demora* (f), *retraso* (m)
delayed *retrasado/a*
depend on: to – *depender de, contar con*
describe: to – *describir*
desk *escritorio* (m), *mostrador* (m)
despite *a pesar de*
dessert *postre* (m)
destination *destino* (m)
diarrhoea *diarrea* (f)
different *diferente*
difficult *difícil*
dining room *comedor* (m)
dinner *cena* (f), *comida* (f)
dinner: to have – *cenar*
disco *discoteca* (f), *disco* (f)
discount *descuento* (m)
district *barrio* (m), *zona* (f)
do: to – *hacer*
doctor *médico/a*
door *puerta* (f)
down: further *abajo: más abajo*
drink: to – *tomar, beber*
drive: to – *manejar, conducir*
driver *conductor/a, chofer* (m)
driving licence *carnet de conducir* (m), *licencia de manejar* (f)
due to *debido a*
during *durante*

each *cada*
early *temprano*
earn: to – *ganar*
eat: to – *comer*
elder *mayor*

eldest: the – *el / la mayor*
else *más*
employee *empleado/a*
end *fin, final* (m)
end: at the – of *al final de, al fondo de*
energy *energía* (f)
engaged *ocupado/a*
engineer *ingeniero/a*
engineering *ingeniería* (f)
England *Inglaterra*
English *inglés* (m) (language); *inglés / inglesa* (m / f)
enjoy: to – *disfrutar*
equipment *equipo* (m)
establishment *establecimiento* (m)
even though *aunque*
evening *tarde* (f early), *noche* (f late)
ever *alguna vez*
every *cada, todo/a*
example: for – *por ejemplo*
exciting *excitante*
excuse: – me *disculpe/a* (pol / fam), *perdone/a* (pol / fam)
executive *ejecutivo/a*
expect: to – *esperar*
expensive *caro/a, costoso/a*
experienced *experimentado/a, con experiencia*
explain: to – *explicar*
extension *extensión* (f), *anexo* (m Chile), *interno* (m River Plate)

fail: not to – to *no dejar de*
family *familia* (f)
famous *famoso/a*
fantastic *estupendo/a*
far *lejos*
fare: air – *pasaje aéreo* (m)
father *padre, papá*
fault *culpa* (f)
February *febrero*
Federal District *Distrito Federal* (m) (Mexico City)
feel: to – *sentirse*
fever *fiebre* (f)
fifth *quinto/a*
fill: to – in *llenar*
finally *finalmente*
find: to – *encontrar*
finish: to – *terminar*
first *primero/a*
fish *pescado* (m)
fish: fillet of – *filete de pescado* (m)

fit: to – well *quedar bien*
fizzy drink *bebida gaseosa* (f)
flat *departamento* (m), *apartamento* (m)
flight *vuelo* (m)
floor (m) *piso* (m)
follow: to – *seguir*
following *siguiente*
food *alimento* (m), *comida* (f)
for *por, para*
free *libre*
Friday *viernes*
fried *frito/a*
fried: – dish *fritura* (f)
friend *amigo/a*
from *de, desde*
fruit *fruta* (f)
fruit: – salad *ensalada de fruta* (f)
full *completo/a, lleno/a*

gate *puerta* (f), *salida* (f)
generally *generalmente, por lo general, normalmente*
gentleman *caballero* (m)
get to: to – *llegar*
get up: to – *levantarse*
get: to – *conseguir*
gift *regalo* (m)
gift shop *tienda de regalos* (f)
girl *niña, chica, muchacha*
give me *deme*
give: to – *dar*
glad: to be – *estar contento/a*
glass *copa* (f), *vidrio* (m)
glory *gloria* (f)
go: to – down *bajar*
go: to – *ir*
go: to – on *seguir*
go: to – out *salir*
good *bueno/a, fino/a*
 very – *muy bueno/a, estupendo/a*
goodbye *adiós, hasta luego; chao, chau* (fam)
grandparents *abuelos* (m, pl)
green *verde* (m / f)
grey *gris*
guest *huésped* (m / f)
guide *guía* (m / f person)

half *medio/a; mitad* (f)
hand luggage *equipaje de mano* (m)
hang: to – up *colgar*
happen: to – *ocurrir, pasar, suceder*
happy *contento/a*

have: to – *tener, tomar, contar con*
have: to – just *acabar de*
heat *calor* (m)
hello *hola*; (on the phone) *aló, bueno* (Mex), *holá* (River Plate)
help *ayuda* (f)
help: to – *ayudar*
help: Can I – you? *¿Dígame?*
help: to – oneself *servirse*
her *la, le* (pronouns), *su, sus* (possessives)
here *aquí*
herself *se*
highway *carretera* (f)
him *lo, le* (pronouns)
himself *se*
his *su, sus, suyo/a*
history *historia* (f)
holidays *vacaciones* (f pl)
home *casa* (f), *hogar* (m)
hope: to – *esperar*
hot *caliente* (m)
hot: to be – *hacer, calor, tener calor*
house *casa* (f)
housing *vivienda* (f)
how? *¿cómo?*
how: are you? *¿cómo está (usted)?*; *¿cómo estás?, ¿qué tal?* (fam)
how many? *¿cuántos/as?*
how much? *¿cuánto/a?*
husband *marido, esposo*

I *yo*
ice cream *helado* (m)
if *si*
immediately *inmediatamente, de inmediato*
in *en, dentro*
in: – any case *en todo caso*
in: – order to *para*
in: – spite of *a pesar de*
include: to – *incluir*
included *incluido/a*
independent *independiente* (m / f)
infection *infección* (f)
inhabitant *habitante* (m)
inside *adentro*
insurance *seguro* (m)
interested *interesado/a*
interesting *interesante*
interruption *interrupción* (f)
interview *entrevista* (f)
introduce: to – *presentar*

January *enero*
journey *viaje* (m)
juice *jugo* (m)
July *julio*
June *junio*

key *llave* (f)
kind *amable*
know: to – *conocer, saber*

label *etiqueta* (f)
lacking: to be – *faltar*
lady *señora*
lady: young – *señorita*
lake *lago* (m)
land (adj) *terrestre*
landscape *paisaje* (m)
language *idioma* (m), *lengua* (f)
last *último/a*
last: – night *anoche*
last: – year *el año pasado* (m)
late *tarde*
learn: to – *aprender*
leather *cuero* (m)
leave : to – *irse, dejar*
left *izquierda* (f)
left: on the – *a la izquierda*
letter *carta* (f), *letra* (f)
lettuce *lechuga* (f)
licence: driving – *licencia de conducir* (f)
life *vida* (f)
lift *elevador* (m), *ascensor* (m)
light *liviano/a*
like *como*
like: to – *gustar*
like: to – very much *encantar*
listen: to – *escuchar, oír*
little *poco/a*
live: to – *vivir*
long *largo/a*
look: to – at *mirar*
look: to – for *buscar, localizar*
lot: a – *mucho/a*
love: to – (to like very much) *encantar*
low *bajo/a*
luck *suerte* (f)
luggage *equipaje* (m)
luggage: hand – *equipaje de mano* (m)
lunch *almuerzo* (m), *comida* (f)
lunch: to have – *almorzar*

majority *mayoría* (f)
make: to – *hacer*

manager *gerente* (m / f), *jefe/a*
many *muchos/as*
many: so – *tantos/as*
March *marzo*
market *mercado* (m)
married *casado/a*
marvellous *maravilloso/a*
matter: what's the – with you? *¿qué le / te pasa?* (pol / fam)
May *mayo*
meal *comida* (f)
meat *carne* (f)
medium sized *mediano/a*
meeting *reunión* (f)
memories *recuerdos* (m pl)
mention: don't – it *de nada*
menu *carta* (f)
message *mensaje* (m), *recado* (m)
Mexican *mexicano/a*
midday *mediodía* (m)
mild *suave*
mileage *kilometraje* (m)
mileage: unlimited – *kilometraje ilimitado* (m)
million *millón* (m)
mind: if you don't – *si no le/te importa* (pol / fam)
mind: I don't – *no me importa*
minute *minuto* (m)
Miss *señorita*
miss: to – *extrañar, echar de menos;* (bus, train) *perder*
mistake: by – *por error*
model *modelo* (m)
moment *momento* (m), (diminutive) *momentito* (m)
Monday *lunes* (m)
money *dinero* (m), *plata* (f)
month *mes* (m)
moon *luna* (f)
more *más*
more or less *más o menos*
morning *mañana* (f)
morning: good – *buenos días*
mother *madre* (f), *mamá* (f)
move: to – *cambiarse, mudarse*
Mr *señor*
Mrs *señora*
much *mucho/a*
museum *museo* (m)
mustard *mostaza* (f)
my *mi / mis* (sing, pl)
myself *me*
myself: I – *yo mismo/a*

name   *nombre* (m)
nationality   *nacionalidad* (f)
near   *cerca*
near here   *por aquí*
nearby   *por aquí*
neighbour   *vecino/a*
neither   *tampoco*
nephew   *sobrino*
never   *nunca*
next   *próximo/a*
next to   *al lado de, junto a*
niece   *sobrina*
night   *noche* (f); *nocturno/a* (adj)
night: at –   *en/por la noche*
noise   *ruido* (m)
noisy   *ruidoso/a*
nor   *ni*
normally   *normalmente, generalmente, por lo general*
north   *norte* (m)
North America   *Norteamérica*
not at all   *de nada*
nothing   *nada*
November   *noviembre*
now   *ahora*
number   *número* (m)

occupied   *ocupado/a*
occur: to –   *ocurrir, pasar, suceder*
October   *octubre*
of   *de*
offer: to –   *ofrecer*
office   *oficina* (f)
official   *oficial*
oil   *aceite* (m)
on   *en, sobre, encima de*
one   *uno/a*
only   *sólo, solamente*
onwards   *en adelante*
open: to –   *abrir*
opportunity   *oportunidad* (f)
opportunity: to take the –   *aprovechar*
opposite   *frente a, enfrente de*
or   *o* (u before o, ho)
orange   *naranja* (f)
origin: place of –   *procedencia* (f)
other   *otro/a*
others   *otros/as*
our   *nuestro(s)/a(s)*
outside   *fuera, afuera*

pain   *dolor* (m)
painting   *pintura* (f)
pair   *par* (m)

palace   *palacio* (m)
parallel   *paralela*
parents   *padres* (m pl)
park   *parque* (m)
passport   *pasaporte* (m)
past   *pasado*
pay: to –   *pagar*
peach   *durazno* (m)
per   *por*
per cent   *por ciento*
per day   *diario, por día*
perhaps   *quizá(s)*
permission   *autorización* (f)
person   *persona* (f)
personal call (telephone)   *llamada* (f) *de persona a persona*
petrol station   *estación de servicio* (f); *gasolinera* (f)
pity   *lástima* (f)
place   *lugar*
place of origin   *procedencia* (f)
plane   *avión* (m)
pleasant   *agradable*
please   *por favor*
pleased to meet you   *mucho gusto, encantado/a*
police   *policía* (f)
possible   *posible*
post box   *buzón* (m)
post office   *(oficina de) correos* (f), *correo* (m)
potato   *papa*
potato: mashed –   *puré* (m) *(de papa)*
prefer: to –   *preferir*
prescription   *receta* (f)
present   *regalo* (m), *presente* (m)
pressure   *presión* (f)
pretty   *bonito/a, lindo/a*
price   *precio* (m)
private   *privado/a*
programme   *programa* (m)
promise: to –   *prometer*
provide: to –   *proporcionar*
psychologist   *psicólogo/a*
pumpkin   *calabaza* (f), *zapallo* (m)
puncture   *pinchazo* (m)
pure   *puro/a*
purple   *púrpura, violeta, morado*

quality   *calidad* (f)
quality: of good –   *fino/a*
quarter   *cuarto* (time (m))
quiet   *tranquilo/a*
quite   *bastante*

raft *balsa* (f)
rain *luvia* (f)
rain: to – *llover*
rainy *lluvioso/a*
read: to – *leer*
ready *listo/a*
real *verdadero/a*
receipt *talón* (m), *recibo* (m)
reception *recepción* (f)
receptionist *recepcionista* (m / f)
recommend: to – *recomendar*
reconfirm: to – *reconfirmar*
red *rojo/a*
registration form *ficha* (f)
relative *pariente* (m / f)
rent *alquiler* (m)
rent: to – *alquilar, rentar, arrendar*
repair: to – *reparar*
repeat: to – *repetir*
report *informe* (m)
reservation *reservación* (f), *reserva* (f)
reserve: to – *reservar*
reserved *reservado/a*
residence *residencia* (f)
responsible: to be – *encargarse*
rest: to – *descansar*
return (something): to – *devolver*
return ticket *boleto de ida y vuelta*
  (m)
rice *arroz* (m)
right *derecha* (f)
right: – away *enseguida*
right: – now *ahora mismo / ahorita*
  (diminutive)
right: on the – *a la derecha*
road *camino* (m)
roast *asado/a*
room *habitación* (f), *cuarto* (m);
  capacidad (f), *pieza*
rucksack *mochila* (f)

salad *ensalada*(f)
salary *sueldo* (m), *salario* (m)
same *mismo/a*
Saturday *sábado* (m)
sauce *salsa* (f)
say: to – *decir*
school *escuela* (f), *colegio* (m),
  instituto (m)
seafood *mariscos* (m pl)
season *estación* (f), *temporada* (f)
seat *asiento* (m)
second *segundo/a; segundo* (m time)
secretary *secretario/a*

section *sección* (f)
security *seguridad* (f)
see: to – *ver*
seem: to – *parecer*
sell: to – *vender*
send: to – *enviar, mandar*
separate *aparte*
September *septiembre*
serious *serio/a*
serve: to – *servir*
service *servicio* (m)
shame *lástima* (f)
share: to – *compartir*
shirt *camisa* (f)
shoe *zapato* (m)
shop *tienda* (f)
shop assistant *dependiente/a*
shopping: to go – *ir de compras*
short *corto/a*
show: to – *mostrar, enseñar*
since *ya que*
single (person) *soltero/a*
single: ticket *boleto de ida* (m)
sister *hermana*
sit: to – *sentarse*
situated *situado/a*
size *tamaño* (m); *talla* (clothes f)
sleep: to – *dormir*
sleeping: – car *coche dormitorio* (m)
small *pequeño/a*
smoke: to – *fumar*
smoker *fumador/a*
snow: to – *nevar*
so *tan; entonces; así que*
so that *para que*
some *algún / alguna* (m / f),
  algunos/as (m / f pl)
something *algo*
sometimes *a veces, algunas veces*
son *hijo*
soon *pronto, ya*
sorry: I am – *disculpe/a* (pol / fam);
  perdone/a (pol / fam), *lo siento*
soup *sopa* (f), *crema* (f)
soup of the day *crema / sopa del día*
  (f)
south *sur* (m)
Spanish American
  hispanoamericano/a
spare time *tiempo libre* (m)
speak: to – *hablar*
speaking: who is –? *¿de parte de quién?*
spell: to – *escribir*
spend: to – (time) *pasar*; (money)

gastar
sport   *deporte* (m)
square   *plaza* (f)
   square: small –   *plazoleta* (f)
stairs   *escalera* (f)
star   *estrella* (f)
start: to –   *empezar, comenzar; entrar*
   (to start work)
station   *estación* (f)
stay   *estadía* (f), *estancia* (f)
stay: to –   *quedarse*
step   *paso* (m)
stewardess   *azafata* (f)
stewed   *guisado/a*
still   *todavía*
stomach   *estómago* (m); (adj)
   estomacal
stomach ache   *dolor de estómago*
stop over   *escala* (f)
   stop: to –   *hacer escala*
store: department –   *tienda de*
   departamentos (f)
straight: to go – on   *seguir derecho*
strawberry   *fresa* (f), *frutilla* (f)
street   *calle* (f)
student   *estudiante* (m / f)
studies   *estudios* (m pl)
study: to –   *estudiar*
subway: *metro* (m), *subte* (m Arg)
such as   *tal(es) como*
suggest: to –   *sugerir*
suggestion   *sugerencia* (f)
suitcase   *maleta* (f), *valija* (f Arg)
summer   *verano* (m)
sun   *sol* (m)
sunbathe: to –   *tomar (el) sol*
Sunday   *domingo* (m)
sunny: it is –   *hace sol*
sure   *seguro*
sure: to be –   *estar seguro/a*
surely   *seguramente*
surname   *apellido* (m)
surprise   *sorpresa* (f)
sweater   *suéter* (m)
swim: to –   *nadar*
swimming pool   *piscina* (f), *alberca* (f
   Mex), *pileta* (River Plate)

table   *mesa* (f)
tablet   *tableta* (f)
take: to –   *tomar, llevar;* (time)
   demorar
tall   *alto/a*
tap: water –   *grifo* (m), *llave* (f),

   canilla (f, River Plate)
tax   *impuesto* (m)
tea   *té* (m)
teacher   *maestro/a, profesor/a*
telephone   *teléfono* (m)
telephone number   *número de*
   teléfono (m)
tell: to –   *contar*
temple   *templo* (m)
tendency   *tendencia* (f)
than   *que*
thank you (very much)   *(muchas)*
   gracias
that   *ese* (m), *esa* (f), *eso* (neuter); *que*
that is to say   *es decir*
the   *el* (m sing), *la* (f sing), *los* (m pl),
   las (f pl)
them   *los* (m), *las* (f); *les*
then   *entonces*
there   *allá, allí, ahí*
there is / are   *hay*
these   *estos* (m), *estas* (f)
think: to –   *creer, pensar*
think: I (don't) – so   *creo que sí (no)*
third   *tercero/a*
this   *este / esta; esto* (neuter); *ello*
   (neuter)
those   *esos / esas* (pl)
Thursday   *jueves*
thus   *así*
ticket   *boleto* (m), *pasaje* (m)
time   *hora* (f); *tiempo* (m); *vez* (f);
   época (f)
time: from – to –   *de vez en cuando*
time: on –   *a la hora*
time: to have a good –   *pasarlo bien*
times   *veces* (f / pl)
times: several –   *varias veces*
timetable   *horario* (m)
tired   *cansado/a*
today   *hoy*
together   *juntos / juntas*
toilet   *baño* (m); *servicios* (m pl),
   sanitario (m)
tomato   *tomate* (m); *jitomate* (Mex)
tomorrow   *mañana*
tomorrow: the day after –   *pasado*
   mañana
too (much)   *demasiado/a*
tour   *tour* (m), *recorrido* (m)
trace: to –   *localizar*
traffic   *tráfico* (m)
train   *tren* (m)
transfer   *traslado* (m)

travel agency   *agencia de viajes* (f)
travel: to –   *viajar*
trip   *viaje* (m)
trousers   *pantalones* (m, pl)
true   *verdad* (f); *verdadero/a* (adj)
try: to –   *tratar, intentar*
try: – on   *probarse*
Tuesday   *martes*
turn: to –   *doblar*
typical   *típico/a*
tyre   *neumático* (m)

underground station   *estación* (f) *de
    metro/subte* (Arg)
United States   *Estados Unidos* (m pl)
university   *universidad* (f)
unlimited   *ilimitado/a*
until   *hasta*
us   *nosotros/as; nos*
use: to –   *usar, utilizar*
usually   *generalmente, por lo general,
    normalmente*

van   *camioneta* (f)
vary: to –   *variar*
vegetable   *verdura* (f)
vegetable soup   *sopa / crema de
    verduras* (f)
very   *muy*
visit: to –   *visitar*

wait: to –   *esperar*
waiter   *mesero, camarero, mozo*
waitress   *mesera, camarera*
wake up: to –   *despertar*
walk: to –   *caminar, andar*
walk: to go for a –   *pasear, dar un
    paseo, ir a caminar*
want: to –   *querer, desear*
warm   *cálido/a*
warm: to be   *hacer / sentir calor*
water   *agua* (m)
weather   *tiempo* (m)
Wednesday   *miércoles*
week   *semana* (f)
week: per –   *por semana*

weekend   *fin de semana* (m)
welcome   *bienvenido/a*
well   *bien; bueno; pues*
well: very –   *muy bien*
what   *que; cual/ cuales; como*
wheel   *rueda* (f)
when   *cuando*
where   *donde*
which   *cual / cuales*
white   *blanco/a*
who   *quien / quienes, que*
whose   *cuyo/s* (m), *cuya/s* (f)
why?   *¿por qué?*
wide   *amplio/a*
wife   *mujer, esposa, señora*
wind   *viento* (m)
window   *ventana* (f)
wine   *vino* (m)
wine: red –   *vino tinto*
winter   *invierno* (m)
wish: to –   *desear*
with   *con*
within   *dentro de*
without   *sin*
work: to –   *trabajar, laborar; trabajo*
    (m)
working hours   *horario de trabajo*
    (m)
world   *mundo* (m)
worry: to –   *preocuparse*
write: to –   *escribir*

year   *año* (m)
yellow   *amarillo/a*
yes   *sí*
yesterday   *ayer*
yet   *todavía*
you   *tú, usted, ustedes* (subject
    pronouns)
young   *joven*
younger   *menor*
youngest: the –   *el / la menor*
your   *su/s* (pol), *tu/s* (fam)
yourself   *se* (pol); *te* (fam)

zone   *zona* (f)

Further study

There are a number of books on sale containing references to Latin American Spanish, which may help you to expand your present knowledge of Spanish and its grammar. The following recommended textbooks may help you to achieve that, but you are advised to consult a specialist bookseller for further titles.

Butt, John, *The Oxford Minireference Spanish Grammar*, Oxford University Press, 1996. (A compact guide to the essentials of Spanish Grammar)

Butt, John, *Oxford Spanish Grammar*, Oxford University Press, 1996.

Kattán-Ibarra, J., Longo, A., and Sánchez, A., *Sueños; World Spanish 2*, BBC Worldwide Ltd, 1996. (Peninsular and Latin American Spanish)

Kattán-Ibarra, J., *Teach Yourself Spanish*, Hodder and Stoughton, 2003. (A complete beginner's course on mainly Peninsular Spanish)

Kattán-Ibarra, J., and Howkins, A., *Spanish Grammar in Context*, Arnold 2003.

Muñoz, P. and Thacker, M., *A Spanish Learning Grammar*, Arnold, 2001.

Sources of authentic Spanish

Newspapers

Latin American newspapers and magazines will be more difficult to find outside each country, but if you have internet facilities you will be able to access their websites, although they may be special net versions. The following is a list of some main Latin American newspapers:

Argentina
La Nación (http://lanacion.com.ar/)
Clarín (http://www.clarin.com.ar/)
Página 12 (http://www.pagina12.com.ar)

Chile
El Mercurio (http://www.emol.com)
La Tercera (http://www.latercera.cl)

Colombia
El Universal (http://eluniversal.com.co/)
El Espectador (http://www.elespectador.com/)

Cuba
Granma (http://www.granma.cubaweb.cu/)

Ecuador
El Comercio (http://www.elcomercio.com)

México
El Universal (http://www.el-universal.com.mx/)
Uno más Uno (http://unomasuno.com.mx /)
La Jornada (http://www.jornada.unam.mx,
http://www.asic-lajornada.com)

Perú
Correo (http://www.correoperu.com.pe/)
El Comercio (http://www.elcomercio.com.pe/online)
La República (http://www.larepublica.com.pe/)

Venezuela
El Universal (http://noticias.eluniversal.com/int.shtml)
La Razón (http://www.razon.com)

Radio and television

An excellent way to improve your understanding of spoken Spanish is to listen to radio and watch television. On medium wave after dark and via satellite you will be able to gain access to Radio Nacional de España, Televisión Española (TVE) and other stations. And for spoken Latin American Spanish, you may like to tune in to the BBC Spanish Latin American Service, which can be heard on short wave.

Travelling in Latin America

Travelling in a Spanish-speaking country is probably the best way to practise what you have learnt and improve your command of the spoken language. If you are planning to do this, there are a number of good guidebooks which will help you to plan your journey. The well-known *Lonely Planet* guides cover not just specific countries, but also main regions and cities, including Latin America and Spain. The *Mexico and Central American Handbook* and the *South American Handbook* have a long tradition amongst travellers in the region. *Time Out, Michelin, Fodor's, Rough Guide*, among several others, have also become well established in the travel market.

Travellers in Latin America will find useful information in Latin America – Travel Notes: http://www.travelnotes.org/ latinamerica; Travel Latin America: http://www.travellatinamerica.com/es/; Travel.org – Latin America (directory of links to cities and regions): http://www.travel.org/latin.html

Culture and history

If you are interested in the culture and history of the Spanish-speaking countries of Latin America, there are a number of publications in English which deal with such matters, some more general than others. Publications in Spanish usually require a much higher level of language than what you may have at present, but some are geared towards students of Hispanic studies and may be easier to follow. The best thing is to seek advice from a specialist bookseller, selling foreign language books.

The following websites contain useful background information on Latin America, including history and current affairs.

Council on Foreign Relations Latin American Studies Program – Country Information: http://www.cfr.org/latinamerica/countries.html; Internet Resources for Latin America: http://lib.nmsu.edu; LANIC, Latin American Network Information Center: (http://www.lanic.utexas.edu)

Spanish language courses

The Hispanic Council, in the United Kingdom, based in London, may be able to help you with enquiries about Spanish language courses and aspects of life in Latin American countries. Alternatively, contact the embassy of the country you are interested in, or visit the following websites:

Spanish Language Schools in Latin America
(http://pages.prodigy.com/studyabroad)

Hispanica – Spanish Studies in Latin America
(http://hispanica.com/english/index.html)

Spanish abroad, Inc.: (http://www.spanishabroad.com)

Worldwide Classroom (http://www.worldwide.edu)

The publisher has used its best endeavours to ensure that the URLs for external websites referred to in this book are correct and active at the time of going to press. However, the publisher has no responsibility for the websites and can make no guarantee that a site will remain live or that the content is or will remain appropriate.

index to grammar